My introduction of the resolution to create a Select Committee of the House of Representatives to reopen the investigation of the assassination of President John F. Kennedy goes back to an event which took place at 9:15 A.M. Tuesday, April 15, 1975. That was when I met Robert Groden and viewed, for the first time, his optically enhanced version of the motion picture film of the murder. It convinced me that there was more than one assassin.

Since that time, I have seen that film innumerable times. Robert has brought it to my office on several occasions for showing to other members of Congress. As a result, many of them have joined in our legislative effort to set the record straight.

If our efforts are successful, if we are able to put to rest for the last time the question, who killed John F. Kennedy?, Robert Groden will have a major share in that success. I am glad that he has put his knowledge of the events surrounding November 22, 1963 on paper. Along with Peter Model, he has put together a story that is captivating and, at times, hard to believe, but it presents the facts which the American people have a right to know.

—Congressman Thomas N. Downing
Virginia
January 1976

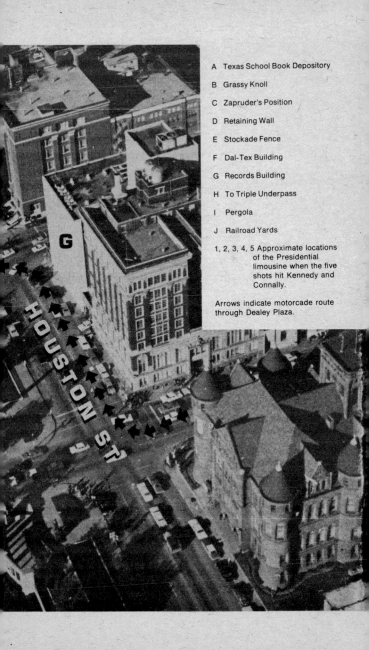

A   Texas School Book Depository

B   Grassy Knoll

C   Zapruder's Position

D   Retaining Wall

E   Stockade Fence

F   Dal-Tex Building

G   Records Building

H   To Triple Underpass

I   Pergola

J   Railroad Yards

1, 2, 3, 4, 5   Approximate locations
of the Presidential
limousine when the five
shots hit Kennedy and
Connally.

Arrows indicate motorcade route
through Dealey Plaza.

JFK:
THE CASE FOR CONSPIRACY

F. PETER MODEL AND ROBERT J. GRODEN

MANOR
BOOKS
INC.

FOR:

ALYNE MODEL & CHRISTINE GRODEN

and four who came after November '63

ALEXA *and* JUSTIN

ROBBIE *and* JOHN

and

*to Harold Weisberg and Sylvia Meagher
(always quoted but seldom credited)*

*and personal thanks to Dick Gregory
from Robert and Chris*

A MANOR BOOK......1976

Manor Books, Inc.
432 Park Avenue South
New York, New York 10016

JFK:
THE
CASE FOR
CONSPIRACY

ABOUT THE AUTHORS:

F. PETER MODEL, 45, is a former magazine staff writer and editor specializing in government, business and the arts. He has been probing the Kennedy assassination for a number of years and has written about the case in *Argosy*, *Oui* and several European publications. He has also been published in *Finance*, *Harvard Business Review*, *Gentlemen's Quarterly*, *Boston Magazine*, *Penthouse*, *In The Know* and *True*. Mr. Model is presently working on his second book, dealing with payoffs of foreign governments. He lives in New York City with his wife, a documentary film editor-producer, and their two children.

ROBERT J. GRODEN, 30, is a multi-media technician specializing in photo-optical image restoration and enhancement. He has been researching the JFK case for ten years, and is best known for his work in clarifying the famous 8 mm. Abraham Zapruder film (which social activist Dick Gregory helped get on coast-to-coast television in March 1975 on ABC-TV's "Goodnight, America"). His private collection of photographs and film footage on the Dallas assassination is perhaps the most extensive single assemblage on the subject next to that found in the National Archives. He lives in New Jersey with his wife, a film archivist, and their two children.

CONTENTS

PROLOGUE

In the year 1963, these events *also* took place:

APRIL 18:

A lurid broadside is distributed to the Cuban exile community of Miami. Literally translated, it declares:

> "Only through one development will you Cuban patriots ever live again in your homeland as free men...[only] if an inspired Act of God should place in the White House, within weeks, a Texan known to be a friend of all Latin Americans...though he must, under present conditions, bow to the Zionists who since 1905 came into control of the United States, and for whom Jack Kennedy and Nelson Rockefeller and other members of the Council of Foreign Relations and allied agencies are only stooges and pawns. Though Johnson must now bow to these crafty and cunning Communist-hatching Jews, yet, did an Act of God suddenly elevate him into the top position, Johnson would revert to what his beloved father and grandfather were, and to their values and principles and loyalties."

The leaflet is signed, "A Texan who resents the Oriental influence that has come to control, to degrade, to pollute and enslave its own people."

NOVEMBER 9:

An emergency meeting takes place in the office of Walter E. Headley, Chief of Police of the City of Miami—"the best damned police chief in the country," former President Harry S. Truman called him. With him is Detective Sergeant C.H. Sapp, head of the Police Department's Criminal Intelligence Division. They are listening to a secret tape recording made the day before in a Miami apartment of a conversation between one of Sapp's undercover people and Joseph Adams Milteer, a 61-year-old wealthy Georgian, a rabid segregationist, suspected Klansman and organizer of a new "American Constitution Party." Discussing plans to assassinate JFK during an upcoming (November 18) trip, Milteer (according to a copyrighted Miami *News* article by Bill Barry in 1967)

> "said that Kennedy would be shot with a high-powered rifle from an office building. The gun would be disassembled, taken into the building (overlooking the motorcade), assembled, and then used for murder. 'They will pick up somebody within hours afterwards—*just to throw the public off.*'" (ital. ours)

The voice on the tape said nothing about disassembling the gun afterwards or taking it out of the building. It was to be left behind. Headley notified the Protective Research Department of the U.S. Secret Service.

> "And when Kennedy did come to Miami, police intelligence took extraordinary steps to guard the President's life. They insisted he abandon the plan to take a motorcade—they put him on a helicopter instead."

NOVEMBER 17:
William S. Walter, on duty as overnight code clerk in the New Orleans field office of the Federal Bureau of Investigation, rips off a teletype alert from FBI headquarters in Washington. It warns of "a threat to assassinate President Kennedy

November 22-23, 1963" in Dallas by "a militant revolutionary group," and instructs all agents in New Orleans, Mobile and Dallas to activate their CI's and PCI's—criminal informants and possible criminal informants—as well as infiltrators into local racial hate groups. Apparently, nobody takes the TWX seriously because it was never produced by the FBI for the Warren Commission. Not until 1975—12 years later—does the TWX come to life, after William Walter, now a Louisiana bank official, is interviewed by CBS News. FBI Director Clarence M. Kelley tells a hastily called Washington news conference that a full check of the files has failed to produce the TWX. He intimates it never existed, although he won't flatly say so. But Walter reads his copy of the famous TWX to a CBS TV network audience, and sticks to his story.

NOVEMBER 23:

According to a partially declassified FBI document (Warren Commission Document 1347) a "reliable" informer places J.A. Milteer at the Union Station in Jacksonville, Fla.

> "...at about 4:35 p.m. on that date...he was very jubilant over the death of President Kennedy. Milteer stated, 'Everything ran true to form. I guess you thought I was kidding you when I said he would be killed from a window with a high-powered rifle.' When questioned as to whether he was guessing when he originally made the threat regarding President Kennedy, Milteer is quoted as saying, 'I don't do any guessing.'"

There is a page missing in CD 1347. It is page 121. By way of explanation there is this note:

> "The Federal Bureau of Investigation has

requested that certain pages of this document not be disclosed. This request was incorporated in a letter of August 13, 1965, to Dr. Wayne C. Grover, Archivist of the United States, from Norbert A. Schlei, Assistant Attorney General, Office of Legal Counsel, Department of Justice."

THE LONGEST
COVER-UP

"What is past, is prologue."
> —William Shakespeare
> Act II, *The Tempest*

One can learn a lot about a government's self-image by reading the inscriptions on its public monuments. Until the National Archives became the official repository for the evidence in the case of United States v. L.H. Oswald (deceased), Shakespeare's line was indeed a fitting one to place beneath a statue fronting its headquarters in Washington D.C.

Since then, it has become singularly inappropriate. And perhaps Congress, in its wisdom, might now wish to replace *The Tempest* with a line from Charles Dickens' *David Copperfield*: "Let sleeping dogs lie—who wants to rouse 'em?"

For it is here at the National Archives at Seventh Street and Pennsylvania Avenue where so much of the current "people's inquiry" into the assassination of John Fitzgerald Kennedy has come to a screeching halt. The huge, bronze doors to our national past may be open, but too many of the filing cabinets remain locked and inaccessible even to the most serious of researchers. The people who hold the keys or know the combinations refuse to surrender them until forced to under the 1966 Freedom of Information Act. That is, should they lose the court battles, which isn't very often.

Still, the fact that they are yielding, if only an inch and a document at a time, is better than last year at this time. But even if these files will one day all be thrown open for us to look at, there's no guarantee that they will contain all the necessary information with which to finally get at the truth of what really happened up to, during and after that fateful November 22, 1963. For in conspiracies, you see, no records are ever kept.

The murder of the 35th President of the United States appears to have been the result of a conspiracy. It is something we shall probably never be able to prove to everyone's satisfaction. But if the murder wasn't a conspiracy, its investigation was, and its certification by the late Chief Justice, Earl Warren, was a palpable fraud.

The Government sought to "explain" the crime, not to "solve" it. There was no way it could have solved so monumental a crime without thoroughly compromising its own law-enforcement agencies. The approach defied all the established rules of criminal investigation—not so much in the casual bending of eyewitness testimony or in the sloppiness of the autopsy or ballistics research, as in the callous, cynical attempt to pervert the truth.

The Commission began with a suspect (conveniently murdered) who appeared to lack both the means and the motive to kill the President and proceeded to drape his corpse with a presumption of guilt handspun out of hearsay and innuendo. On this rickety proposition it built so shoddy a case that, under any other circumstances and at any other time, it would have been thrown out by any backwater village judge for lack of credible evidence. We swallowed it whole. The alternatives were just too unthinkable.

Unthinkable for the Government as well. Fearful that a *real* investigation, with all the stops pulled out, would reveal its sordid clandestine activities—especially those it conducted in concert with organized crime—the Government undertook a grand deception. It deliberately reversed the natural order of inquiry: instead of starting out by determining which of the victim's enemies might have had the motivation, the means and the opportunity to kill the President—and the clout with which to escape detection—it chose to grapple with the occult. The result was a massive cover-up that not only involved but has now clearly tarnished the very highest levels of Government.

Today, four out of five Americans will no longer buy the verdict that Lee Harvey Oswald shot and killed John F. Kennedy. According to a 1975 Cambridge Survey Research poll, only 18% still cling to the "lone assassin" conclusion reached in September 1964 by The President's Commission to Investigate the Assassination of President Kennedy—the so-called Warren Commission. Fifty-one percent feel Kennedy was killed by "a conspiracy", and 13% feel the CIA was part and parcel of that conspiracy. Not exactly reassuring thoughts as we enter the third century of American progress.

To the millions of Americans who first came to political maturity during the brief Kennedy years, the assassination was and continues to be the watershed of their lives. Few will ever forget precisely where they were and what they were doing when the first news bulletins came in from Dallas that Friday afternoon. It was an event so traumatic, so profoundly wrenching, that its impact shattered political barriers. Even those who despised Kennedy, and there were many, were moved in the aftermath.

In its way, the New Frontier was a mirage, a brief, exciting interlude between the dull grayness of the Eisenhower years and the volatile divisiveness of a decade of Lyndon Johnson and Richard Nixon. It was a romantic, ephemeral period of much hope, great promise—and empty rhetoric. The political bedrock was found to be barren.

Lyndon Johnson pledged continuance—but of what? He rammed through a spate of civil rights and social welfare bills in memory of the slain King of Camelot. But there was no way he could stem the tide of seething black militancy that came out of anger and frustration. Johnson further activated Kennedy's promise to "let every nation know that we shall pay any price, bear any burden, meet any hardship to assure the survival and success of liberty." After all, the license to intervene in Vietnam had been issued during the Kennedy Administration. It had been good for travel to Cuba, and it would also be used in the Dominican Republic.

Nonetheless, Dallas remains for most of us the end of The American Dream—the dividing line between the best of times and the worst of times. It would take about a year for the realization to set in—the time the Government took to bank and default on two hundred years of accumulated public respect bordering on veneration. Say what you will about Watergate and all of the assorted "White House Horrors" that have surfaced in its backwash. The alienation of the American voter began years before Nixon began contaminating the nation.

If any justification is needed for re-opening the JFK case, look no further than the dismal voter turnout during the 1974 Congressional elections. Nixon was gone, banished to San Clemente, yet of the 141 million Americans eligible to vote, only 62% had bothered to register, and less than 45% of these actually shuffled off to the polls. And if the Government persists in disparaging the assassination/conspiracy movement as a misguided Children's Crusade, it should be reminded that after all the hue and cry for lowering the voting age to 18, only 21% of the new eligibles bothered to vote. We may well be in for a long siege of minority presidents and unrepresentative legislators.

The voters are plainly troubled. To Senator Richard S. Schweiker of Pennsylvania, one of a growing handful of Congressmen who want to re-open the case, it's "a big, public boil that's going to burst," and the Warren Report "a house of cards that's going to collapse."

This much is sure: in the eyes of most of its citizens, the Government of the United States stands indicted for first degree perfidy. That it persists in copping a plea that whatever it did was done in the "national interest" is an obscenity that must be called.

That excuse may have been valid for a short time afterwards, when there was a genuine fear that the assassination was perhaps the first round of an international *coup d'etat* engineered by "foreign powers"—Russia, Cuba, or Red China. But as we now know from reading various political memoirs and all those declassified documents the FBI and CIA have been forced to release lately, before another week had passed, Johnson had been completely reassured: the assassination had been planned not in Moscow, or Havana or Peking. It was a home-grown affair.

In December of 1974, the day after he was fired by his chief, William E. Colby, a high-ranking CIA official named James Jesus Angleton was bluntly asked by newsmen: was the CIA "involved" in the assassination?

Angleton could have laughed. He could have shot back, "are you mad?" But no. Cryptically, and in a line that might have jumped from the pen of John LeCarre, this veteran of The Company's lethal services branch replied: "There were many rooms in the mansion. I was not privy to who struck John."

My God! "Who struck John." Who *would* strike John?

The list of potential suspects was long, but it would start with certain CIA agents at Langley. Long before Kennedy assumed the Presidency, CIA agents had been quietly running amok, defying a succession of presidents and quite possibly, its own hierarchy. "A rogue elephant," Senator Frank Church would call the agency in 1975. As we shall see, it had made its compact with the Mafia long before Cuba became a national obsession. It would shock the American public to realize that the two organizations were not strange bedfellows at all, but shared a commonality of interests. Harrison Salisbury, in an article in *Penthouse* magazine, described it as "a true brotherhood—one for all and all for one—except that, in the clutch, alas, everyone is expendable."

Certainly that included the President of the United States. And perhaps even his brother, the Attorney General. For the Kennedy brothers reached the top with more enemies than even they might have imagined. And they compounded the number during the next one thousand days.

John and Robert Kennedy interacted to try and reshape the country in their image. In the process, they managed to arouse just about every single powerful pressure bloc that preferred the *status quo*.

Where John Kennedy tussled with the "military/industrial complex," Robert Kennedy rumbled with organized crime and the rackets-infested Teamsters of his arch-enemy, James R. Hoffa.

John Kennedy urged Defense Secretary Robert S. McNamara to try to reassert civilian control over the Pentagon and called upon Congress to end the 27.5% oil depletion allowance that—had Congress passed the bill, which it didn't—could have cost the Texas oil barons at least $1.4 billion a year in additional taxes.

Bob Kennedy had begun to overhaul the Justice Department for an all-out war on the Mafia, launching organized Strike Force after organized Strike Force, and bringing the list of Mafia figures scheduled for prosecution up to 2,000 and more. More often than not, he would dispense with the niceties of constitutional law by illegally deporting "alien" *capos*, indulging in wiretaps without court order and other extra-legal activities. J. Edgar Hoover of the FBI was not impressed; he'd always felt the enemy was not within but in Moscow. Jimmy Hoffa vowed to kill the Attorney General. So did one of the deportees, New Orleans Mafia boss Carlos Marcello who, upon returning to the U.S. to successfully contest the order, was said to have screamed: "*Livarsa na petra di la scarpa!*" or "Get that stone out of my shoe!" Marcello, who was closely linked with the anti-Castro Cuban exiles, also said, "Don't worry about that little Bobby son-of-a-bitch. He's gonna be taken care of."

Jack Kennedy, meanwhile, was infuriating the generals, admirals and the spooks of Langley as he found the suit of the eternal cold warrior too confining. Burned by the Bay of Pigs fiasco and checkmated by Castro in the ensuing "secret war" on Cuba (of which more later), he met Khrushchev eyeball-to-eyeball during the October 1962 missile crisis and called the game a tie. He would recognize Fidel Castro as the legitimate head of the Cuban government—which meant no return to Havana for either the CIA's rag-tag army of partisans or the disenfranchised casino operators of the Mafia. He engineered the first workable nuclear test ban treaty with the Soviets. Seven weeks before his death, he had McNamara come to the South Portico of the White House and there announce to the press that the Administration would be recalling the first 1,000 of some 16,500 military advisors that were then in Vietnam. His aide, Kenny O'Donnell, later recalled JFK was—in Kennedy's own words—"prepared to take the risk of unpopularity" by effecting a total Vietnam withdrawal by the end of 1965 and then trying for *rapprochement* with Mao Tse-tung and Chou En-lai.

Whom had the Kennedy brothers not offended? But were these offenses so great as to warrant assassination? Rogue elephants and other animals do not reason.

Who struck John? While it is highly inconceivable that the CIA as an institution had its hand in the killing, no such assurances can be extended on behalf of individual CIA contract employees, past or present. In fact, it now seems highly probable that a number of aberrant agents, deeply involved in the Cuban situation, may have gone off half-cocked. And that, upon realizing that probability, John McCone and his key CIA hierarchs laid down a massive cover-up blanket—even to the extent of trying to wash their hands of the early Lee Harvey Oswald's entire Russian adventure.

And if only the CIA had the clout and the means with which to undertake so vast a "protective reaction," then it is equally certain that only its partners-in-crime, the Mafia, had the machinery to take on the operation with such surgical precision, leaving the motive to its anti-Castro Cuban wards. The fiery Cubans could well have conceived the idea, but only the mob had the experience to set it in motion, and see to it that in the aftermath, sufficient dust and doubt would be generated to send investigators off, groping in the wrong direction. Thus, we now know that even Lyndon Johnson was convinced that the Cubans were involved—but *Castro*'s Cubans, not ours.

Logic, in short, played no role in this particular crime. Thus, there is another school of thought that believes JFK's murder may actually have been the means to a greater end: the elimination of Attorney General Robert Kennedy. To these theorists, it's the only "logical" explanation for the Mafia's possible role in the assassination. For the mob to have shot RFK outright while his brother survived in the White House would have quite literally unleashed the full might of the United States against organized crime. The ensuing bloodbath would have been unimaginable. But by killing the President first, this reasoning goes, the Attorney General would have been effectively neutralized, his anti-crime campaign dismantled. Which, of course, is precisely what did happen soon after the assassination. "Bobby Kennedy," exulted Hoffa on November 24, "is just another lawyer now."

Another theory, in which logic plays little part, is that the two invisible brotherhoods—Mafia and CIA—got together as a means to overthrow Castro and recapture Cuba. This makes a little more sense, incredible as the scenario may seem. That faction within the CIA that seems to have grown critical of the Kennedy administration was the very group that "ran" the Cuban exiles, before, during and after the Bay of Pigs operation. When it was denied further Government support following the resolution of the missile crisis, it looked to the Mafia and other extremists for the required monetary and logistical aid. To the Mafia, these renegade CIA men might yet pull it off. What was needed was a provocation that would enrage the United States into launching a second strike at Cuba—this time with its full military might totally committed. Which may explain the necessity of Lee Harvey Oswald, professed pro-Castro propagandist, ex-Marine turncoat, suspected *agent-provocateur*. With the mob providing the manpower and the hardware, and the spooks providing the scapegoat, the plan could hardly miss.

Ironically, the reason it did fail was that Lyndon Johnson conjured up a different kind of scenario, suspecting CIA duplicity, and convened the Warren Commission without telling Warren what he suspected. In its eagerness to provide LBJ with a *prima facie* case against Oswald, the Commission searched for a palatable political truth. It rejected political motive and attributed Oswald's act to sheer mindlessness. But in finding Oswald guilty, it had to exonerate Dr. Castro. And once that was done, there was no longer any reason to attack Cuba.

Of course, all this is in the realm of speculation, where it must remain until such a time as we are given a more believable accounting than we have received up to now. Therefore, we are still just about where we were in late 1964, playing with what little we know—and all that we can only suspect—on the chance that by moving enough of

24

the pieces around long enough, the puzzle may no longer seem so puzzling. The problem, of course, is that the puzzle is incomplete: the Government is holding some of the pieces. Others that they have let go don't quite fit.

Let us therefore begin with what we do know to be established and incontrovertible fact:

• That at about 12:30 p.m., CST, on Friday, November 22, 1963, as their motorcade was passing in front of the Texas School Book Depository on Dealey Plaza, the President, his wife Jacqueline, and their hosts, Governor and Mrs. John B. Connally Jr., were caught in a fusillade of rifle fire. The President was mortally wounded, the Governor critically. One half hour later, at nearby Parkland Hospital, chief neurosurgeon Dr. William Kemp Clark pronounced the President dead. Emergency life-saving procedures had been futile for Kennedy. Connally survived and resumed an active political life.

• That at the precise moment of impact, Lee Harvey Oswald, hired the month before as a laborer in the Depository, was either perched in the southeast corner of the sixth floor, firing his gun (the Government's version), or standing in the doorway of the Depository's main entrance, watching the motorcade (according to eyewitnesses and photographic evidence). Oswald was a former U.S. Marine who had defected to Russia and had returned the year before. Less than two hours after the shooting, he was arrested at a movie house, not for killing the President but for murdering a Dallas policeman, Officer Jefferson Davis Tippit. (The Kennedy charge would come later that day.) When arrested, the Dallas police

25

said, the suspect was carrying a snub-nosed .38 calibre pistol and false identification cards for an Alek J. Hidell, a non-existent person.

• That Jack L. Ruby, the 51-year-old stripjoint owner who was to kill Oswald on November 24, in full view of 70 cops, 65 newsmen and a coast-to-coast television audience, claimed to have been blocks away from the assassination scene, placing a classified newspaper ad. But a famous photo, cropped by the Warren Commission, shows him standing outside of the Depository, either during or moments after the assassination. He was also seen right afterwards at Parkland Hospital for reasons unknown (only suspected). Ruby, who died in jail in January 1967, was not the harmless, bumbling character he made himself out to be, but a member of the Dallas underworld, an occasional police informer, and bagman for the anti-Castro partisans in the Dallas-Fort Worth area.

• That Officer Tippit's movements seemed to be rather suspicious at that particular time. Even before the first radio alert went out, Tippit had been cruising four miles from Dealey Plaza. At 12:45 his dispatcher instructed Tippit to proceed to Oak Cliff and "to be at large for any emergency that might arise". His last word to central was at 12:54. He was "moving into position". Thereafter silence. At 1:00 p.m. the dispatcher tried to contact Tippit, but there was no acknowledgement; at 1:08 Tippit tried to contact the dispatcher but this time there was no answer at the other end. Minutes thereafter, Tippit was shot dead, about one mile from Oswald's rooming house. There were scores of eyewitnesses, some of whom saw two men, one tall, one short. None could reliably pull Oswald out of the line-up. The ballistics tests were equally inconclusive.

• That the alleged assassination weapon, an eccentric Italian-made war surplus Mannlicher-Carcano 6.5 mm. bolt action rifle with scope (known to the Italian Army as "Il Umanio" or "the humanitarian" gun for its lack of power and accuracy), had been ordered on March 13, 1963, by a man in Dallas named A. Hidell, who enclosed a U.S. Post Office money order (#2202130462) in the amount of $21.45, including postage and handling. The mail order was in response to a magazine ad taken out in *The American Rifleman* by Klein's Sporting Goods Inc. of Chicago. On March 20, the gun #C2766 was shipped to Hidell c/o Dallas post office box 2915. There was no signed receipt indicating it had ever been picked up. The post office box had been taken out on October 9, 1962, by Oswald, but an FBI report states, "Our investigation has revealed that Oswald did not indicate on his application that others, including an 'A. Hidell', would receive mail through the box in question." We now also know that according to postal inspector Harry D. Holmes, the law firmly states that records on all post office boxes *must* be kept for two years after a box is closed. In this one instance, the records were thrown away "accidentally" right after Oswald closed the box on May 14, 1963.

And we know—though the Warren Commission didn't mention it—that there could have been any number of Mannlicher-Carcanos with the number C2766, since the Italian manufacturer did not brand the rifles with individual serial numbers.

• Now, of course, we also know that on November 12—ten days before the assassination—Oswald was supposed to have delivered a "threatening note" to thirty-five-year-old Special Agent James Patrick Hosty, Jr., who had apparently been keeping an eye on Oswald's Russian-born wife Marina. Two hours after Ruby killed Oswald, Dallas FBI head Shanklin ordered the note destroyed. Hosty flushed it down the toilet.

In late October 1975, three months after the story first broke in the Dallas papers, FBI officials said the note read, "Let this be a warning. I will blow up the FBI and the Dallas Police department if you don't stop bothering my wife." But agent Hosty, who had been demoted after his 1964 appearance before the Warren Commission and transferred to Kansas City, recalls it as much milder: "If you have anything you want to learn about me, come talk to me directly. If you don't cease bothering my wife, I will take appropriate action and report this to proper authorities." Both versions sound suspicious in light of the note's inexplicable destruction; more so because the FBI admitted it contained no threat on Kennedy's life.

(Some say the order to destruct came either from Hosty's superior, Dallas bureau head J. Gordon Shanklin, or *his* boss, FBI chief of administration John P. Mohr, acting on instructions from J. Edgar Hoover. Hoover is dead, Shanklin and Mohr are retired, and Hosty is sticking to his story. William C. Sullivan, the FBI's #3 man until Hoover forced his premature retirement in 1970 after a falling out, thinks more than just this letter was destroyed.)

With the FBI and other law-enforcement agencies going about burying or destroying evidence, it is no wonder we know as little as we do.

For that we may blame, among others, Johnson and Warren. It was they who mandated that certain documents pertaining to the case should not be seen "in our lifetimes". Their lifetimes or ours? They are dead and we are not. Only God knows how many *other* papers, not accounted for in any inventory, have been stashed away by the FBI, CIA, ONI, NSA and the countless other agencies who might have had a hand in the investigation—their existence unknown perhaps even to their present directors. Intelligence, after all, is a highly compartmentalized craft, and those who speak darkly of some tight-knit "intelligence community" are victims of their own paranoid cliches.

No, there is just too much in this case that defies logic, that takes it out of the ordinary realm of regicide. There's too much that we don't comprehend—too many discrepancies in the historical recapitulation, too many irrelevancies in the evidentiary research, too many contradictions and inconsistencies in the eyewitness and other testimonies, too many unexplained "coincidences".

Perhaps it's in the way these "facts" were elicited, or in the way they were finally reported by the Gilbert & Sullivan version of an "impartial" fact-finding panel.

So that, for example, we learn that when the assassin's rifle was first discovered in the Book Depository, the two police officers who found it testified it was a 7.65 mm. German-made Mauser, only to abruptly change their story a day later, raising the possibility that there may have been, in fact, *two* rifles found. Or that a switch had been made for some insidious purpose. Or that the rifle held up as the Mannlicher-Carcano measured 40.2 inches, while the one that was advertised by Klein's Sporting Goods measured 36 inches.

Or why Oswald would bother to wipe his

fingerprints off a gun that could be so easily traced—too easily—or why he would have been so stupid as to order the gun by mail in the first place, when it would have been far more intelligent to have walked into some Dallas gun store and paid cash, signing nothing.

Or why, assuming the FBI knew all along about post office box 2915, it did nothing about Oswald's *incoming* mail, such as the .38 pistol ordered in January 1963 from a Los Angeles firm, and the rifle ordered two months later. Or why, when the FBI agents received the Oswald palm-print that the Dallas police lab had taken from the rifle, it did not question the fact that the lines and loops were flat (as if taken from a police blotter) instead of distorted, as they would have been from a curled palm?

Or why, in the most celebrated murder case of the twentieth century, in which every bit of evidence counted, someone had taken Governor Connally's bullet-torn jacket and thoughtfully had it cleaned and pressed before submitting it as an exhibit? Or why neither federal, state or local investigators could find so much as a single additional 6.5 mm. bullet on Oswald's person, in his Dallas rooming house or in the garage in Irving where, the cops said, he'd stashed the gun until he was ready to use it on Kennedy?

The only bullet ever linked to the Mannlicher-Carcano, the famous "superbullet" (of which more later), was found at Parkland Hospital. Since they don't sell ammunition as they do eggs—a half-a-dozen at a time—this assassin must have covered his tracks exceedingly well. As the noted Warren Report critic, Sylvia Meagher, facetiously points out:

"Oswald squandered more than $20 of his

meager earnings for a rifle but—unwilling or unable to spend a small additional sum for ammunition—stole, borrowed or found on the street five cartridges that just happened to fit the weapon; and that those five cartridges sufficed, from March through November 1963, for dry runs, attempted murder [of retired Major General Edwin A. Walker] and successful assassination.... And that he loaded four cartridges into a clip-fed rifle which can hold seven, firing three times with such phenomenal skill as to make the fourth cartridge superfluous."

Ridicule may therefore be the only way of looking at this particular aspect of the investigation, because it's obvious that none of these explanations make much sense. And yet, so much time, and so many critiques, later, all these now seem *technical* questions that tend to confuse rather than clarify the issue of who did what to whom, when and how. For they bring us no closer to the most elusive question of all, one that the Warren Commission never really got around to asking. Namely, *why*? Not why was John F. Kennedy killed? But why would Lee Harvey Oswald want to kill him?

The answer may be inferred from posing another set of questions. Such as, how was it that within ninety minutes of the assassination, minutes after Oswald's capture, so much "evidence" had been marshalled against the accused? How was it that the Dallas Police department had access to certain vital information about Oswald that could *only* have come from the FBI—*before* the FBI ever entered the case? Thus, the first police alert, at about 12:45 p.m., described the unknown assailant as a "white male . . . slender build...height five feet, ten inches...weight 165 pounds...gray eyes"—pretty close to how the FBI dossier described Oswald. The stunning speed with which the local officials put together the case hasn't been equalled since.

And why was it necessary for the FBI to destroy the now-famous Oswald-to-Hosty letter of November 12 if it contained no threat on the President? What was *really* in that letter? Might it have confirmed the equally famous TWX of November 17—an alert the FBI ignored out of sheer laziness or indifference, which certainly *would* warrant its destruction?

If so, it would tend to confirm the belief that Oswald *was* an FBI informer—and it would, moreover, lead impartial investigators to conclude that there may have been collusion between certain FBI officials and the Dallas Police department, and between the Dallas Police department and the genial proprietor of the Carousel Club, Jack Leon Ruby. And that this might even explain the seemingly unrelated murder of Officer Tippit, who might have been lured to Tenth Street off Patton so that the conspirators might have the additional insurance of branding Oswald a "cop-killer".

The root question, though, remains the enigmatic figure of Oswald himself. We may assume he was no innocent bystander; that he was somehow caught up in the conspiracy, as an informer or as a fall guy (or "patsy", as he himself insisted after his arrest).

Until the Government deals with *this* question in a more forthright manner than it's done up to now, it will continue to enlarge the credibility gap in which demonologists thrive, spinning their wild and reckless headline-making tales that only end up impeding any kind of rational search for the truth. As Professor Mark Harris of the University of Pittsburgh recently wrote:

"The exploitation of paranoia is easy enough. It's an old political and oratorical trick, and anyone can do it whose objectives are sufficiently self-serving. Orators of conspiracy are eloquent. Why not? They are unrestrained by doubts, hesitations or the absence of facts. They have settled upon theories. They intend to qualify nothing, retract nothing, amend nothing. They charge guilt by association by means of connections from person to person, though the connections may be irrelevant even if true....Real conspiracies have occurred. But not all occurrences are conspiracies....Not all crimes are solved, as they are on television."

Another academician, Brandeis University history Professor Jacob Cohen, finds incomprehensible

"the extraordinary degree of political distrust, and beyond that, the pervasive taste for mystery and conspiracy which is everywhere so conspicuous."

He believes

"we are dealing with habits of mind...which positively revel in mystification, which do not wish to know the truth, and perhaps could not recognize it if they saw it."

Whose truth? Dr. Cohen obviously has not troubled himself to read the entire Warren Report and its contradictory appendices. One who has is Sylvia Meagher, the U.N. World Health Organization researcher who spent *years* poring through the 888-page Report and its 26 volumes of eyewitness testimony, inter-agency memoranda, photo

33

exhibits, tax returns, dental charts, truancy reports and other minutiae. Long before Watergate raised the conscience of the nation, Meagher found the lack of correlation so staggering that she wrote (in *Accessories After the Fact*):

> "the [Report] pronounces Oswald guilty; the [Appendix], instead of corroborating the verdict...creates a reasonable doubt of Oswald's guilt and even a powerful presumption of his complete innocence of all the crimes of which he was accused."

Mrs. Meagher wrote those words in 1967. Now, of course, public opinion is clearly on her side, not Cohen's, Harris' or the Government's. Conspiracy fever *has* gripped us, and it will not subside simply by throwing more cold water on the critics.

Since Watergate, people have a pretty good idea of what makes a conspiracy—two people or more. So even if it should come out one day that—yes, by God—Lee Harvey Oswald *did* fire a gun from the Depository, but that someone *else* had brought the gun in the day before, that *alone* would totally wreck the Government's carefully contrived case. It would *have* to start all over again.

Actually, as even some of its own people now suspect, the case was built on sand and, as will be noted in the next chapter, political expediency. It started with a presumption of guilt, and worked downhill from there, not merely denying the accused his posthumous constitutional rights but, in the process, perverting history by striking the word "conspiracy" from the American political dictionary.

Until the Warren Report was published, the conventional wisdom was that, in America at least, political assassinations were mostly carried out by madmen possessed by real or imagined causes. They performed acts of which they made no secret and which they would not deny when caught. With the exception of only two known conspiracies (the assassination of Abraham Lincoln in 1865 and the 1950 attempt on Truman by Puerto Rican separatists), presidential murder or attempted murder was always the act of a loner. Each had a grievance to voice, including the Lincoln and Truman plotters and the two most recent would-be assassins, Lynette (Squeaky) Fromme and Sara Jane Moore.

But not Oswald. When arrested, he carried no petition, issued no proclamation, offered no shopping list of complaints against the system and its leader he had just eliminated. No John Wilkes Booth, he. No cry of *"Sic Semper Tyrannis!"* from him. Merely a cry to the cops and bystanders of "I am not resisting arrest, I am not resisting arrest."

And afterwards, in a city where—as Meagher so trenchantly points out—"his political convictions [as an admitted Marxist-Trotskyite with pro-Castro leanings] were perhaps more damning than the crime of assassination", Oswald did nothing to hide or deny his past. Quite the contrary, he directed his captors to his wife's residence where they would find all his personal possessions, including such incriminating evidence as the famous Commission Exhibit 133-A— the photo showing Oswald posing with the Mannlicher-Carcano—and negatives of what the cops said were forged Selective Service and U.S. Marine Corps cards in the name of Hidell.

Another critic, former CIA man George O'Toole, observes (in *The Assassination Tapes*):

"He could have drafted [a manifesto] and mailed it to the press on the morning of

November 22.... He could have carried it on his person and gone out in a blaze of glory by barricading himself in the Book Depository and shooting it out with the police and FBI. He could have surrendered himself to a local newspaper or television station where he would have received an immediate forum."

He most certainly could have done so during that extraordinary midnight "press conference" the Dallas Police arranged that night. He'd obviously been beaten by the arresting officers: his face was bruised and puffy. His hands manacled, he'd just undergone non-stop interrogation by a platoon of cops, Secret Service and FBI agents. He'd been charged with Tippit's murder (but not yet with Kennedy's). He'd been denied legal counsel, even so much as the nicety of a single phone call to his wife. This was serious, heavy stuff.

Yet, he showed not the slightest amount of fear, nervousness or whatever else one experiences in such a similar situation. Without so much as a tremor in his voice, he told reporters, "I positively know nothing about this situation here." Earlier, he'd told his interrogators that he liked the Kennedys ("they are interesting people") and that he certainly was no "malcontent".

His conduct during the interrogation, at the press conference, and afterwards, was not that of a wild-eyed, defiant anarchist, but of a bewildered, somewhat obsequious, not terribly bright individual who apparently knew his legal rights and expected eventually to be rescued by someone, or if not that, at least given a trial where he would surely be exonerated of whatever dreadful charges these people had brought against him. Newsmen who were there were struck by the appearance of genuine shock when he was finally told of the assassination charges.

And the next day, visited by his mother Marguerite and his older brother Robert, and told that the "evidence" against him was overwhelming, Oswald said, "Do not form any opinion on the so-called evidence". As his brother would later recall before the Warren Commission:

> "All the time we were talking, I searched his eyes for any sign of guilt or whatever you call it. There was nothing there—no guilt, no shame, no nothing. Lee, finally aware of my looking into his eyes, said, "You will not find anything there."'

At midnight, Oswald coolly told reporters:

> "I would like to have legal representation. . . . I really don't know what this situation is all about. Nobody has told me anything except that I'm accused of murdering a policeman. I know nothing more than that. I do request someone to come forward and give me legal assistance."

Through an intermediary—his wife's great and good friend, Ruth Hyde Paine (whom we'll meet later)—Oswald, the next day, asked to get hold of noted American Civil Liberties Union lawyer John Abt, but Abt could not be reached. By this time, he obviously perceived he was in a police trap, that no Dallas lawyer would be of much help. He told Secret Service Inspector Thomas J. Kelley he would only talk in the presence of a lawyer, but the cops may not have *wanted* him to talk. When the local ACLU people came by police headquarters and asked to represent Oswald, they were waved off with the absurd comment that "the prisoner has been informed of his rights."

This was utter nonsense, since during all of

twelve hours of interrogation, no transcript, no notes, not even a tape recording, was made. So everything the Commission would have to work with later was pure hearsay, which would have been admissible in any court of the land.

Either Oswald was a brilliant performer, or supremely convinced of his innocence. When the police finally allowed Oswald to be interviewed by H. Louis Nichols, head of the Dallas Bar Association, the prisoner implored him to intervene. "If I can find a lawyer here who believes in anything I believe in," Oswald told Nichols, "and believes as I believe, and believes in my innocence as much as he can, I might let him represent me."

Even as he lay bleeding to death slowly on the floor of the police station—unbelievably, the cops had given him artificial respiration, thus insuring his death from a gunshot wound in the stomach— he protested his innocence, shaking his head when asked for a "dying confession".

On Friday night, the reporters put it to him straight. Did you kill the President? He hadn't yet been notified. But that afternoon, as he was being arrested at the Texas Theatre, he'd heard at least one cop yell at him, "kill the President, will you?" and another tell a bystander, "we've got him on both accounts" (sic)—although *at the time*, the arresting officers were not supposed to have connected Oswald to both killings. Someone had obviously flubbed their lines.

Standing there, under the hot lights of the TV cameras, Oswald unhesitatingly answered:

"No, I have not been charged with that. In fact, nobody has said that to me yet. The first thing I heard about it was when the newspaper reporters in the hall asked me that question."

What starts out like something out of Dostoyevsky by way of Franz Kafka—the hapless, confused *petit bourgeois* trapped in some huge, governmental vise, but assured that somehow the mistake will be recognized and rectified—ends up smacking of a Len Deighton spy story with a tragic ending. *Nothing* is recognized, and the vise closes.

And Ruby, the instrument of his death, is similarly depicted—the victim of psychomotor epilepsy (according to defense lawyers Melvin Belli and Joe Tonahill), a Kennedy-lover freaked out (according to Ruby), concerned only with wanting to spare the widow Jacqueline the ordeal of having to testify at Oswald's trial. Jack Ruby also expected to be rescued. And so he was, cruelly so. His death sentence was suspended, his conviction overturned, and Ruby was only a month away from getting a new trial well outside of the Dallas jurisdiction from where, it was assumed, he would walk away, a free man. Then he too died. During the fall of 1966, Ruby was dying, but his jailers called him a malingerer and refused to give him needed medical attention. It turned out that he'd been suffering not from psychomotor epilepsy or concern for the First Family, but from a cluster of brain tumors that had metastasized, with death brought on by a blood clot in the leg.

We still don't know the whole truth about Ruby, of whether he pulled the trigger out of a misguided desire to be universally proclaimed as the avenger, or on specific orders from persons unknown. By the time the Warren Commission got down to asking him what was what, Ruby had already become spaced out. During his trial, according to Dallas newsman Gary Cartwright, writing in the *Texas Observer*, "he was forced to sit as a silent exhibit while psychiatrists called him a latent homosexual with a compulsive desire to be liked and respected." Cartwright in 1975 wrote of a talk he had with Joe Tonahill, Ruby's defense counsel. Recalled Tonahill:

> "In the beginning, Ruby considered himself a hero. He thought he had done a great service for the community. When the mayor...testified that the act brought disgrace to Dallas, Jack started going downhill very fast. He got more nervous by the day. When they brought in the death penalty, he cracked. Ten days later he rammed his head into a cell wall. Then he tried to kill himself with an electric light socket. Then he tried to hang himself with sheets."

Tonahill doesn't believe to this day that there was a conspiracy ("that's a bunch of crap") but Ruby obviously became convinced there *was*, and that part of it was directed at him as a Jew and as a scapegoat.

In June 1964, interviewed in the Dallas County Jail by Chief Justice Earl Warren and Congressman Gerald R. Ford—one of the Warren Commissioners—Ruby told them flat out that as long as he remained in Dallas, he could not talk.

> "Gentlemen, unless you get me to Washington you can't get a fair shake out of me. If you understand my way of talking, you have got to bring me to Washington."

But neither Warren nor Ford would rise. Justice Warren mumbled something about there being too many "procedural details" involved in such a transfer, conveniently forgetting that Congress had empowered the Commission to subpoena witnesses to Washington, if needed. He told Ruby he would "think it over" and see if "something could be done," to which Ruby replied, all too prophetically:

> "Well, you won't ever see me again, I tell you that....Maybe certain people don't want to know the truth that may come out of me. Is that plausible?"

It certainly was. And still is.

Is it any wonder that reasoned doubt *had* to give way to collective paranoia? Author Norman Mailer, not the most sober or reasoned of the assassinologists, ten years after the assassination compared the obsessed critic of the Warren Report to a jealous lover who, "in his affliction, careens between the two extremes of hating his unfaithful wife for her unspeakable conduct and hating himself for his unspeakable imaginings."

The Government's conduct up to now has clearly been unspeakable. Perhaps Earl Warren should have prevailed when he argued against publishing the 26-volume Appendix on grounds of economy. For the two months between the publication of the Warren Report and the release of the Appendices, we were all willing to believe its conclusions. But then, starting in 1965, what the *Wall Street Journal* had hailed as "a believable detective story—a tale told not to entertain but to persuade," fell apart before our very eyes.

One couldn't go back to the authors: in indecent haste, the Commission had disbanded, its offices closed, its files locked up. The publisher, the Superintendent of Documents hid behind the Great Seal of the United States and shrugged off all responsibility as if to say, "don't blame us, we're just the printers." There was no one to explain the overwhelming number of discrepancies, no one to hold accountable except the ubiquitous Government.

The Government, in all its myopic majesty, thus created the assassination/conspiracy movement, and for the longest time, has seemed determined to accord it perpetual life.

Unlike the "Society of the Friends of King Richard III," organized 450 years *after* his death by history buffs seeking, they say, to redress the calumny heaped upon their hero, the last of England's Plantagenets, the society of the latter day friends of Lee Harvey Oswald is far less frivolous in its quest.

It maintains that the Government, having conducted a legal lynching, is now obligated to make available *acceptable* proof in support of its verdict, or if unable to do so, the exculpating evidence that Oswald didn't do it. Until this is done, the critics feel, you might as well suspend presidential elections.

The Kennedy assassination, they say, based on the "evidence," could not have been the solitary act of a desperate madman. It had all the characteristics of a conspiracy, and conspiracies of this magnitude have a way of disrupting the electoral process. And they make a pretty good case for the argument that the last three presidential elections were really decided by bullets, not ballots.

Lyndon Johnson in 1964 was the incumbent-by-murder. There was simply no way Barry Goldwater could have campaigned against the ghost of John F. Kennedy. It was a forlorn, quixotic try, and he knew it, which may explain his kamikaze slogan of "extremism in the pursuit of liberty is no vice." And the 1968 campaign may have, in fact, been decided as early as April 4, with the assassination of Dr. Martin Luther King and the ensuing ghetto riots, the birth of the "law 'n order" approach and the Lazarus-like reappearance of Richard M. Nixon. Any question of his ultimate triumph was settled in June, with the murder of front-running Democratic candidate Robert F. Kennedy, and the lamentable Chicago Convention that produced Hubert H. Humphrey's singularly inappropriate "politics of joy". And the 1972 election, as we remember all too clearly, was decided not so much by George McGovern's ineptitude or Edmund S. Muskie's tears as by Arthur Bremer's shooting of Governor George C. Wallace and CREEP's Donald Segretti and his "rat-fuckers."

Ten days before the shooting at Laurel, Md., the Gallup election polls had shown Nixon dropping to 44% of the popular vote, McGovern moving up to 41%, and Wallace holding 13%—the swing conservative vote that could either cost or clinch Nixon the election.

Now, with a riled-up Congress pressing for answers to questions nobody has asked for the longest time, the Government may no longer be so quick to denigrate the Original True Disbelievers as dingbat heretics, or "assassination freaks". Some may be, but most are not.

A year ago, before Sam (Momo) Giancana had his last midnight snack and before the Abraham Zapruder film was finally seen by a network TV audience, the critics were generally thought of as just that, members of a toothless Dealey Plaza Debating Society. Now, with the FBI beginning to yield a little, and the CIA yielding a lot, the Government may actually be looking for some sort of accommodation by which it will give the critics what they want without the Government's having to lose face in the process.

Thus, on the twelfth anniversary of Dallas,

former Warren Commission staff attorney David W. Belin—the movement's most aggressive and intractable antagonist—executed a surprising pirouette. After years of insisting there was no need to do so, he now called upon Congress to reopen the inquiry and for the Government to unlock the files in order to "restore trust and faith". Like so many other of Belin's public statements, this one, too, was artfully contrived.

It could hardly be a coincidence of timing that Belin would find religion the day after the Senate Intelligence Committee released its long-awaited, 347-page indictment of the CIA's "Mongoose" assassination program—a report, incidentally, made necessary by Belin's pointed failure, as Executive Director of the Rockefeller Commission, to get at the truth the first time around.

Now, Belin seemed to say, in light of that report, Dallas might very well turn out to have been a conspiracy; even so, a re-inquiry would still support the original Warren Commission conclusion that Oswald acted alone to kill JFK.

Disingenuous. Since we're a nation of headline readers, with little time or patience to read the entire story, Belin suddenly seemed the most reasonable of counter-critics: "Warren Commission Aide Calls for New Inquiry." And people might now forget his persistent name-calling of the critics as "grubby sensation-seekers," and might even overlook his disreputable tactics as head of the Rockefeller panel.

Early in 1975, he sought to once again discredit the entire movement, this time by feigning to respond to charges that the CIA might have had a hand in the killing. Instead of seriously studying the new evidence, he artfully directed his people to disprove "evidence" that Watergate conspirators

E. Howard Hunt and Frank (Fiorini) Sturgis were in Dealey Plaza masquerading as tramps at the time of the assassination. The fact that the "evidence"—the photos of the "Dealey Plaza Tramps"—had been bandied about the underground press by the Yippies and other kooks suited Belin's purposes just fine. By purporting to take these absurd photos seriously so as to knock them down and out, Belin figured to restore the public's sagging faith in the Warren Report's veracity.

But the effort was too heavy-handed, too blatant, too clumsy. It only made the Rockefeller Commission look twice as silly for having resorted to such a shallow subterfuge. And it is in this light that one must now interpret Belin's latest gambit: not a reasoned quest for accommodation but a clever attempt to extricate himself from the political limb onto which he'd climbed. The best defense is always offense.

As for the other side—the critics—this time they want to proceed with a great deal more care than the last time their challenges aroused the Government to intervene. That was back in 1967-8, during the so-called "Garrison Affair".

In December 1963, a few weeks after the assassination, the office of New Orleans District Attorney Earling Carothers (Jim) Garrison got wind of "a very unusual type of person who made a very curious trip at a very curious time"—from New Orleans to Ft. Worth the night before the assassination. The name of this person was David William Ferrie. This bizarre-looking man—totally hairless from a disease called alopecia—was not easily a victim of mistaken identity: he wore a red mohair wig which he glued to his scalp with plastic cement. His large and uneven "eyebrows" were painted on with greasepaint. But this clown-like appearance belied the man within: a bi-lingual dangerous oddball who'd been thrown out of the priesthood, the Civil Air Patrol and Eastern Airlines for various kinky sexual perversions; who'd then turned to pornography, private-eye work, a private religious mysticism and cancer research—an eccentric Jack-of-all-trades, master of none.

But he was also something else. Garrison's office had learned he was a CIA contract employee, who'd flown in the Bay of Pigs invasion, and who afterwards had become mixed up with the anti-Castro Cubans as a paramilitary instructor in secret training camps in St. Tammany's Parish. And when Garrison learned that Oswald had served with Ferrie in the CAP, and that Ferrie had gone to Ft. Worth before the assassination and returned to New Orleans the following day, he ordered Ferrie held for the FBI. Only the FBI didn't seem to want Ferrie; it insisted he be let go.

Four years later, largely at the urging of Senator Russell B. Long and a group of fifty New Orleans businessmen (incorporated as Truth and Consequences Inc.), Garrison decided to move against Ferrie. He felt he had enough hard evidence to link him to organized crime and the CIA and with which to force Ferrie to talk about the assassination. But hours before Garrison was to formally charge Ferrie and bring an indictment against him, the prime suspect was found dead in his hotel apartment. The coroner said death was from a cerebral hemorrhage but Garrison suspected suicide or foul play.

Enter a 25-year-old Baton Rouge insurance salesman, Perry Raymond Russo, with a penchant for fantasy. His lurid revelations, true or not, triggered an investigation that ran for over a year, and resembled a Barnum & Bailey circus featuring the Spanish Inquisition. Charging that the "American Power Elite had a vested interest in creating historical mythology," Garrison weaved his own. He implicated Maj. Gen. Charles P. Cabell, whom Kennedy had fired as Deputy Director of the CIA after the Bay of Pigs, maintaining that Cabell (whose grandfather and father both had been Sheriffs of Dallas, and whose brother Earl was mayor of Dallas in November 1963) had orchestrated the breakdown of presidential security. He named Richard Helms and accused him—most presciently, it now appears—of having turned the CIA into a *domestic* warfare unit.

But it wasn't until he trained his guns on an effete New Orleans businessman, Clay L. Shaw, that he over-reached himself. Shaw, former director of the New Orleans International Trade Mart and a prominent member of the city's Establishment, was fingered by Garrison's weird "sources" as a CIA executive and the mastermind behind the assassination. Garrison promised he would show the world that this fey and mysterious man was at the core of a cabal involving Texas oil barons, Cuban sugar tycoons, the ex-Nazi rocket experts of NASA, and all others interested in the elevation of Lyndon Johnson. Mind-boggling as this skein was to begin with, it would grow even more absurd by the time Garrison managed to indict Clay Shaw.

For his "raw data", Garrison and his investigators would come to depend on the demonologists who flocked to New Orleans from all over the country, eager to stoke the fires of paranoia. It was to be expected, therefore, that the entire case would end up jerry-built on links, coils and conundrums. And as things got out of hand, and Garrison sensed it, he unhappily lapsed into demagoguery, citing chapter and verse from "documents" he had not seen nor could he produce.

A compliant press went along, selling papers and catering to the American public's insatiable appetite for "facts". But when those "facts" had to be weighed by a jury of Shaw's peers, they found them badly wanting, and so acquitted Clay L. Shaw.

Where Garrison had set out with the quite-logical premise that everything argued against Oswald's lone "act of madness", therefore demanding the presence of more than one other gunman, before long two gunmen had become sixteen, with the conspiracy so ubiquitous as to make the July 20, 1944 plot on Hitler's life an innocent escapade of a few misguided generals. And when a few doubters began making themselves heard over the wild charges coming out of New Orleans, Garrison self-destructed. He saw massive Government-inspired "counterplots" directed against him personally. At that point, he'd crossed the line. The public clicked off, just as it had thirteen years earlier after Wisconsin's Senator Joseph R. McCarthy finally short-circuited its overloaded critical faculties.

The media, which had left town when Ferrie died, and then returned after Garrison had unleashed his demons, now turned on the D.A. Hell hath no fury like a conman conned: the reporters tore into the movement with unrestrained bitchiness, calling the critics "scavengers" and worse. A typical response was that of *Newsweek* (which, by its current coverage, seems not to have forgiven past transgressions).

"...the assassination industry's products would never stand the scrutiny of Consumer's

Union. Consumers buy its products as they buy most trash: the package promises satisfaction but the innards are mostly distortions, unsupported theories and gaping omissions."

Which is precisely what the critics have been saying all along about the Warren Report.

Garrison, who set out looking for the truth, suffered the consequences. Having trampled the sensitivities of the CIA and the FBI, it was inevitable that with the Nixon Administration now in power, he would get his due. In July 1971, the Justice Department set after him on trumped-up charges of having taken bribes from pinball-machine operators, and the following year, the IRS hit him with income-tax evasion (on the purported bribery "income"). Garrison easily beat both raps, but by then, the voters had tired of their flamboyant District Attorney, and turned him out of office.

The irony, of course, is that the early Jim Garrison may have been on the right track, even if Ferrie's untimely death sent his investigation careening into limbo. Interestingly, the long FBI interview with Ferrie on November 24 is one of the few documents still embargoed at the National Archives. Its contents might conceivably dovetail with the recent remarks by defected CIA agent Victor Marchetti to the effect that Helms seemed more than routinely interested in the Garrison investigation, and that at Langley he'd been informed that David Ferrie had at one time been a CIA contract employee, and that Shaw was still on the payroll. We know for a fact that New Orleans was a principal CIA base of operations for the Caribbean; we also know Ferrie was closely allied with Mafia kingpin Carlos Marcello and with Guy Bannister, former head of the FBI's Chicago field office and CIA operative during the 1954 Guatemalan coup, and that Bannister was involved with the far-right Minutemen and that, according to one unsubstantiated report, after Bannister's death his widow found a desk-drawer full of Oswald's Hands-off-Cuba leaflets. Last of all, we know that the dark allusions linking the CIA to the Mafia and the Cubans—links that no one took seriously back in 1967 and 1968—have now born bitter fruit.

Garrison still believes he was onto something, still believes the reason the CIA "is now willing to 'fess up to smaller crimes is to keep us from seeing the biggest crime of all."

Perhaps. Perhaps Garrison is right when he insists that "if outsiders—people outside of the Government—had really done this, the Government of the United States would have been far more aggressive in hunting down the killers. Pinning it on Oswald was too easy, *too* easy."

To be sure, there is a case to be made for what Mark Harris calls "the momentum or accident of history". It could well be that it was fate that brought Jack Kennedy together with Lee Harvey Oswald that November noon on Dealey Plaza. But was it also fate that drew Jack Ruby to Parkland Hospital just after they brought in the President's moribund body, perhaps to casually drop that 6.5 mm. Mannlicher-Carcano bullet in the stretcher area where some attendant would be sure to find it? Was it just an accident that Oswald's transfer from the city to the county jail was delayed by one hour and twenty minutes? What sort of momentum drew Oswald to New Orleans just around the time that the CIA, by its own admission, had lost control of "its" Cubans and their CIA overseers?

It's hard to believe this was all some sort of grotesque accident of history in which human calculation played no part whatsoever. Why is it, for example, that at no point during the entire ten months of deliberation, did the Warren Commission ever once openly discuss the possibility of a "Cuban Connection"? Why is it that during the entire time Oswald was in custody, from 1:51 p.m., Friday, November 22, to the time he died at 1:07 p.m., Sunday, November 24, there isn't one scrap of paper to tell us what the man told his captors?

One does not have to be paranoid to sense the possibility of calculated deceit on the part of the various authorities. This would evolve into a pattern with the way the Government and the State of Tennessee handled Dr. King's accused assassin, James Earl Ray. Or later, the disposition of the Sirhan Bishara Sirhan and Arthur Bremer cases.

In all four instances, crucial records were withheld or locked away; evidence conveniently lost or destroyed; ballistics mangled; eyewitness testimony either suborned or dismissed as "mistaken"; transcripts doctored or censored. Even the assailants were gagged, or as the case may be, executed before their time.

In the two Kennedy assassinations as well as that of King and the attempt on Wallace, the authorities seemed to grope for rational explanations to apparently *ir*rational acts. In all four cases, little or no consideration was given the possibilities of (a) motive and (b) conspiracy. At least, we now know the Government's position on assassination conspiracy: it's something decadently European, a dirty word that has no place in the political language of this nation.

"All four shootings," observes scraggly New

Left theoretician Carl Oglesby, one of the charter members of The Assassination Information Bureau, the movement's *Agitprop*, "involve a lone, half-mad, disassociated radical, fuming in demented solitude, stalking his prey like in some cheap spy thriller. Each assassin has his diary, his secret notes from the underground, and each has been silent. Why?"

Another student of conspiracy is Professor Richard H. Popkin of Washington University in St. Louis. Before he, too, flaked out like Garrison—warning President Ford that the CIA has turned loose upon the land a platoon of computer-programmed robot-assassins—Popkin shrewdly observed that the Establishment in this country suffers from a "lone-nut fixation." Where is it written, asked Popkin, "that only *politicians* are killed by solitary psychopaths, while the rest—people like Jimmy Hoffa, Jock Jablonsky or Joey Gallo—are always victims of conspiracies?"

"Assassination," asserts Harold Weisberg, the dean of the critics, "is a political crime, a theft of sovereignty." As we know all too well from our own experience in Vietnam under Johnson and Nixon, assassinations invariably produce wrenching shifts in foreign policy.

But let us, for a minute, give the David Belins their due and say that the Government was right, that there was no conspiracy to kill John F. Kennedy. Can the same be said for the alleged cover-up? If there was no conspiracy cover-up, how can the Government account for its stonewalling for all these years, for the fact that its citizens have to *sue* their way into the National Archives? If everything was open and above board, and if the Oswald inquiry resulted in an open-and-shut case, why all the persistent secrecy?

Either the Government of the United States lied, or itself was lied to by the people who provided most of the raw input, the various intelligence agencies and as many as 28 other government units.

"Once a lie is floated," writes the conservative political pundit, Garry Wills, "it must be protected long after its first use has become irrelevant, if people are to believe future lies."

There will always be a need for governments to float lies if they are to function in a global society of warring ideologies. It would be naive to assume otherwise, and that as a result of Watergate and the CIA-FBI revelations of 1975, ours will henceforth be 99 and 44/100 percent pure. Unlike Ivory soap, truth doesn't always float.

So the cover-up conspiracy is still locked in place, even if it's no longer as secure. Its own people are beginning to wonder out loud if it's not time to call a halt.

Former Dallas Chief of Police Jesse E. Curry, who was in the vanguard of the Oswald lynching party, now admits, "We don't have any proof that Oswald fired the rifle, and never did. Nobody's yet been able to put him in that building with a gun in his hand."

Thank heavens for small favors. This, at least, means that in this book we will be able to spare the reader the mind-boggling exercise of having once again to go through all of the Dealey Plaza testimony—of who did or did not see "Oswald" on the sixth floor of the Book Depository—and focus instead on what happened afterwards.

Curry is not the only one. Former Dallas District Attorney Henry Menasco Wade, he of the "airtight case", now says that had Oswald lived to stand trial, he would never have been convicted, so circumstantial was the evidence. Even Gerry Ford, the most zealous of the seven Warren Commissioners in his determination to crucify Oswald, is beginning to waffle. He now favors a Congressional inquiry, although he adds, "I still believe the Report was correct—at least, to the evidence we *saw*." (ital. ours).

That evidence which was shown, recalls former Commission assistant counsel Burt W. Griffin, was capriciously selective and may *now* be considered wholly suspect. Currently a trial judge in Ohio, Griffin wants the investigation reopened because "I never thought the Dallas police were telling us the entire truth. Neither was the FBI."

Oh, now he tells us. Why didn't he speak up then? They were not the best of all possible times in which to question the wit and wisdom of J. Edgar Hoover—for any challenge of the vaunted FBI would have been interpreted as a direct assault on his simon-pure integrity. "Back in 1964," says Judge Griffin laconically, "that was something one didn't do."

Back in 1964, researcher O'Toole reminds us, Americans still revered the FBI, which was "staffed by infallible and benevolent Eagle Scouts". Less than ten years later, these same sleuths would be turned loose on the Watergate. Richard Nixon promised that it would be "the most exhaustive investigation" since Dallas. That should have been a tip-off. "The official truth," O'Toole writes, "was that the Watergate burglary was the unauthorized act of a handful of misguided zealots, a 'seven lone nuts' theory. But then, one of the zealots decided to talk, and eventually the world was given an unhurried view of the crawling colony that lives beneath the rock-like edifice of the federal government."

As Mark Lane, one of the earliest of the Warren Report critics, likes to remind his $1,500-a-shot lecture audiences, "It's no longer a question of convincing people that the Report was a fraud. They know that. They're now ready to believe almost *any* explanation, however crazy—just as long as it doesn't come from the Government."

So thank you, Mr. Nixon, for crystallizing all our doubts. The American people have at last lost their political virginity. They might have lost it sooner, of course, had they not been lulled to sleep by the pious homilies of Dwight Eisenhower, dazzled by the *elan* of Jack Kennedy and conned by the impressario of the cover-up, Lyndon Johnson.

The jig is up. It's safe to say that most Americans now feel the Government has forfeited their trust. That the Government is perfectly capable of lying, even if it doesn't have to. That the entire bureaucratic infrastructure routinely and systematically commits constitutional crimes, then denies them when caught flat-footed with the skag, and then unblinkingly proceeds to cover up not just the crimes but the cover-ups as well.

The Europeans and the Asians have been at it for centuries. It only took Americans two centuries to get wise.

FRAUD IN THE ANNALS OF MEDICINE

"This medico-legal proceeding was a tragic, tragic thing..."
—Dr. Milton Helpern
Former Medical Examiner,
City of New York

The killing took place in Dallas at around 12:30 p.m. C.S.T. The official cover-up began shortly after 8:00 p.m. E.S.T. in Bethesda, Maryland.

The purpose of an autopsy in a case of homicide is to determine how, precisely, the victim died—thus aiding the criminal investigators in reconstructing the murder, thereby making their case against the accused killer stick. If the medical findings do not sustain the assumptions of the investigators, the assumptions are invariably thrown out, and a new explanation is sought.

But in this instance, there was no room for objectivity. By the time the President's body had been flown up to Washington and sent over to the U.S. Naval Medical Center at Bethesda, the assumptions of guilt had long since been hardened into presumptions; the investigators only sought confirmation. Thus, if the autopsy had been just a little bit honest, it is conceivable that Lee Harvey Oswald might have had to be let out on bail the next morning—a most intolerable thought.

The autopsists began not just with a famous corpse but with their hands tied. The result was a travesty in established forensic medical practices, a report that was little more than a rickety concatenation of physiological absurdities.

To begin with, the two chief autopsists—Commander James J. Humes and his deputy, Commander J. Thornton Boswell—were not experts in forensic science but hospital pathologists. And the man who was called in as an afterthought to assist them—U.S. Army Colonel Pierre A. Finck—was only a provisional member of the American Academy of Forensic Sciences, and an administrator at that. Humes was the Director of Laboratories at Bethesda, and Finck, Chief of the Wound Ballistics Pathology Branch of the Pentagon's Armed Forces Institute of Pathology. Former New York City Medical Examiner Dr. Milton Helpern felt sorry for Finck, and still refers to him as having played "the role of the poor Army bastard child foisted into the Navy family reunion".

None of the three had had much experience dealing with gunshot wounds, and the victim was clearly a gunshot case. Nor were the spectators of much help, either. There were three Secret Service agents, witnesses of the assassination, Roy H. Kellerman, William R. Greer (both of whom were in the front seat), and William O'Leary (from the back-up car). Two FBI agents from the Baltimore office—James W. Sibert and Francis X. O'Neill Jr.—had not been witnesses. Later, Kellerman summoned a fourth Secret Service agent, Clinton J. Hill, to come in to look at the wounds.

Before Humes even made the first incision, eleven X-rays were taken, as were forty-five pictures. Medical photographer John T. Stringer shot twenty-two (4x5) color transparencies, eighteen (4x5) black-and-white negatives, and for good measure took five exposures on a roll of 120 b&w film. The X-rays were developed at the hospital, but Stringer's pictures were not. He turned them over, undeveloped, to the Protective Research section of the Secret Service—and they now repose in the National Archives, under lock and key, apparently not even having been seen by Humes, Boswell, et. al.

Even at this earliest of stages, it was apparent that the autopsy was to be a vital part of the prosecution's case.

At Bethesda, they knew that the President had been hit twice and that Connally had been hit once. They also knew that the man in the Dallas jail was accused of shooting both from behind. Period. They would learn a lot more the next day from speaking with the emergency surgeons at Parkland Hospital in Dallas, but by then, the body had long since been sewn up, sent to Joseph Gawler's Sons funeral home for embalming, and placed on the Lincoln catafalque in the White House.

In unwrapping Kennedy's body from the bloody sheets in which Parkland had wrapped the corpse, they found a wound in the front of the throat. They paid it little mind, assuming—as Humes was to testify four months later—it was "a surgical tracheotomy wound". They were far more interested in the massive skull and back wounds.

First they removed the President's brain and placed it in a Formalin solution to study two weeks later, as per established practice in such cases. Then they proceeded to the back wound.

Agent Kellerman described this wound to have been "just below the large muscle between the shoulder and the neck". Agent Hill observed it as "a wound about six inches down from the neckline on the back, just to the right of the spinal column". There was only one thing wrong: the wound went nowhere and the bullet could not be found.

Commander Humes probed it with his finger and felt the end of the wound after his finger had gone in up to the first or second knuckle, a penetration of, at most, two inches. Then Finck probed with an instrument, and Kellerman asked, "Colonel, where did it go?" Mystified, Finck answered, "there are no lanes for an outlet of this entry in this man's shoulder." Further exploration proved equally fruitless and frustrating. This left the FBI no choice but to report to the Warren Commission that "medical evaluation of the President's body revealed that one of the bullets had entered just below his shoulder to the right of the spinal column *at an angle of 45 to 60 degrees downward*, that there was no point of exit and that the bullet was not in the body." (ital. ours).

As we shall see in our detailed look at the Zapruder film, this would become one of the major discrepancies in the Warren Report.

While Humes and Finck were probing the wound that went nowhere, word came to the attending FBI team from their colleagues in Dallas that a 6.5 mm. bullet had miraculously been found falling out from under a stretcher mattress at Parkland Hospital. When told minutes later, the autopsists were mightily relieved. They had deduced that while applying cardiac massage to the near-lifeless body of the President, the Parkland emergency staff must have forced the bullet out of Kennedy's back. That made sense, as far as it went. But later, it was learned that the bullet fell out from under a stretcher that wasn't the President's at all. But by then, as far as the autopsy was concerned, it had become a moot point.

Armed with that deduction, the autopsists saw no reason to further probe the back wound. Since the bullet was now accounted for, they did not perform the customary tracking procedure. Obviously, there was no need for wasted motion.

The next morning, however, they sky fell in on Dr. Humes. He'd telephoned Dr. Malcolm Perry at Parkland to review his findings, and in the course of the conversation casually mentioned the tracheotomy incision. And that's when Humes learned for the first time that Perry's incision had obliterated a tiny "circular, symmetrical and uniform" hole the Parkland people had perceived to be a frontal bullet puncture. Perry recalled there had been an "injury to the right lateral wall of the trachea," that there had been "blood and air in the upper mediastinum". Commander Humes was stunned, for this "entrance wound" immediately raised the possibility that Kennedy had been wounded in a cross-fire, which meant the involvement of a second gunman!

At this point, of course, there was no way of retrieving the body for another look, much less to do the tracking procedure they would have done the night before had Humes known about the frontal wound. The telephone call to Dallas thus invalidated a substantial part of the autopsy report Humes had drafted. At the same time, Dr. Perry's bombshell raised an entirely new possibility: that the throat wound he and Dr. Charles Carrico had enlarged from 3 to 5 mm. was actually the point of exit for the bullet that could not be found. And since no one in their right mind would ever call for an exhumation that might eventually dispute this notion, Humes—possibly in consultation with Boswell and Finck—decided to re-write the autopsy. Over the weekend, he burned not only his notes but the draft of the autopsy, and produced a new one embodying the back-to-front bullet trajectory. The new autopsy report would disregard the official death certificate signed by Admiral George G. Burkley, the President's personal physician ("...a second wound occurred in the posterior back at about the level of the third thoracic vertebra") since it was obvious—with the frontal "exit" being at a higher plane than the back entrance—the latter wound would have to be moved up.

Later, Humes would have great cause to regret his hasty revision, because by the time the Warren Commission met to examine the medical evidence, Parkland's Perry had filled in some crucial details. Among them: that the tear in the trachea was on the front or "anterior lateral right side", destroying the possibility of a back-to-front transit. Moreover, since that puncture was considerably *higher* than the wound of entry, and since the bullet found appeared not to have struck bone that might have deflected the missile *upwards*, Humes found himself in a deep dilemma. Had he been experienced in the behavior of gunshot wounds, he'd have known that exit wounds tend to be *twice* as large as entrance wounds—but that's getting ahead of ourselves.

What makes this seemingly trivial part of the autopsy report so pivotal is that, in the hands of an ambitious Warren Report staff counsel, Humes' verbal and artistic surgery would form the foundation of the so-called "single bullet theory" by which the Government would posthumously frame Lee Harvey Oswald for all time.

The attorney was Arlen Specter, then a 33-year-old former Assistant District Attorney from Philadelphia. In January 1964, when Assistant Commission Counsel Specter came to work, he found both Humes' handwritten draft of the revised autopsy and the official copy waiting for him. Where Humes' draft described the throat wound as one "*presumably* of exit," the official version had deleted the qualifier, and as assassination critic Josiah Thompson points out in his landmark study, *Six Seconds in Dallas*, "[the hypothesis] had (now) achieved a remarkable solidity and firmness; it was not to be doubted."

In fairness to Specter, when he set out on his

quixotic trip into supernaturalism, he was probably as confused as anyone. The Government had said the bullet had gone through Kennedy, but where did it go? It wasn't found in the limousine, nor was it picked up in the street afterwards. *Ergo*, there was only one place it could have gone: into Connally.

To prove this contention, Specter would spend a week at Parkland Hospital, interviewing various doctors and nurses with the clear intent of turning Humes' hypothesis into indisputable fact. His questions, according to the people at Parkland, were by and large hypothetical—of the "what-if" school of logic—and not surprisingly, so were the responses. But by that time, Specter had become a man possessed: he simply ignored the hedges and presented the replies as solid testimony.

As he presented it to the Commission, that back shot was actually a *neck* shot, entering the President at an angle of 15 degrees, exiting *downward* from his throat, nicking the left side of his necktie knot, and leaving a 5 mm. wound.

At this point, it hovered in the air for 1.8 seconds and then, with sharp, angular deviation—like a bumblebee—zig-zagged into Connally's back, below the right armpit. (Connally, at this instance—according to the Zapruder film—is shown turning around to his left to see what the commotion is all about.) Maintaining its downward flightpath, the bullet now shattered his fifth rib, causing bone fragments to penetrate and collapse his right lung, exiting below his right nipple and leaving behind a 5 cm. sucking wound. Next, this "superbullet" penetrated Connally's right wrist from the back, shattered the radial wristbone into seven or eight pieces, and upon exiting, entered his left thigh five or six inches above the knee, penetrating to a depth of about three inches. Finally, *mirabile dictu*! this bullet still had sufficient energy left to work its way out of the thigh and to burrow itself under the stretcher mattress at the hospital, where a maintenance engineer found it less than an hour after Connally had gone into emergency surgery.

Even more wondrous, this bullet—marked Commission Exhibit (or CE) 399—emerged in near-pristine condition. Having inflicted this simply awesome damage—seven wounds in two people—CE 399 seemed to have lost only 1.5% of its substance. When new, a 6.5 mm. bullet of this make weighs 161.5 grains; when found, CE 399 weighed 159 grains.

Specter's account of CE 399's incredible journey was postulated not because it was supported by any kind of evidence, but because without it, the Government's case would have collapsed then and there like Senator Schweiker's "house of cards". The crime could not have been pinned on just one assassin.

It would have been simple for both the FBI and the Secret Service to ridicule Specter's "magic bullet theory". After all, they both had reported that Kennedy and Connally had been hit by separate bullets. On November 28, the Secret Service reported that:

> "at a point approximately 200 ft. east of the triple underpass... President Kennedy... was shot. Immediately thereafter Governor Connally was shot once. The President was then shot the second time..."

And on December 9, the FBI reported that:

> "...three shots rang out. Two bullets struck President Kennedy and one wounded Governor Connally."

Both the Secret Service and the FBI had seen and studied the Zapruder film, which showed that the maximum time that had elapsed between the wounding of Kennedy and Connally was less than half a second, *less* than the minimum firing time of the kind of single-shot, bolt-action rifle found in the Depository. But Specter's theory gave them a Hobson's Choice: either stick to their reports, which would have been tantamount to admitting two gunmen were involved, or go with Specter's oddball explanation.

Not only did the FBI and Secret Service go with Specter, but to do so, they would now have to begin reshuffling a great deal of the evidence they'd accumulated since the assassination. And if the agencies at times seemed embarrassed to do so, the Commission itself felt no restraint.

Thus, the Warren Report states that FBI ballistics expert Robert A. Frazier "testified that [the bullet] probably struck Governor Connally", when in fact, Frazier had specifically testified:

"We are dealing with a hypothetical situation...so when you say it would probably have occurred then you are asking me for an opinion on a whole series of hypothetical facts which I cannot substantiate."

To Specter, this was hairsplitting. What mattered was that once certified, the Government's explanation could not be disproved through reenactment, and the burden of disproof would lie with the critics, few of whom were in the position to challenge an autopsy.

But the Commissioners did hedge a bit. After all, how to explain that, without hitting bone, the bullet could have sharply altered its course, the Report noted:

"...the alignment of the points of entry was only indicative and not conclusive that one bullet hit both men. The exact positions of the men could not be recreated; thus the angle could only be approximated...if the President or the Governor had been sitting in a different lateral position, the conclusion might have varied. Or if the Governor had not turned exactly the way calculated, the alignment would have been destroyed."

In other words, as if the bumblebee-bullet story isn't outrageous enough, we are now expected to believe that if, perchance, Kennedy had sneezed or Connally had scratched his armpit simultaneously, the assassin would have missed them entirely!

Not until 1968, when Jim Garrison put Colonel Finck on the witness stand in New Orleans, did it come out that no tracking procedure had ever been done. The FBI, of course, knew it all along but decided not to rock the boat. In two of its reports to the Commission, written well after it had gone over the official autopsy, the Bureau reiterated the 45-to-60 degree angle of entry, stating "there was no point of exit...the bullet was not in the body," and that the bullet "had penetrated to a distance of less than a finger's length". Only later, in 1966, after critic Edward Jay Epstein (in *Inquest: The Warren Commission and the Establishment of Truth*) reminded Hoover that "consistency with the evidence does not necessarily prove validity, but inconsistency does prove invalidity," did the FBI fall into line. In an extraordinary about-face, it belatedly discovered that its men on the scene, agents Sibert and O'Neill, had been out of the room when the tracking procedure was done. Clearly, this was a bald lie, since several Secret Service agents had earlier testified, under oath, that at no time was the FBI not represented: only one agent had left the room to take a message, not two.

But, as they say, memory is a magnificent filter, and by then—two years after the publication of the Warren Report—only the gadfly critic would remember: over 200 million Americans would not.

Speaking of memory, it was most helpful to Specter that no tracking had ever been done, because in appearing before the Commission, the autopsists had to rely on recall, and on medical drawings of the body and the wounds. They were denied access to the photos and the X-rays, and instead were told to work from new drawings made by a medical artist who, likewise, had never seen the photographs—or the body. He had simply been told what to draw and how to depict the wounds. It was a charade. Humes was asked if the drawings were accurate. No, he said, they were not, but then again, they could not be without having let the artist see the photographs. The question was then quickly dropped.

One famous drawing showed the bullet path traversing 15 degrees down, towards Connally, not at the 45-to-60 degrees the FBI said it did. No wonder: following the FBI's flightpath, the bullet would have exited Kennedy well below the breastline and would have "entered" Connally's right buttock.

Another drawing showed the bullet's point of entry. Now, at least four Secret Service agents, who had either seen JFK get shot (from the back-up car) or seen his body on the autopsy table, had testified that he'd been shot in the back. So had FBI ballistics expert Frazier. He'd described the bullet hole in Kennedy's shirt as being five and three-quarter inches below the top of the shirt collar and one and one-eighth inch to the right of the shirt's middle seam.

That hole, Frazier testified, was unquestionably the point of entry: the shirt fibers had been pushed in, and showed traces of copper. Not so the hole in front of the shirt. It was more of a slit, and revealed no metallic residue.

> "I could not actually determine from the characteristics of the hole whether or not it was caused by a bullet. However, I can say that it was caused by a projectile of some type which exited from the shirt at that point."

Not surprisingly, while Frazier's testimony is contained in the 26-volume Appendix of the Warren Report, his equivocation was left out of the Report itself.

Aside from the shocking breach of accepted legal proceedings that the employ of unsubstantiated medical drawings represented in this "trial", equally shocking was the way the lawyers manipulated the testimony to shore up their scenario. Thus, to reconcile the disparity between where the agents had actually seen the bullet hole and where it appeared in the drawings, the Commission insisted Kennedy's shirt had actually crept up. In other words, the hole in the shirt may actually have been where Frazier had said it was, but when worn by the President, that hole lined up with the "hole" shown in the drawing. Clever, but too clever: if that had been the case, the shirt would actually have had to double up, producing *three* holes in the back of the shirt. Nor would the photographs taken by spectators support the Commission's contention that Kennedy took the neck shot because he'd been leaning forward so that his shoulder was higher than his throat, a swan-like posture.

But then, the Commission didn't want to see any amateur photographs that would dispute its "findings", nor would it brook any opposing arguments in the hearings. It was a closed court, not a court of inquiry.

Still left unanswered is how that "puncture wound" came to be in Kennedy's throat. Could he have been shot at precisely the same moment the bullet entered his back—even if the Zapruder film suggests this to have been a physical impossibility?

The Parkland Hospital medical staff ultimately thought not, seeing as how the puncture wound had actually been too small to account for even a high-velocity bullet fired from the railroad overpass over the front windshield of the oncoming car.

The answer may have been there all along, as early as the afternoon of the assassination, when Parkland's Dr. Robert N. McClelland, in an admission note, described the President as being at the time "comatose from a massive gunshot wound of the head with a fragment wound of the trachea." What kind of fragment?

In 1966, Professor Thompson, the Haverford critic, came up with an interesting bit of conjecture, for lack of a more plausible explanation. The hole had been made by a bone fragment from the skull, driven downward and out by the impact of one of the fatal headshots. It was, he said, "a hypothesis that accords with all the known facts surrounding the throat wound. The absence of copper traces on the shirt fibers would indicate that bone fragments did the major work of disruption."

As hypotheses go, this one is refuted by the Zapruder film, which shows Kennedy clutching his throat well *before* receiving the first head shot. And regardless of what Arlen Specter may have said, in no way could the hole have been a bullet-inflicted exit wound. Early in 1964, in tests conducted at the Army's Edgewood Arsenal, Dr. Alfred G. Olivier fired three 6.5 mm. bullets through 14 cm. of goat meat held between goat skin and clothing—simulating the President's neck. The entrance wounds in the back of the simulator matched the size of Kennedy's back wound, but the smallest exit hole was 10 mm.— almost three times as large as the "small puncture" wound that Dr. Perry had enlarged in his tracheotomy procedure.

The point is that for every shot but this one, there was a logical and exact explanation. In the absence of such, speculation thrives. Thus, it has been suggested by more than one researcher that a small-calibre, low-velocity bullet fired by a silencer-equipped weapon, struck the President from the right front, hit bone and buried itself in the mid-neck, inaccessible to the probing fingers of Doctors Humes and Finck. Or, perhaps the missile deflected upwards into the head, whence it was blasted out by the subsequent headshot. If these postulations sound convoluted, they are no less so than Specter's "magic bullet" theory.

Aside from CE 399, the only links between the wounds and Oswald's gun were the bullet fragments that the Secret Service discovered the night of the assassination while going over the limousine at Bethesda. Because the fragments were too deformed to produce meaningful ballistics comparisons, the Warren Commission asked the FBI to go to the Atomic Energy Commission and have the fragments tested by what was then the brand-new method of Neutron Activation Analysis in order to determine whether the fragments had been fired from the same gun as CE 399.

NAA calls for the irradiation of a specimen in a nuclear reactor in order to produce a characteristic radiation "pattern" that either matches or doesn't match that of the secondary specimen. It is so exact a test that it's possible to detect and measure trace elements down to parts-per-billion. (Recently, NAA performed on the preserved hair of Napoleon Bonaparte, 140 years after his death in exile on St. Helena, suggested that the Emperor may have been assassinated by his British jailers: an ever-increasing level of arsenic in his hair follicles indicated a slow and gradual introduction of poison into his food.)

The FBI's Neutron Activation Analysis report is one of the documents that has never been published, one possible reason being that the test tended to undercut the relationship of the "magic bullet" found at Parkland Hospital to the fragments found in the limousine. All we have to go on is a July 1964 memo from Hoover to the Commission's Executive Counsel, J. Lee Rankin. The FBI, said Hoover:

> "...found no significant differences within the sensitivity of the spectrographic method ...and while *minor variations* in composition were found these were not considered sufficient to permit positive differentiation among the larger bullet fragments and thus positively determining from which of the larger bullet fragments any given small lead fragments may have come." (ital. ours).

The fact that "minor variations" were detected should have alerted the Commission, for what makes NAA such a definitive technique is that specimens either match or don't match: there can

This photo of the Texas School Book Depository was taken
from the motorcade press car by *Dallas Morning News*
staff photographer Tom Dillard seconds after the fatal shots.
The arrow points to the alleged sniper's lair in the southeast
corner of the 6th floor where Oswald worked.

The close-up of the "sniper's lair" (top left) shows the window sash raised approximately 15-16 inches—a position verified by a Government official (top right) during a reconstruction of the crime. The bottom photo, taken on the afternoon of Nov. 22 by the late Jack Beers of the *Dallas Morning News,* was snapped from inside the southeast corner 6th-floor window. The window had been raised. However, the dotted line shows the window height at the time of the shooting. Had the sniper rested his gun on the carton (foreground), the telescopic sight would have been blocked by the window sash. Clearly, JFK was not shot from this point.

With the Dillard and Beers photos proving the impossibility of a gunman's ability to target JFK in a moving limousine, a crucial Beers photo taken that same afternoon inside the "lair" (top left) was conveniently ignored by the Warren Commission. Instead, it relied on Dallas police recreations (top right, bottom left and right) that are all contradictory to each other. Note the varying stackings of boxes in order to make the corner of the box match the view recorded by Dillard's camera.

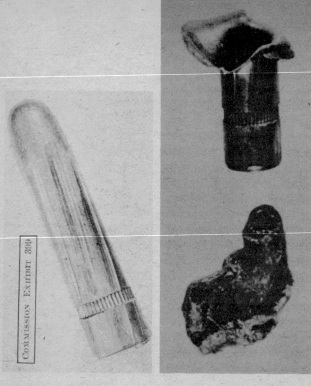

CE-399—the so-called "magic bullet"—as offered in evidence by the Warren Commission (top left) had a most remarkable flight path. It emerged virtually pristine after inflicting a total of seven wounds in its two victims. According to the Commission (opposite page), it entered JFK's neck (disregarding the back wound) at a downward angle on a right-to-left trajectory, exited the throat, hovered in the air for 1.8 seconds, made a sharp, upward right-hand turn, then a downward left-hand turn and entered Connally below his right armpit. Then it shattered the Governor's fifth rib, with bone fragments collapsing his lung and exiting his chest. Next, it made a right-hand turn, shattering his radial wrist bone, exiting, making a U-turn and burying itself in his left thigh. There it remained until forced out by cardiac heart massage —of the President! Had it, indeed, made this extraordinary journey, it would have emerged looking much more like the FBI test bullet (top right). During the crime's recreation, the FBI demonstrated it knew the truth about the wound locations, but the Commission Report did not see fit to reproduce this photograph (below opposite).

President

Governor

Jack Ruby is shown in better days with some of his girls at the Carousel (top left) and as a self-styled newshound with members of the Dallas press corps at the jailhouse the night of Nov. 22 (top right). Another friend was the late Officer J.D. Tippit (below left). Few Dallas cops admitted they had ever known Jack Ruby following his arrest for the death of Oswald on Nov. 24 (bottom right).

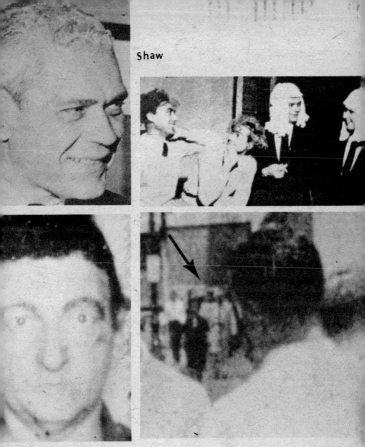

Shaw

Ferrie

PROOF OF PERJURY: D.A. Jim Garrison linked Clay Shaw and pilot David Ferrie as co-conspirators in the assassination. Shaw swore under oath that he had never met Ferrie or Oswald. But in the photo at the top, Ferrie is on the left and Shaw is the second from the right. At the bottom, Oswald is on the right and Shaw (note arrow) is walking towards him.

The "umbrella man" by the Stemmons Freeway sign (at Z-228) is said by some critics to have given the signal to fire. As JFK approaches, the umbrella opens, twirls clockwise, and pumps up and down. After the shooting, the man furls the umbrella, calmly observes the panic around him, and slowly walks back up Elm St. and disappears into the throng. He has never been identified, and has never come forward.

be no variations of *any* kind, minor or otherwise.

Allegheny County (Pittsburgh) coroner Dr. Cyril H. Wecht, one of the few forensic pathologists in the country who have joined the movement disputing the Warren Report, has an explanation of why the Commission didn't jump on the FBI. "By July of 1964, the Commission's staff had already missed one deadline...and was told by Rankin that, at that stage, it should be 'closing doors, not opening them'."

Dr. Wecht, who by his badgering of the Government was finally invited by then-Attorney General Ramsey Clark to look at classified medical data, also managed to start a ruckus by reporting that some of the crucial tissue slides made during the autopsy had mysteriously disappeared from the National Archives, as had Kennedy's preserved brain. Over a year later, the archivist reported that, by golly, his people had come across a cannister, labeled simply "gross material" and that therefore Kennedy's brain hadn't been lost, simply misplaced. Still, no independent researcher has been allowed to see what's in the cannister, possibly because of recurring rumors that there might be an "unidentifiable foreign object" in the brain that could be a spent bullet, and something the Warren Commission hadn't been told about.

Such bureaucratic sloppiness would be shocking were it not for the fact that the Government was merely being consistent with its entire medico-legal approach to the assassination. Take, as an example, its attempt to have us accept the incredible contention that CE 399 had emerged clean from Connally after riddling the Governor in several places.

In March 1973, the National Archives released a

heretofore "Confidential" ballistics report by the Edgewood Arsenal showing what happened to 6.5 mm. bullets after they'd been fired into the wrists of human cadavers. Photographs showed them to have been grossly deformed just by striking wristbone—without first having to shatter a human rib! Naturally, the Warren Report made no mention of this finding, just as it ignored the testimony of Colonel Finck who, when asked whether CE 399 could have actually caused the wrist wounds replied: "no, for the reason that there are too many fragments described in the wrist".

A possible reason, and one that none of the medical authorities ever considered, was that the alleged assassination weapon either lacked the power to inflict so massive a sequence of wounds, or that the ammunition employed was defective.

Numerous ear-witnesses reported hearing not the sound of gunshots but of "firecrackers". This sound is consistent with what rifle experts know about the behavior of the Mannlicher-Carcano. In his 1975 book about Oswald's weapon (*The Gun*), author Henry S. Bloomgarden quotes a veteran of the Fifth Army campaign in Italy who fought alongside the partisans. When they fired their Mannlicher-Carcanos, the sound was "much like a firecracker. I couldn't believe they were serious... I thought the bullets would poop out and drop harmlessly, no trajectory... it sounded like the Fourth of July."

This, of course, fits one school of thought that claims Oswald was framed; that the Mannlicher-Carcano found on the sixth floor had, indeed, been fired, but merely as a diversion, to establish yet another link in the frame-up. And that the magic bullet, CE 399, had been test-fired into cotton waste, retrieved and then planted at Parkland

Hospital by—they say—Jack Ruby (whose presence at the hospital was clearly established by sworn testimony from Scripps-Howard newsman Seth Kantor). A somewhat less sinister explanation, of course, could be that some ghoulish spectator at the hospital that afternoon (and there were many) may have snatched it up as a souvenir and later—realizing its importance—snuck it onto a nearby upright stretcher where it might be found by the authorities.

But then, it's never really been proven to anyone's satisfaction, not even the Commissioners, that the "pristine" bullet actually fell from a stretcher. Hospital engineer Darrell C. Tomlinson, who claimed to have found the bullet at 2:40 p.m. C.S.T., wouldn't swear that the stretcher was Connally's. "I am going to tell you all I can and I am not going to tell you something that I can't lay down and sleep at night with, either," Tomlinson told the Commission.

A good thing he did. Because some of the triage orderlies insisted that the stretcher hadn't even been the one on which Connally was transported to surgery; it was used to carry a two-and-a-half-year-old black child, Ronnie Fuller, who had been brought into emergency after a bad and bloody fall.

One thing is certain: CE 399 didn't "fall" out of Connally. Nurse's aide Rosa Majors, who had removed Connally's pants, shoes and socks, said she held up the patient's pants to go through his pockets for valuables. Had the bullet worked its way out of Connally's thigh, as Specter said it did, that would have been the time it would have had to come clattering out into public view. So much for Specter's magic bullet.

CE 399 was a military projectile, a hard-jacketed bullet. But such bullets, which are designed for maximum penetration, rarely fragmentate. The only time they become deformed is when they strike a hard surface such as armor plate—or human bone. How, then, could CE 399 inflict its fractures and emerge clean? And more to the point, where did all those metal fragments dug out of Connally come from?

In February 1968, fifteen months after he had ordered the transfer of all Warren Commission data to the National Archives, Ramsey Clark secretly convened a panel of top-flight pathologists to look at the X-rays, thereby hoping to allay some of the suspicions generated during the previous three-and-a-half years. Alas, just the opposite happened as the pathologists discovered small, metallic fragments in Kennedy's throat. The discovery ripped apart the Commission's argument that CE 399 was a "clean" projectile: it had to be if the 3 mm. "exit wound" was to stand up. Had it not been "clean", the "exit wound" would have been much larger.

So where did all those metal fragments come from? And why did this distinguished panel describe the entrance to the rear skull shot as being four inches higher than the autopsy? The answers would not be forthcoming from anyone in the Government: there was no more Warren Commission, and none of the participants would dignify the questions. All the doctors could do was describe *two* shots striking Kennedy's head almost simultaneously—a belief unquestionably strengthened by the grisly tableau of the Zapruder film.

The first shot entered Kennedy from the rear, blasting out a substantial chunk of the right skull—and making it so easy to remove the brain during the autopsy, Commander Boswell testified, that no surgery was required: "we simply lifted it out." The second head shot was frontal, the one the critics now say was fired from the "grassy knoll".

As far as the Commission was concerned, the second shot was never fired, because to have said it was would have recognized the existence of a second gunman. For that reason, we are told only selectively about the fatal skull injuries. Dr. William Kemp Clark, the Parkland Hospital neurosurgeon had pronounced the President dead at 1 p.m. A few hours later, at a press conference, he described the head wound as "tangential"—as opposed to straight-on. At the press conference, Dr. Clark had said "a missile had gone in and out of the back of his head causing external lacerations and loss of brain tissue". Before the Commission, Specter asked him to differentiate between "tangential" and other types of wounds, which he did. But what Specter didn't ask Clark was *why* he thought the wound was tangential—hardly an accidental omission. Had he done so, Dr. Clark undoubtedly would have had to describe a shot originating from the front—and Specter must have known it.

Specter knew fully well what others at Parkland had seen—to a man, the emergency staff had cited a massive *exit* wound in the posterior (back) portion of the skull, with brain substance protruding. The best summary was provided by Dr. McClelland. From where he was standing, at the head of the emergency table:

> "I was in such a position that I could very closely examine the head wound, and I noted that the right posterior portion of the skull had been blasted. It had been shattered, apparently, by the force of the shot so that the parietal bone was protruded up through the scalp and

seemed to be fractured almost along its posterior half, as well as some of the occipital bone being fractured in its lateral half, and this sprung open the bones that I had mentioned in such a way that you could actually look down into the skull cavity itself and see that probably a third or so, at least, of the brain tissue, posterior cerebral tissue and some of the cerebellar tissue, had been blasted out."

In everyday English, McClelland's testimony, put next to Dr. Clark's, had clearly described a shot on the frontal right side of the head (tangential) that blasted open the *rear* of Kennedy's skull.

The fact that Ramsey Clark's panel found the rear skull wound to have been four inches higher than the Commission's Report placed it, simply reinforces suspicion of a cover-up. For as Professor Thompson of Haverford notes, "the precise character of the brain tissue is important, for only a deep-ranging shot could have blown out cerebellar tissue, which is located *very low* in the brain." (ital. ours). This would certainly be consistent with the testimony of the motorcycle policemen who were splattered by the President's brains and by Jacqueline Kennedy's unexpurgated testimony, released years later: "I was trying to hold his hair on. But from the front, there was nothing. I suppose there must have been. But from the back, you could see, you know, you were trying to hold his hair and his skull on..."

Such fearful damage as was done to the President's skull does not seem to be consistent with the behavior of high-velocity, hard-jacketed military bullets, the kind the Commission said Lee Harvey Oswald fired from his Mannlicher-

Carcano. It certainly wasn't consistent with the Commission's own tests.

To duplicate the head wound(s), U.S. Army Wound Ballistics experts fired a number of 6.5 mm. rounds into ten reconstructed human skulls, covered with simulated skin, scalp and hair, and filled with a gelatinous substance—"the brain". Only *one* of the ten reenactments produced the desired results of a small entrance wound and a large, gaping exit wound. But even then, the gelatin stayed pretty much intact, offering little resistance to the speeding projectile. Nor did the skulls evidence much scalp damage.

This, of course, immediately begs the question: what kind of bullets could have wreaked such havoc? The answer, of course, is "soft" ammunition, the kind of hollow-nosed bullets that are designed to cause the maximum internal damage. Upon striking a hard surface, the lead mushrooms outward and furthermore, it fragments, often ending up unrecognizable as having been a single projectile.

The Bethesda autopsists noticed a substantial number of "dust-like (metallic) fragments" in the oozing brain matter, but they didn't see what the Ramsey Clark panel saw on the X-rays: a 6.5 mm. fragment lodged in Kennedy's skull, at the bottom of the rear entrance wound—a phenomenom clearly inconsistent with the behavior of a copper-jacketed bullet but quite consistent with that of a *soft, lead* bullet.

Had the autopsists been familiar with gunshot wounds, they would have surely been alerted by the extent of the skull fractures, again, so characteristic of a soft bullet-caused wound. Commander Humes testified that when examining the skull, pieces tended "to come apart in our hands, very easily".

Last, virtually all the doctors who examined the President's body—at Parkland and at Bethesda—concur that so massive a skull implosion could have been the work of a high-velocity round. The Mannlicher-Carcano is a *medium*-velocity weapon. It is therefore much more likely that the fatal head shot(s) came from a hunting rifle—a precision hunting rifle, firing dum-dum (soft-nosed) bullets.

This much is sure: none of the fragments dug out of Kennedy's head or Connally's body have been satisfactorily shown to have come from bullets fired by the Mannlicher-Carcano. And the only fragments that were said to have been linked did not seem to have passed the Neutron Activation Analysis test.

We are left with the distinct feeling that the Government was fortunate to have entrusted so important an autopsy to pathologists who were clearly professionally *un*qualified to do the job properly. It is equally significant that so much of its defense in the media—since the publication of the Warren Report—comes from "medical specialists" who never saw the actual body (as did the Parkland Hospital emergency surgeons). Dr. Olivier of Aberdeen Proving Grounds is a *veterinarian*, not a forensic pathologist. And Dr. John K. Lattimer of the College of Physicians & Surgeons at Columbia University, who appears to have appointed himself as the Kennedy family's unofficial medical theoretician, is a *urologist* specializing in adrenal gland disorders, not gunshot wounds.

(Newest of the medical "experts" is Dr. James Weston, Chief Medical Examiner of the State of

New Mexico, who says he's willing to "stake his reputation" on the belief that Kennedy was hit by two bullets only—one of them being Arlen Specter's CE 399. Commissioned by CBS News to review autopsy photos and X-rays for its TV series, "The American Assassins", Weston must think very little of his reputation: he places the back bullet wound five and a half inches higher than the death certificate did because, he said, otherwise it would have had to penetrate Kennedy's lung and collapse it. Since it wasn't collapsed, it didn't enter there. Of course, he totally ignored the fact that when Humes and Finck probed the wound, it went nowhere—certainly not deep enough to enter the rib cage. Likewise, in describing the head shots, he ignored the findings of the Parkland Hospital emergency staff. One can therefore assume that the only reason CBS News picked Dr. Weston was that he is the new president of the American Academy of Forensic Sciences, an evolutionary post. Interestingly, Dr. Cyril Wecht, the Pittsburgh coroner with whom CBS News did not agree, is a *past* president of the American Academy. He was not asked whether he, too, would stake his reputation on *his* interpretation. Curious.)

When he returned to Philadelphia from his stint on the Commission, Specter told his boss, District Attorney James C. Crumlish, "I don't think the people are going to believe the single bullet theory this year, next year or a hundred years from now. This thing will be challenged today, tomorrow and forever." It was the only accurate thing Specter ever came out with.

Graceless to the bitter end, and having beaten Crumlish to become District Attorney two years later, Specter would turn on his unwitting allies, the Bethesda autopsists, by telling reporters "the issue rests squarely on the integrity of Humes, Boswell and Finck."

More recently, a cornered Arlen Specter has begun to speak ill of the dead. By challenging him, he says, you are merely suggesting "that Chief Justice Warren perjured himself when he signed the Report."

Clearly, it's not just Richard M. Nixon who gives lawyers a bad name.

A VERY SPECIAL
LAW FIRM

"The monumental record of the President's Commission will stand like a Gibraltar of factual literature through the ages to come...."
—Rep. Gerald R. Ford (1965)

Gerry Ford never was one for understatement. But as a team player, even with gum in his mouth, he could always be relied upon to say the right thing. Maybe that's why Lyndon Johnson chose him to be the seventh member of his very special law firm. One can think of no other reason.

By no stretch of the imagination could the President's Commission to Investigate the Assassination of President Kennedy be considered anything else. It certainly was no impartial fact-finding panel. Even if, as Earl Warren told the press, the Commission would "evaluate all the facts and circumstances surrounding the assassination and the subsequent killing of the alleged assassin," it would soon be made abundantly clear to all the senior and junior partners that the Commission wasn't interested in facts. Not *real* facts.

Of course, the American public had no way of knowing it then, or even after the Report came out in September of 1964. After all, who in his right mind would spend $79.50 for a set of twenty-seven books when the *New York Times* had set the world's speed-reading record and the day after the twenty-six Appendices came out in November, pronounced them a masterpiece of jurisprudence?

That the Commission would be a victim of its own mind-set should have been apparent to anyone reading the ground-rules of the investigation. It would conduct no adversary proceeding, brook no arguments for the defense, and operate *in camera*, behind closed doors. A hanging court by any other definition. There would be only one defendant, the late Lee Harvey Oswald. He would be represented by his wife Marina, to whom it had been made perfectly clear by the FBI during her "protective custody" following the assassination that the price of non-cooperation could be a one-way return ticket to the Soviet Union.

Witnesses who were called by the Commission were really not expected to tell what they had *witnessed*. What the Commission wanted were "facts" with which to shore up its institutionalized presumption of Oswald's guilt. The Warren Report, thus, is noteworthy more for the witnesses who were not summoned, or who were not asked such crucial questions as, from where did *they* think the shots came? More ominous, perhaps, is that a number of people whose recollections contradicted the preconceived verdict seemed to disappear or even die mysterious deaths during and after the Warren Commission hearings.

Critic Sylvia Meagher, for example, discovered that of some eighteen witnesses who died within the three years following the assassination, only five died of natural causes. The rest were murdered, committed suicide or otherwise met sudden, unexplained death. Thirteen of them figured in the official Report, seven as primary witnesses, six as "secondary" (interviewed by the FBI, Secret Service and Dallas Police). Two were direct eyewitnesses to the killing, whose stories shattered the "lone assassin" myth; two had contact with Oswald after the assassination; three figured in the Tippit shooting; ten knew or dealt with Jack Ruby. Eight died during the ten months the Commission sat, the other ten died afterwards. Texas newspaperman Penn Jones, Jr. put these grisly statistics together, and when the *London Sunday Times* asked an actuary to determine the likelihood of all eighteen being dead by February of 1967, the odds were one hundred thousand trillion to one *against*.

Witnesses who did appear and who generally tried to reconstruct all they had seen and heard were generally dismissed as "unreliable", their testimony dismissed as "mistaken". Many were not allowed to complete their remarks, finding themselves cut off in mid-sentence by rude and meaningless interjections whenever they seemed to be veering dangerously close to something the staff did not want to hear. Those who refused to be badgered were close to vilified on the stand, and their testimony thoroughly mangled and deliberately distorted in the Report itself. Thus, only by a careful reading of the individual testimonies in the Appendices will one find the painstaking recollections of those witnesses who swore, under oath, that they had discerned activity behind the wooden stockade fence atop the grassy knoll—clusters of footprints, cigarette butts and the acrid smell of gunpowder, tell-tale marks of gunmen who may have just done their work and fled in mud-streaked automobiles that had been seen moving into the parking lot moments before the shooting. Even then, the Appendix contains not a word from Mrs. Carolyn Walther, who stood across the street from the Book Depository and told the FBI she had seen two gunmen in one of the upper stories of the building, one of them—a blond-haired man wearing a white shirt—cradling what she thought to be a machine gun. She was never called.

Some witnesses, on the other hand, people who could be depended upon to tell the Commission what it wanted to hear, were intensively prepped in advance of their appearances. Usually, that's done in full-fledged, *open* murder trials where aggressive cross-examination by the opposing side might cause such witnesses to buckle. Only here, there was *no* opposing side. There was only the Government of the United States and the ghost of Lee Harvey Oswald, so dishonored in death that vandals had even stolen his tombstone.

It would have been, frankly, impossible to have returned an honest verdict. None was called for. One can imagine, but not very easily, Justice Warren calling on President Johnson with a working draft of the Report, saying something to the effect of, "look, Mr. President, my people and I have studied this case in great length and at enormous expense to the taxpayer and, uh—well, Mr. President, I don't know how you're going to like this but—well, there's just *no* way this chap Oswald could have done it."

The 14th Chief Justice of the United States,

whatever else he may have been throughout his long and distinguished career, was no Thomas Becket, even though there were times Johnson fancied himself to be King Henry II reincarnated.

Which explains why the Warren Report told us that Oswald, an unhappily married drifter, re-defected turncoat and left-wing radical—worse, a crypto-Communist—was the "lone and unassisted assassin". That he had earlier in 1963 attempted to kill right-wing Major General Edwin A. Walker ("thereby demonstrating his disposition to take human life"). That he had threatened to do likewise to former Vice President Nixon. That in a fit of despondency over his tottering home life, his inability "to enter into meaningful relationships", his penis envy of the all-powerful President, he had taken his rifle to work and there, had fired three shots in rapid succession, killing Kennedy, wounding Connally and doing inordinate violence to the theory that the assassination was premeditated.

That afterwards, he fled the Book Depository, took a highly irregular and astonishingly circu-itous route to his boarding house, where he picked up a jacket—having left one in the Depository—a revolver and planned to leave town. That about ten minutes later, stopped by a suspicious police officer, he gunned the man down in cold blood (muttering "dumb son-of-a-bitch cop") and high-tailed it to a nearby movie house. That he crashed the gate, so alerted the cashier that she called the police, and that they came, quick as a flash, to subdue, disarm and arrest him. And that, after being arraigned for double murder, but before confessing, an enraged Dallas citizen took the law into his own hands and killed the assassin.

All of which, of course, was more than amply supported by the "evidence", painstakingly pieced together by a consortium of law-enforcement and investigative agencies who, like Caesar's wife, were quite simply beyond reproach.

Well, now that the patriotic bunting in which the Warren Report originally came wrapped has been shown to be made of whole cloth, we might now logically ask, for what purpose did the Government spend ten months doing what it did, when it must have known that sooner or later, it would have to be found defective?

The answer is elementary. To get Lyndon Baines Johnson off the hook, and accord him an unimpeded run for the Presidency on his own.

Johnson, the compleat and consummate politician, knew that no matter *how* much good will might be showered on him in the wake of Kennedy's funeral cortege, the period of national mourning would last just so long, after which there would be business as usual. That is to say, the 1964 presidential election.

As Hugh Sidey, *Time*'s White House correspondent, was to remind us after LBJ's death in January 1973, he "was a man who believed there were no accidents in politics, only conspiracies."

Dallas, to Johnson, was no accident—that much he knew after the first shot rang out. In an extraordinary segment of a far-ranging television conversation with Walter Cronkite in April 1972 (one which LBJ embargoed and CBS released only in 1975), the ex-President declared: "I never believed Oswald acted alone." And to a former White House aide, Leo Janos, visiting the ranch that same year, Johnson invoked the "Cuban Connection" by musing, "we were running a damned Murder Incorporated down in the Caribbean."

Now, of course, we all know to what Johnson

referred. As the first Vice President in U.S. history who had actually been brought into top-secret deliberations by his President, LBJ quite obviously knew about the arrangements Washington "consultant" Robert A. Maheu had made on behalf of the CIA with the Mafia. Just as certainly, he must have been familiar with the post-Bay of Pigs paramilitary actions against Cuba sanctioned by the White House.

One of LBJ's closest confidantes, Joseph A. Califano, Jr.—now a law partner of Edward Bennett Williams—recalled in 1975 that "on more than one occasion" Johnson voiced "a very strong opinion, almost a conviction," that the Kennedy assassination was a "response and retaliation" by Castro to the myriad provocations instigated by the Kennedy brothers. (Castro himself feared this interpretation. The week after the assassination, he told a French journalist that now the U.S. would try and implicate him *personally* by branding Oswald a Cuban agent gone haywire.)

The plotters must have been similarly inspired. According to the Commission's Appendix, the Secret Service in Dallas early in December intercepted a letter to Oswald, postmarked November 28 and signed by one "Pedro Charles", in which the sender indicated he'd paid Oswald to "carry out an unidentified mission [involving] accurate shooting". That same volume contained reference to another letter, this in the FBI's possession, from one "Mario del Rosario Molina" to Attorney General Kennedy, alleging that Oswald had been hired by Pedro Charles for the sum of $7,000, the hiring having taken place in Miami early in 1963.

Since Oswald's movements were pretty much

accounted for all during 1963, it was established that (a) he had never been in Miami and (b) both letters were frauds, elaborate plants by an anti-Castro splinter group, the International Anti-Communist Brigade. (Dr. Peter Dale Scott of University of California at Berkeley, one of the keener students of assassination/conspiracy, suggests the letters were designed not so much to implicate the now-deceased Oswald as to create a case for U.S. intervention. He further raises the intriguing hypothesis of a "two-tier conspiracy", namely that the fraud was *meant* to be discovered and exposed and in so doing, debunk the Cuban angle and force the investigators to revert back to the "lone nut" theory.)

LBJ's man Califano also remembers Johnson telling him, with astounding prescience, "in time, when all the CIA activities are flushed out, then maybe the full story of the assassination will become known."

But on the afternoon of November 22, aboard Air Force One on the melancholy flight back to Washington, Johnson probably wasn't thinking about Castro at all. Intimates remember him at this time as a man quietly obsessed by the legitimacy of his succession—or at least, what he perceived to be the one issue that could render him politically impotent and even cost him the 1964 election.

Namely, the *Cui Bono* theory—or, who would have profited most from Kennedy's removal? After all, JFK had been murdered *in* Texas *by* a Texan and had now been succeeded by *another* Texan, one who had long hankered after the Oval Office.

And Johnson was all too aware of the political gossip. The scandal involving his former Senatorial aide, Robert G. Baker, could have cost him the Vice-Presidential renomination. Why, even that "chronic campaigner", Nixon, knew it. Nixon had been in Dallas the previous day, as had Johnson, attending the convention of the Associated Bottlers of Carbonated Soda on behalf of his law client, the Pepsi-Cola Company. And in a newspaper interview on the 21st, Nixon claimed to have the inside word that JFK would be dropping LBJ in '64. The story was splashed in headlines all over the state; even Kennedy had seen it.

Like his namesake, Andrew Johnson, who was first suspected of complicity in the murder of *his* President, Abraham Lincoln, the new President was haunted by the fear that cruel history would now repeat itself. People *would* talk.

Upon arriving in Washington, Johnson learned that Oswald was a "Communist". The fears of *Cui Bono* faded as new fears emerged. Was the Soviet KGB involved? He now had the defection folder before him. How would the Soviets react if they felt the U.S. suspected *them*? Would they consider a pre-emptive strike? Even if the "hot line" cleared that up, the country demanded an answer. The murder would have to be solved, and fast. There could be no questions left dangling, otherwise he— the usurper of Camelot—would not be able to govern at all.

Legally, the assassination was wholly a jurisdictional matter for the state of Texas. Presidential assassination, in 1963, had not yet become a federal crime. And so, while the Secret Service had acted precipitously by rushing the body of the President out of the state over the protest of local authorities, on Monday, November 25, Texas Attorney General Waggoner Carr announced his office would conduct "a court of inquiry...to develop fully and disclose openly" details of the triple murder—Kennedy's, Tippit's and Oswald's—and the relevant background.

The notion of a Carr investigation panicked the White House. It was apt to be far-reaching, clear up to Washington D.C., and would most assuredly drag out in the open the internecine political wars that had prompted the Texas junket in the first place. For Johnson, there would be no hope of avoiding entanglement.

Already, before the assassination, there were several ongoing Congressional investigations into the way the Convair Division of General Dynamics of Ft. Worth got the lucrative TFX-11 experimental jet fighter contract from the Navy. One subcommittee had already compromised Jackie Kennedy's good friend, Deputy Defense Secretary Roswell Gilpatric. His New York law firm, Cravath, Swaine & Moore, represented General Dynamics. And the man Johnson had urged upon JFK to succeed his protegee, John Connally, as Secretary of the Navy—Fred G. Korth—had been forced to resign after Congressional investigators found Korth's bank had made substantial loans to General Dynamics.

Another subcommittee, on the very afternoon of November 22, had been taking testimony from LBJ's former insurance agent, Don Reynolds. Reynolds testified that as the price for getting the lucrative Johnson insurance business—land, cattle, TV stations, the works—Bobby Baker had exacted a $100,000 kickback. How much, wondered the Congressmen, had gone back to LBJ?

In time, Johnson might show the world his abdominal surgery scar but he'd be damned if he wanted to bleed in public. It was plain he'd have to head Waggoner Carr off at the old corral, before he could saddle up.

The decision may actually have been made for Johnson by his old Senate colleague, Everett M. Dirksen of Illinois. On Tuesday, the 26th, Dirksen proposed that the Senate Judiciary Committee undertake an investigation, and the next day, New York's Representative Charles E. Goodell chimed in with a call for a *joint* Congressional blue-ribbon panel, which would *have* to include some of LBJ's old enemies.

Both Truman and Ike had taught Johnson a valuable lesson: to cool potentially embarrassing inquiries, convene a *presidential* commission. They worked for them, why not for him?

Why not, indeed? On November 29, seven days after taking office, Lyndon Johnson signed Executive Order #11130, establishing the Warren Commission—the *President*'s Commission, if you will. Not America's Commission, but *Lyndon*'s.

As he'd anticipated, the two Congressional inquiries sputtered out. After all, Congress couldn't very well accuse the new President of malfeasance when there was no Vice President waiting in the wings. The thought of an aging President John McCormack, then Speaker of the House, sent shudders throughout the Hill. And a few well-placed telephone calls later, even Waggoner Carr fell into line. He would call off his dogs on the understanding that Texas could assign two liaison lawyers to the Commission—Southern Methodist University Law School Dean Robert G. Storey, and a Houston attorney by the name of Leon Jaworski—yes, the same.

At first, Earl Warren balked mightily. His involvement, he told Johnson, would surely compromise the High Court should the Jack Ruby case come up for review and appeal. But Warren hadn't reckoned with the "Johnson Treatment", complete with tear-filled eyes appealing to this decent man's patriotism, and the implied threat that if the Chief Justice failed him in this hour of need, the country might well be plunged into a war costing forty million lives.

Warren, of course, gave in. The President then hand-picked the members of his Commission—men chosen, according to *The New Yorker*'s astute Washington observer, Richard Rovere, "more for their known probity than for their mastery of probative techniques". He began with two senior Senators—Georgia's conservative Richard Brevard Russell and Kentucky's liberal John Sherman Cooper, and in the same bipartisan breath, two from the House: Majority Whip Hale Boggs of Louisiana and Ford, then Chairman of the House Republican Conference. Presumably for their expertise in foreign affairs, he added former World Banker and U.S. High Commissioner, John J. McCloy and the deposed CIA Director, Allen W. Dulles.

(Dulles, of course, knew all about the CIA attempts to assassinate Castro, having authorized it as far back as December 11, 1959. As the Senate Intelligence Committee report on CIA assassinations revealed in November 1975, the Castro operation was "completely authorized at every appropriate level within and beyond the Agency" and that it fell "within the parameters of permissible action". But just as "the doctrine of plausible denial" may have kept Dulles from telling Kennedy about the details, so did he keep his own duplicity from his fellow Warren Commissioners. He ought to have had himself disqualified as hopelessly compromised, for as it turned out, the Commission never looked for *any* Cuban connection.)

The seven wise men met for the first time on December 5, and agreed to hire as Executive Director and General Counsel, J. Lee Rankin, the former U.S. Solicitor General. They also solemnly pledged themselves "to insure the truth [be] known so far as it can be discovered... and report [our] findings and conclusions to the President, the American people and the world".

They oughtn't to have taken the pledge. Even before Rankin had been sworn in or had started to build his staff, J. Edgar Hoover let the world know that his people had already solved the crime. On December 5 he gave Deputy Attorney General Nicholas DeB. Katzenbach a preliminary report for transmission to the Warren Commission. Why the big rush? The answer only came out in 1975 when columnist Jack Anderson reported that secret memoranda in Hoover's own handwriting showed he wanted to get the Bureau's version on record before a mourning Bob Kennedy resumed his post. Hoover figured that once the Commission had the FBI's version of the "facts", there'd not be much RFK could do to change it. But whether Hoover actually believed in Oswald's guilt, is something else; in one memo the Commission didn't see, he wrote, "with that background, O. could have hollered false arrest if we had arrested him."

The "Summary Report" from the FBI was a work at once brilliant in detail and obfuscation. It showered the Commissioners with reams of irrelevancies such as the dental charts of Jack Ruby's mother and the medical records of Marina Oswald's second pregnancy, but withheld from them such crucial memorandae as the June 3, 1960 (!) alert from Hoover to the State Department in which he raised the possibility of a Soviet impostor using the passport of an American defector named Lee Harvey Oswald. (This memo would finally only surface in the summer of 1975.) This FBI report would not only dominate the entire proceedings for the next ten months, but would also greatly influence the rendering of the verdict. And just to make sure the Commission meant business, Hoover's flacks were all over the Washington press corps, dropping tantalizing hints here and there. So that by the time he'd actually read through the four volumes, a plainly irked Earl Warren snapped at Rankin: "I have not seen anything in there yet that has not been in the papers."

Later in the inquiry, in an executive session, the transcript of which had been suppressed until flushed out into the open in 1974, irritation with Hoover's antics reached the sparking point.

RANKIN: "Part of our difficulty is that they [FBI] have no problem. They have decided that it is Oswald who committed the assassination, they have decided that no one else was involved, they have decided..."

RUSSELL: (interrupting) "...they have tried the case and reached a verdict on every aspect."

McCLOY: "Yes, 'We know who killed cock robin.' That is the point. It isn't only who killed cock robin. Under the terms of reference, we have to go beyond that."

On December 18, the Secret Service weighed in

with *its* 4,600-page report, supporting the FBI's finding that three shots were fired—the first shot hitting Kennedy, and a *separate* shot hitting Connally. File that for future reference.

Six days earlier, Congress passed Joint Resolution #137, submitting for Johnson's signature Public Law 88-202, giving the Commission its unlimited subpoena power.

Actual staffwork began January 11, 1964, when six study areas were delineated: the basic facts about the assassination, the identification of the assassin, Oswald's background and motives, possible conspiratorial relationships, the Ruby role and how to improve presidential protection. From this it may be readily seen that there was no need to identify the assassin when the next study area had already named him.

It was equally apparent, from the start, that the Commissioners would be little more than figureheads—a part-time board of directors or executive committee of elders who would meet only when necessary and only when it suited their schedules. The High Court was in session, as was Congress; Dulles was writing his memoirs and McCloy had pressing Wall Street business to tend to.

"Let's not kid anyone," recalls Wesley J. Liebeler, one of the fourteen assistant counsels hired by Rankin to oversee the daily work-load, "the Warren Report was a staff job." With Rankin operating as *major domo*, the staff consisted of $100-a-day part-time lawyers and their full-time juniors, young, top-of-their-law-school-class beginners willing to put in sixteen-hour days at a measly $4.68 an hour. The part-time lawyers were ambitious men, eager to advance in the interlocking worlds of law and government, and in their eagerness to please, they garnished the head of Lee Harvey Oswald and outdid the legendary Salome. As the old saying goes, to get along, go along.

When Rankin set up the staff, the Report insists, he "did not select people who had ties or allegiances to the Government, or who might have been beholden to some department or another for their jobs". Strictly speaking, this was true. But well over one-third of the staff had direct or indirect *past* Government connections. (One assistant counsel had been Earl Warren's law clerk on the Supreme Court, another had served as an Assistant U.S. Attorney in Ohio, and the one who singlehandedly plucked out of thin air the controversial "single-bullet-*ergo*-lone assassin" theory, 33-year-old Arlen Specter, had been Assistant District Attorney in Philadelphia.

Rankin also overlooked, perhaps inadvertently, the compromising symbiotic relationships of some of his staffers. Thus, assistant counsel Albert E. Jenner Jr.—the same Jenner who would emerge ten years later as minority counsel to the Nixon impeachment committee—was a Chicagoan whose biggest client then (as now) was Colonel Henry Crown, the largest individual shareholder in General Dynamics. And Liebeler, who would go on to become planning director of the Federal Trade Commission before becoming a law professor at UCLA, had come from the New York law firm of Carter, Ledyard & Milburn. The late Stewart Alsop once described CL&M as "perhaps the most conspicuously CIA-linked law firm in the country".

Guilt-by-past association may be patently unfair, especially in the case of Liebeler, who seemed to be the most objective of the bunch. Still, he may not have been Rankin's most inspired choice to head that part of the inquiry dealing with Oswald's alleged CIA links.

Rather quickly, the Warren Commission seemed to evolve into a high-priced, prestigious law firm whose only client was Lyndon Baines Johnson. For the young lawyers, to want to be part of a history-making project of this magnitude was certainly understandable. So is the fact that for their investigators, they had to rely on some of the very government agencies that had been most severely compromised by the assassination, most notably the FBI and the Secret Service.

The nearly thirty agencies churned out enough paper to fill three hundred cubic feet of filing space in the National Archives. The FBI alone sent in 2,300 reports toting up to 25,000 pages, much of it, according to assassination researcher Harold Weisberg, "worthless and of no consequence". Weisberg finds it replete with "the customary FBI doubletalk and filtering-out of what was actually said, adding, "working in that tremendous accumulation is like walking in quicksand. There's an enormous amount of trivia and unrelated material and diversions in every file. The sheer bulk defeats scholarly effort and hides official transgressions."

Case in point: whenever the investigation veered into the role of organized crime, the transcribers seemed to lapse into stenographic jabberwocky. Thus, dealing with Jack Ruby's ties to Hoffa, the Report's FBI memo has him placing a call to Murray (Dusty) Miller, now secretary-treasurer of the 400,000-member Teamsters union and even then a trustee of the union's $2.3 billion Central States Pension Fund. But that's not the way Miller's name appears in the official hearings: there, he becomes "Deutsch I. Maylor". Even accounting for Ruby's adopted Texas accent, it's easy to see why tracking down non-existent people like "Maylor" proved a little difficult. It seemed to happen an awful lot, almost as if it was deliberate.

As far as the CIA was concerned, staff relations were more than strained; they practically didn't exist. The CIA, its paranoia up, was to Wesley Liebler "so secretive as to be virtually useless". The FBI wasn't much better. The Bureau clearly resented the intrusion onto their turf from those Hoover derisively called "these amateur sleuths". Agents made it exasperatingly hard to get information on time, and when they finally came through, the staff found it—putting it kindly— "less thorough than it appeared to be". One junior attorney went so far as to come right out and dismiss the FBI's fabled field work as "not immediately relevant to the assassination". We can understand why.

As early as its December 9 "Summary Report," the FBI had one overriding concern: to cover its tracks. Later that month, it handed over to the Commission a list of the names, addresses and telephone numbers from Oswald's notebook. Conspicuously missing was that of agent James Patrick Hosty Jr., the FBI agent assigned to keep an eye on Oswald's wife and possibly, Oswald's FBI connection.

The Secret Service, too, was mighty vulnerable. As will be seen, it had been inexcusably lax in establishing presidential security in Dallas, a seething hot-bed of right-wing, anti-Kennedy passions. The Commission staff also had to rely, to a staggering degree, on what the Dallas Police department had fed both the Secret Service and the FBI. Although Police Chief Curry's men seemed to have the case all wrapped up minutes after Oswald's arrest—and perhaps even before—

their investigatory work struck one Commission staffer as "looking like Swiss cheese and smelling like Limburger". Even the State Department's Bureau of Intelligence & Research was all thumbs when it came to explaining why it was that Oswald's passport file had never been "flagged".

True, it was incumbent upon the staff to persist, to ask and ask again, and not simply to take the word of the investigators at face value. But here, too, one encounters the basic flaw in the very premise of the inquiry. No matter how hard the lawyers will *now* insist that they approached their assignments with "independence of mind"—even the recalcitrant David Belin asserts "I would have loved to nail the FBI in a lie"—it is quite apparent they didn't, or couldn't. They were, after all, Government *employees*, and in the heady environment of Washington, one simply doesn't bite the hands that feed the body, or in this case, the ego.

Thus, Commission critic Edward Jay Epstein (in *Inquest*) reports on the colloquy between two staff lawyers arguing a sensitive point in the draft report. One of them "explained that he had written the chapter exactly the way the Commission wanted it written. He said, "The Commission judged it an easy shot, and *I* work for the Commission.'"

Appearing on a TV-panel discussion on the assassination movement, Belin and Liebeler agreed that if they knew then what they know now about the transgressions of the FBI and CIA, they'd have moved in an entirely different direction. But whether they'd have worked with different assumptions, or come up with different interpretations, remains highly improbable. They would still have had to nail a coonskin to the wall to please their client, Lyndon Johnson.

"There was a dualism in its purpose," writes Epstein. "If the explicit purpose of the Commission was to ascertain and expose the facts, the implicit purpose was to protect 'the national interest' by dispelling rumors.... But what if the rumors proved to be true?"

Why then, the Commission would simply ignore them—if it could.

No better illustration of this exists than in the way the Commission closed its mind to the possibility that Oswald was a government agent, a spy left out in the cold.

The rumor first surfaced on New Year's Day, in a story appearing in the Houston *Post* under the byline of Alonzo ("Lonnie") Hudkins. Based on a tip from Allen Sweatt, Chief Criminal Deputy Sheriff of Dallas County, and Dallas Assistant District Attorney William F. Alexander (who must have gotten it from D.A. Wade), the story said that when Oswald was arrested, he was on the government payroll as a $200-a-month informer; that Oswald had been recruited in September of 1962 by agent Hosty, and that he had been assigned informer number S-179 (or S-172)—a far cry from the "Marxist" the FBI had reported less than a month earlier.

Alexander held no great sympathy for Kennedy: on St. Patrick's Day, 1964, learning that the march was to follow the same route as the presidential motorcade had taken the previous November, Alexander tastelessly cracked, "don't you think we're pushing our luck a little having another parade for an Irishman in Dealey Plaza?"

Henry Wade knew all about FBI informers. He'd been an FBI agent and had used them. He was well aware of the Bureau's *modus*: pick your informers from the movement you want to infiltrate; don't worry about them being of sound mind and sterling character, all we want is information. Also, be sure to give them a cover number and a code name, arrange to contact them through various postal box "covers". Pay them in cash through Western Union money orders, and if possible, hold something over their heads to keep them in line.

In Oswald's case, Wade felt, all conditions were met. Now that the word was out, thanks to Lonnie Hudkins, Wade met with Texas A.G. Waggoner Carr. On January 22, Carr telephoned Rankin in Washington.

That same day, Rankin called an emergency meeting. The Commissioners were stunned, and Warren insisted that Carr, Wade and Alexander, as well as Dean Storey and Leon Jaworski, fly up two days later for a face-to-face report. By the time they got to Washington, the rumor had grown somewhat: Oswald had also been a CIA informant, code number 110669. Worse, at the January 24 meeting Rankin learned also that Sheriff Sweatt had initially tipped off the Secret Service in mid-December, but that the agency, on the pretense of checking it out, hadn't bothered to inform the Commission.

Convening a full meeting of the Commissioners and the staff on the following Monday (27), Rankin let it all hang out, revealingly so.

"We do have a dirty rumor that is very bad for the Commission . . . and very damaging to the agencies that are involved in it, and it must be wiped out as it is possible to do so by this Commission."

The rumor was "dirty" not because it was necessarily false but because it would clearly compromise everything and everybody, and the only way of dealing with it would be to "wipe it out".

Not to do so would bring down the wrath of the House of Hoover. Not that there was anything wrong with the FBI using informers, but that J. Edgar Hoover—the man Nixon would eulogize as "the symbol and embodiment of courage, patriotism, dedication to his country and a granite-like honesty and integrity"—would hire a man who had just assassinated the President. Too much.

How, trembled the Commission, would Hoover react when confronted with this little gem? And who would be the messenger of doom?

Senator Russell still had his head screwed on right.

> "It seems to me we have two alternatives. One is we can just accept the FBI's report [of Dec. 9 and Jan. 13] and go on and write the Report based on their findings and supported by the raw materials they have given us, or else we go and try to run down some of these collateral rumors that have just not been dealt with directly in this raw material that we have."

Banker McCloy shook his head. "We don't want to be in the position of attacking the FBI," said he. Rankin favored talking to Hoover before attempting to investigate the rumor—as if permission was needed. He felt it was. Were the Commission's eager-beaver staffers to undertake their own inquiry into this rumor, word would flash back to Hoover and create all sorts of ill-will—the inference being that then the FBI agents would all go on strike and leave the Commission without input. The alternative would be to confront him point-blank with the rumor, take two steps back for the explosion, and then jot down the Instant Denial. A pretty scene this couldn't have been.

Puffing thoughtfully on his pipe, retired spymaster Dulles allowed as how such a rumor would be "a terribly hard thing to disprove" since written records are rarely kept on undercover agents. What's more, he noted, their recruiters would almost certainly lie, even under oath.

BOGGS: (exasperated) "you...make our problem utterly impossible because you say this rumor can't be dissipated under any circumstances."

Note the operational word here—"dissipated". The Commission just didn't want to grapple with the remote possibility that the "rumor" wasn't a rumor at all, but hard fact.

McCLOY: "Allen, suppose somebody, when you were head of the CIA, came to you and said specifically...or suppose the President of the United States comes to you and says, 'Will you tell me, Mr. Dulles?...' "

DULLES: "I would tell the President of the United States anything, yes, I am under his control. He is my boss. [But] I wouldn't necessarily tell anybody else, unless the President authorized me to do it."

Heavy. They had the full subpoena power of the United States Congress, and still, they recoiled from using it. Why? Perhaps at that point, they caught Dulles' hint: Hoover would feel unrestrained from lying under oath to protect his men— or his own reputation. Dulles would, and probably did, just as his successors have—Richard Helms and William Colby.

McCloy was suddenly incensed. He was an old government hand, going back to FDR, when J. Edgar Hoover still knew his place in the hierarchy of the Department of Justice. He asked, acid and anger dripping:

"Just why would it be embarrassing to the *Attorney General* of the United States to inquire of one of his agencies whether or not this man who was alleged to have killed the President of the United States was an agent? Does the embarrassment supersede the importance of getting the best evidence in such a situation as this?"

Ordinarily, the Attorney General would probably delight in calling in the FBI head for an accounting. But this was no ordinary situation: the assumption still was, informer or not, Oswald had killed the Attorney General's brother.

The upshot was predictable: the FBI ended up investigating itself and to nobody's surprise, came up empty-handed and squeaky clean. Concludes Epstein: "the surest and safest way to dispell [a] rumor [is] not to investigate it but to keep secret the allegations and publish only the affidavits of denial."

This whole episode might never have come to public attention had it not been for Harold Weisberg and his skillful use of a law that goes back to 1946.

That year, emerging from a war that had given unbridled reign to wholesale governmental secrecy, Congress enacted the "Administrative Procedures Act." Part of the law held that government records be opened to people "properly and directly concerned ... except [for] information held confidential and for good cause found." Naturally, the Government for the next twenty years found all sorts of "good causes" to deny the public access.

In 1966, Congress tried again, this time producing S-1160, by which—effective July 4, 1967—*any* citizen, without having to give a reason, could demand access to Government files, thus placing the burden of denial on the affected agencies or departments.

Enter Weisberg, the Kennedy-assassination movement's "man you love to hate". A pre-war investigator for the late Wisconsin Senator Robert LaFollette, and a wartime OSS operative who spent years tracking down cleverly hidden Nazi assets in this country, Weisberg may be everything his friends and enemies say he is—cantankerous, obstreperous, infuriating—but he also happens to be bullheaded, a man obsessed with uncovering Government chicanery. He's been studying the Kennedy assassination ever since November 23, 1963, and to date has written six privately published books on his researches into Dallas (and a seventh on the King-Ray case, on which he is working as an official investigator for the defense team that's trying to get Ray a trial, something the Government never gave him).

He is clearly not in this for the money. In fact, it is no credit to the assassination/conspiracy movement that all of Weisberg's works have been ripped off, almost word-for-word, by his fellow researchers, and then recycled as their own brilliant discoveries.

No single American has made greater or better use of S-1160 than Weisberg. Even before the law was drafted, Weisberg had asked the FBI for the spectrographic (bullet) evidence. The FBI didn't respond. Then came the Freedom of Information Act, and four years after the first attempt, in 1970, Weisberg once more asked the FBI. This time, at least, it responded: *no*. Weisberg teamed up with Washington attorney Bernard (Bud) Fensterwald and sued the FBI. Two years later, in 1972, the decision came down in favor of Weisberg. But John Mitchell's Justice Department appealed, and in October 1973, the Weisberg ruling was overturned. The FBI ballistics files would remain inviolate.

The next month Weisberg was back again. This time, he knew precisely what he was after: the transcript of the January 27 executive session. He'd first come upon it, as did others, in Congressman Ford's 1965 book, *Portrait of the Assassin*. Gerry Ford and his ghost-writer, John R. Stiles, had simply paid no attention to the "Top Secret" stamp atop every page of the minutes of that heated session, and had excerpted portions of it. (Worse, in his confirmation hearings as Nixon's appointed Vice President, Representative Ford denied under oath having done so, which effectively made him guilty of contempt of Congress, if not of perjury).

So instead of taking on J. Edgar Hoover, Weisberg went after the General Services Administration, custodian of the National Archives, where the full January 27 transcript was under lock and key.

In his suit against the GSA, Weisberg charged that "neither Executive Order 11130 nor Senate Joint Resolution 137...authorized the Commission to classify documents" at will.

He'd learned that a *private* court transcription service had routinely slapped the "Top Secret" stamp on *all* transcripts from January 21 to March 4, 1964, regardless of what was discussed. He also reminded the court that even if the "Top Secret" stamp was valid, the very fact that the Government simply allowed Representative Ford and his ghost-writer to appropriate classified material nullified the classification. In effect, Weisberg said, the GSA had "sold" to Simon & Schuster and to Bantam Books, Ford's publishers, material that was still marked "Top Secret".

The GSA's response was predictable. The January 27 session had been embargoed "in the interests of national security", even though, as Weisberg was to learn later, Rankin had written New York's Senator Jacob K. Javits in mid-1964 that "at this point in the investigation, there appears to be nothing of significance which should not be revealed to the American public because of national security or any other consideration." But by the time he learned that, he'd lost the case.

The presiding judge was Gerhard A. Gesell, whose moment in history was soon to come. Weisberg took the appeal straight up to the Supreme Court, which upheld Judge Gesell. Or, as Weisberg puts it, "on May 13, 1974, the Supreme Court converted S-1160 into a law for the suppression of public information that could not otherwise be suppressed."

Then, inexplicably, a month later, Archivist James B. Rhoads contacted Weisberg at his home in Frederick, Md., and told him he could have his lousy transcript after all. Just send the money.

What had happened, of course, was Watergate.

Apparently, indicted White House Domestic Affairs Counselor John Ehrlichman, appearing before the very same Judge Gesell, had argued disingenuously that Richard M. Nixon's presidential files were essential to his defense. This naturally put Gesell into the unenviable position of (a) denying access to Erlichman, thus (b) throwing the indictment out for lack of evidence and (c) having to charge the President with obstruction of justice. It is by no means certain whether, at the time, such a charge would have forced a divided Congress to expedite its impeachment proceedings. But Erlichman's message filtered down to the White House bunker—"give me what I need to make a defensible case, or I'll sing my head off". An inspired thought must have crossed Nixon's mind: perhaps there was enough negative material in some of the old assassination transcripts to besmirch the FBI's and CIA's so-called competence, thereby justifying Nixon's decision to set up the White House's own Gestapo. A call went out from the White House to GSA Administrator Arthur Sampson: *let go.*

Which is why we now know that Oswald was an FBI informer. Simple?

That wasn't the end of it, though. This ungodly fear the Commission held of incurring Hoover's displeasure permeated virtually all the proceedings, clear through the end. It's as if under the unwritten FBI motto of "Don't Embarrass The Bureau", some flunky had added a post-script, "and don't bother J. Edgar, either".

Thus, pressed to account for the strange deletion of agent Hosty's name from Oswald's notebook, the FBI memoed Rankin: "The circumstances under which Hosty's name, et cetera, appeared in Oswald's notebook were fully known to the FBI". Period. Don't ask us anything else about this. And the Commission didn't.

By the time six months had passed, Hoover had taken measure of the Commission. So he felt pretty safe in dispatching Assistant Director Alan H. Belmont to the Massachusetts Avenue offices with an offer from the Godfather the Commission simply could not refuse: the complete Oswald file. But it did. Predictably so.

Earl Warren felt that once the Commission saw the file, why, then anyone else might want to see it, too. Rankin, a little more (but not much) pragmatic, said he wanted to keep the Oswald file on tap just so that nobody could say the Commission hadn't seen everything the FBI had on Oswald. Yet—Rankin promised Belmont that he wouldn't peek inside the file. Ahh, that *rumor*. It was still safe. One assumes Belmont kept a straight face as he left the Commission's offices.

The net effect of such non-confrontation with the investigatory agencies is that the Commission never even came close to what Epstein aptly calls "The Threshold Question". Namely, the question of conspiracy.

Though "possible conspiratorial relationships" was to be one of six major study areas, little more than lip service was actually given this part of the investigation. Not that there wasn't an abundance of material to work with.

Take the business of the rifle shots. The initial FBI and Secret Service reports insisted that at least three shots were fired and that Kennedy and Connally *each* received a bullet, before the fatal head shot. The Warren Report said that wasn't so, that Kennedy and Connally were *both* wounded by *one* shot—the so-called "superbullet" or CE 399.

In any other homicide case involving two victims shot while riding in an open car, were it to become known that the two successive shots were fired within 1.8 seconds of each other by a gunman using a defective, sluggish bolt-action gun, there would be no question of more than one gunman having been involved. But not in this instance. There *could* be no conspiracy: such a finding would have been intolerable to the client—and the client, no matter how often Earl Warren might insist, was not "the truth".

In the context of conspiracy, it might be worth looking at one aspect of the famous "grassy knoll" story that seems to have gotten less attention than it should have all these years. And that has to do not with "puffs of white smoke" but the flash of badges.

There were about 400 people lining both sides of Elm Street, including children under the age of five. The Commission knew the names of at least 266, of whom testimony was taken from 259. Ninety of them were asked from where they thought the shots had come. Fifty-eight said the grassy knoll—that sloping expanse of lawn, trees and bushes between the Book Depository and the triple underpass. These 58 were dismissed, their recollections "mistaken".

They had to be "mistaken" if the preordained scenario were to remain on track: the shots *had* to have come from the Book Depository, not somewhere else, and they had to have been fired by *one* gunman, not two. A ratio of 58:32 eyewitnesses pointing in an opposite direction was not very reassuring to the advocates of the "lone nut" concept.

The Commission really didn't have to ask the 58 who had pointed to the grassy knoll; if they wanted to find conspiracy, it had been staring them in the face. All they had to do was believe a couple of local lawmen.

The Warren Report makes unmistakable the fact that all Secret Service agents who were with the motorcade accompanied the dead or dying President to Parkland Hospital. "None stayed at the scene of the shooting," insists the Report, "no one entered the Texas School Book Depository at or immediately after the shooting." The head of the Secret Service's small Dallas office, Forrest V. Sorrels, the Report tells us, came back to Dealey Plaza twenty-five minutes later.

Yet... when Dallas Deputy Constable Seymour Weitzman, right after the last car in the caravan had disappeared from view on its way to the hospital, charged up the grassy knoll, he testified having run into "other officers, Secret Service as well". Dallas Police Officer Joe Marshall Smith ran into one man he didn't recognize in the parking lot behind the Depository, about to get into a Chevrolet sedan, pulled his gun, then put it away. "I felt awfully silly," recalled Smith to the Commission, "when he showed me he was a Secret Service agent." And Sergeant D.V. Harkness, wanting to make sure the Depository was sealed (in the event a gunman was still inside), at 12:36 p.m.—six minutes after the first shot rang out— "encountered some Secret Service there. I didn't get them identified. *They told me* they were Secret Service agents." (ital. ours) Three reliable law-enforcement officers seemed to be tripping over Secret Service agents that, the Secret Service insists, weren't there, *couldn't* have been there.

Then there's the unexplained presence in Dealey Plaza of a West Coast hoodlum named Eugene Hale Brading. His name has cropped up innumerable times in various Congressional investigations into racket domination of certain labor unions, mostly as a courier taking "skim" money out of Las Vegas to the Bahamas and Switzerland. If Brading hadn't insisted on giving the Dallas cops a fake name, he might never even have been mentioned in the Appendix. Mr. Brading was found in the Dal-Tex Building (across

Houston Street from the Book Depository), coming off the elevator just as the cops arrived to seal off that building. He lacked identification but produced a credit card. His name, he said, was "Jim Braden" and he'd come in from Beverly Hills to conduct some "oil business" with Donald D. Ford, Vice President of Tidewater (now Getty) Oil Company. So his West Coast parole officer confirmed: Brading required his approval to leave the state.

During his three-hour detention in the Sheriff's office, Brading-Braden claimed he'd been walking up Elm, away from Dealey Plaza, when he heard the President had been shot. He asked a spectator which way to the nearest phone, and, Brading told the Sheriff's office, he was pointed up to the third floor of the Dal-Tex Building. Plausible. Except for one thing: Photos taken show Brading-Braden in a crowd lining Elm Street, well *past* the Depository, closer to the underpass, at the precise moment of the assassination.

Questions the Commission didn't ask: why was it necessary for Brading-Braden to walk all the way back up Elm Street to get to a phone? Why not a public phone, if that's indeed what he was looking for? Might he have met someone on the third floor of Dal-Tex? Last, and hardly least, Mr. Ford of Tidewater had no appointment scheduled with Mr. Brading-Braden at any time from November 15 on. Exit Brading-Braden; two months after the assassination, he shows up as a charter member of the alleged Mob-linked La Costa country club in Carlsbad, California.

By not asking such pertinent questions when it had the chance, the Commission plainly seemed less fearful of encountering a conspiracy than it seemed to be of exploring the unknown. To have posed the "threshold question" would have meant redirecting the entire thrust of the investigation.

"Once across the threshold," Epstein points out, "the investigation would enter a new dimension of uncertainty. No one could know where it would lead, when it would end nor what would be its ramifications."

In one respect, the Commission did live up to its promise to dredge up facts. But facts, as the noted social critic Dwight Macdonald is fond of saying, aren't necessarily factual or truthful. A year following the Report's publication, Macdonald, writing in *Esquire* Magazine, said:

"Americans often assume that facts are solid, concrete (and discrete) objects like marbles, but they are very much not. Rather are they subtle essences, full of mystery and metaphysics, that change their color and shape, their meaning, according to the context in which they are presented."

Even if the Commission had set out to be painfully honest with itself and with the American people, and genuinely quested after the truth, it would have failed. The very idea that it lacked its own investigative apparatus and was forced to rely for its input from people with something to hide also meant that it *had* to set out with a presumption of guilt.

The day after the assassination, Dallas Police head of homicide Captain J. Will Fritz told reporters, "we are convinced without any doubt he did the killing." The media quickly picked up the refrain. By Sunday, it stopped referring to Oswald as the "alleged" or "accused" assassin. On the same day, November 24, that its editorial pages called for a "presumption of innocence," the *New York Times* headlined

PRESIDENT'S ASSASSIN SHOT TO DEATH

By April 1964, it was all but codified. Even the flaming liberals were now convinced. Norman Redlich, the noted civil libertarian who was a law professor at New York University before joining the Commission—he is now Dean of the NYU Law School—memoed Rankin:

> "Our intent is not to establish the point with complete accuracy, but merely to substantiate the hypothesis which underlies the conclusions that Oswald was the sole assassin."

Only one element was missing: motive. The Commission seemed incapable of adequately dealing with motive. It preferred groping. And so it reached all the way back into Oswald's childhood, calling upon—for example—New York psychiatrist Dr. Renatus Hartogs, the same Hartogs who in 1975 would be hauled into court on the charge of treating a woman patient horizontally. Dr. Hartogs had examined Oswald as a thirteen-year-old truant during his brief residence in New York City. He remembered Oswald as a love-starved child who slept with his domineering, embittered, much-married mother until he was a teenager. Very simple, concluded the shrink, Oswald suffered from an Oedipal Complex. And in his repressed lust for the unlovely Marguerite, his rejection by the materialistic Marina, he killed the King of Camelot.

Such errant nonsense, of course, suited the Commission fine. Clearly unwilling to look for a plausible political motive, it embraced Dr. Hartog's hogwash and reduced motivation to psychological mumbo-jumbo. No evidence is better than some evidence.

So here they sat, these unrepresentative seven Commissioners—"white, gray, middle-aged, fleshy, male affluent Americans," in Mark Harris' description—having had little or no contact with the real world outside, mulling over input provided by highly suspect sources, lapped up and processed by a bunch of ambitious lawyers out to make a name for themselves, and as a kangaroo court, rendering its verdict ten months after having reached it.

Maybe, Mark Harris says by way of mitigation, "their own useful paranoia was down, their belief shrunken, their experiences limited." Maybe. More likely, though, it was the monkey on their back, the client, the 36th President of the United States. There was no way the "client" could be the truth, because the truth would not set Lyndon Johnson free.

In hindsight, the Commission vote was not unanimous. Four favored crucifixion, three did not—the "nays" being Senators Russell and Cooper and Representative Boggs. None of the three would buy Arlen Specter's "magic bullet" theory, and so they argued right down to the wire on how to couch the language of the conclusion.

Ford insisted the evidence was "compelling", but Russell said, no, it was "credible". McCloy arbitrated and came up with the nice, inoffensive "persuasive", watering this down even further by getting the Report to state that Governor Connally's testimony "gave rise to some differences of opinion as to this probability".

It was obvious it could not be what Johnson wanted, a strong, unanimous Report. Earl Warren, the good soldier, insisted it be just that.

Say what you will about Senator Russell's die-hard stand on racial integration; at least the man was honest. No, said Russell, he would not make it unanimous. During the last executive session, on

122

September 18, 1964, Russell told Warren, "look, you just put a little asterisk up there and a footnote down at the bottom of the page, saying 'Senator Russell dissents to this finding as follows ...'"

Afterwards, when the Report had come out, and reporters would ask him what he thought, Russell minced few words: "We have not been told the truth about Oswald by the Federal authorities. I never believed that he did it without any consultation or any encouragement whatsoever. Too many things caused me to doubt that he planned it all by himself." He was even harsher privately, scorning the Report to which he had signed his name as "a sorrily incompetent document".

What about Russell's footnote?

It would only be towards the end of his life that Russell would learn he'd been tricked. It was Harold Weisberg who discovered this ultimate indignity, and then took it upon himself to bring it to Russell's attention.

Warren had simply waited until afterwards, and then—before the minutes were to be officially transcribed—struck Russell's footnote, and even deleted any reference to his request.

The revelation so anguished Russell, who had spent the past thirty-six years in what he thought had been honorable give-and-take between the three branches of government, that he openly broke with his old comrade, the President. And he did so in the only way that Johnson would recognize. He resigned as chairman of the all-powerful Senate Armed Services Committee, thereby divesting himself of further "oversight" responsibilities over the CIA, whose man, he felt, Oswald was. And Johnson did, indeed, get the message. Only he would deny Russell the ultimate dignity of acknowledgement. The Senator had resigned, Johnson told the press, for reasons of health.

He was dying of emphysema and lung cancer. But for the remaining twenty-six months, Richard Brevard Russell would not speak again to, or of, Lyndon Baines Johnson.

Instant Replay: Zapruder's Little Home Movie

> "They talk about the 'one-bullet' theory but as far as I'm concerned there is no 'theory'. There is only my absolute knowledge..."
>
> —John Bowden Connally Jr.

Not long ago, a reporter ran into Senator Edward M. Kennedy up at Martha's Vineyard, and asked him how he felt about the idea of reopening the Dallas investigation.

"Obviously," said he, "it is painful for the family. But the first consideration ought to be on the basis of what new evidence is available."

New evidence? What's wrong with the *old* evidence?

The oldest evidence, of course, is photographic: this was the most visually recorded assassination in history. There were at least 510 different photographs taken before, during and after the shooting by as many as 75 people, mostly amateurs. The record embraces just about every mode of film—Polaroid, 35 mm., and 8 mm. motion picture, the most famous of which is a six-foot-long strip of color home movie film lasting twenty-two seconds, the famous "Zapruder film".

This macabre film strip—Grand Guignol *cinema verite* in living (and dying) color—exposes the Warren Commission cover-up even more vividly than the Nixon tapes did the Watergate cover-up.

The late Abraham Zapruder, who died in August 1970, was a children's dress manufacturer, whose firm (Jennifer Juniors) was based in the Dal-Tex Building at 501 Elm Street, across Houston Street from the Texas School Book Depository.

Late on the morning of November 22, at the urging of his secretary, Lillian Rogers, Zapruder went home to retrieve his 8 mm. Bell & Howell camera (model 414PD, serial #AS 13486). Around noontime, with his receptionist, Marilyn Sitzman, Zapruder stationed himself on top of a four-foot concrete pedestal, part of an ornamental pergola on the sloping "grassy knoll", 200 feet to the west of the Book Depository and 72 feet from the middle of Elm Street.

As the presidential motorcade made the slow turn off Houston and onto Elm at precisely 12:29:50, Abe Zapruder activated his Bell & Howell, and for the next few seconds, captured what may well be the single most dramatic piece of documentary footage of modern times. And as one of history's more ghastly episodes unfolded before his horrified eyes, Zapruder numbly kept his trigger finger pressed down on the shutter release.

Of all the people gathered in Dealey Plaza at that moment, Zapruder—his eye locked into the viewfinder—may have been the only one not distracted. He saw it all and missed nothing. It made such an indelible impression on his mind that, in testifying before the Commission *eight* months later (the first time this all-important eyewitness was called), Zapruder broke out in tears and wept unashamedly. "I have seen it so many times," he sobbed, "that I used to have nightmares. The thing would come every night..."

The evening of the assassination, he told Secret Service agent Max O. Phillips that he remembered:

"...cops running right behind me...in the line of shooting. I guess they thought it came right behind me. I also thought it came from back of me."

Abraham Zapruder was a reliable witness. Perhaps *too* reliable. Because, under very clever questioning by one Commission staff lawyer, Zapruder finally was led to say that he had "no opinion about the directions from which the shots came". It was an incredible performance by the Commission since the film offers absolute and incontestable proof of crossfire. *Ergo,* conspiracy.

What it shows is a planned execution in broad daylight. It also casts a mighty shadow of doubt on the keystone of the Government's case—namely that Kennedy and Connally were hit by the same bullet, and that Oswald and only Oswald fired all three shots within a 5.6 second time frame. Unmistakably, we see Connally hit *at least* 13 frames after Kennedy, too late for the same bullet, too soon to have been a bullet fired from the same rifle.

The Zapruder film is the kind of document one can see time and again, each time catching a detail or a nuance overlooked the previous time. It bedevils even the most impartial of historians who see things in the film that, on scientific examination, appear impossible (but then turn out not to be). Thus, John Wolf, President of the Optical Systems Division of Itek Corporation, which was hired by CBS News to examine the Zapruder film by use of computer analysis and image integration, said "I don't know what I see, I know only what I measure."

According to Itek's measurements, there was no frontal or tangential headshot; according to the human eye—Wolf's as well as the Parkland doctors—there most certainly was. Even so, it is worth noting that only four of the Warren Commissioners saw the film run through *once*, and the staff, which wrote its Report based on the film, did so not on the *moving* footage but on an examination of *still* slides.

Until April 1975, the film was owned by Time Incorporated, which had paid Zapruder somewhere between $150,000 and $250,000 for all commercial rights. *Life* magazine, now defunct, had made extensive use of the individual frames over the years, but single freeze shots, taken out of context, are generally meaningless. Finally, with bootleg copies of the film popping up all over the country, and concerned that its retention could make it a party to the cover-up, Time Inc. sold the film back to Zapruder's heirs for the sum of $1.00.

To fully understand how this little piece of film could demolish the Government's painstakingly contrived case, let us review, briefly, the Commission's version of the events:

- The assassin fired his first shot between Zapruder frames #210 and #224, the camera running 18.3 frames-per-second. This was a safe assumption to make since during the entire time span the President was hidden from Zapruder's lens by a large road sign. Therefore, the exact moment of impact is not shown. The interval between firing and impact could only be a maximum of one frame. Thus an error in so vague a statement would be difficult to argue either way.

- The second shot, missing completely, was fired at an unmentioned moment sometime "later".
- Finally, the third and last shot, at frame #313, was the one that entered the back of the President's skull, ending his life.

Now, to prove the Government's argument that the lone assassin fired all three shots in the prescribed 5.6 seconds, as called for by the Zapruder film, FBI ballistics expert Robert A. Frazier and two associates, Charles Killion and Cortland Cunningham, went out to a U.S. Marine Corps firing range five days after the assassination. They fired the obligatory three shots at a target 15 yards away—which was not moving, and not 60 yards away as Kennedy had been. All shots were high and to the right, and none matched the assassin's time. Frazier took six seconds, Killion nine and Cunningham eight. Later that day, Frazier brought his time down to 4.8 seconds—"as fast as the bolt can be operated" without aiming. Four months later, they tried again, and again they all missed widely. By now, the Commission was perturbed, and called in three other sharpshooters. They did even worse.

And unlike the assassin, whose time sequence began the minute "he" must have sighted the lead car, the sharpshooters timed their shots only from the *sound* of the first to the sound of the last shot. Also, unlike the assassin, they used *accurate* sights, and even at that they missed their *stationary* targets. (One Commission lawyer finally sighed in despair that the sight on the Oswald rifle was so out of kilter that "if he'd centered the cross-hairs on Kennedy, he'd have missed.")

Yet, the Commission persisted in its hopeless

Z-225
JFK reappears from behind Stemmons Freeway road sign . . .

Z-228
. . . and responds to the first shot that hit him at Z-189.

Z-230
Now JFK is struck in the back.

Z-237
Connally is about to be struck. Note his right shoulder.

Z-238
". . . I felt like somebody had hit me in the back," Connally later said.

Z-274
Connally is still holding his hat; there is no blood on his cuff. His wrist is not yet hit.

Z-413
Could this be an assassin? Z-413 is the clearest of 18 frames revealing the back of a man's head through the foliage in front of the pedestal where Zapruder was standing.

Nix sequence 3

Nix sequence 4

Another assassin on film? This film by Orville Nix shows the distinct shape of a man who appears for an entire sequence (top). Seconds later, the man is gone (center). As can be seen from the blow-up, he appeared to be in a classic military firing position.

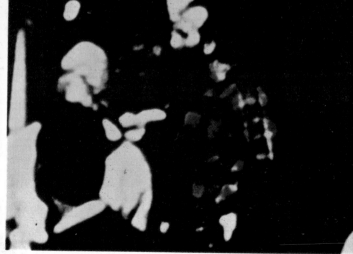

quest by citing ex-Marine Oswald's rifle scores. During his three years in the service, he'd only been tested twice, scoring 212 ("fairly good") and 191 ("rather poor"). No matter, said the Commission, the tests were conducted under "poor" conditions. The testimony of Marine buddy Nelson Delgado, who recalled Oswald's alleged marksmanship "a pretty big joke", was ignored. So was a report from the Soviet KGB file on Oswald, furnished by defector Yuri Nosenko, in February 1964. It seems when Oswald went hunting in Russia, others had to shoot his rabbits so he wouldn't come back empty-handed.

Even if Oswald's Mannlicher-Carcano had been in perfect operating condition, the fastest two successive shots could have been fired would be 2.3 seconds—without fixing the target in the sights. But the two shots were fired in under 2.3 seconds. Two gunmen or one?

The Commission deliberately refuted the obviously crystal clear recollection of those in the best position to recall what happened.

On April 21, 1964, Specter asked Gov. Connally *which* bullet had caused his chest injury, though by this time Specter "knew" the answer:

> "Well, in my judgment, it just couldn't conceivably have been the first one, because I heard the sound of the shot... and when I heard the sound of that first shot, that bullet had already reached where I was... and after I heard that shot, I had time to turn to my right, and start to turn to my left, before I felt anything. It is not conceivable to me that I could have been hit by the first bullet."

But why believe Connally? He was only a victim, hardly trustworthy as an "eyewitness".

So then, Specter asked Connally's wife Nellie,

who was not hit but had been sitting next to Connally. Her trauma was only emotional.

"...I heard a noise, and not being an expert rifleman, I was not aware it was a rifle...I turned over my right shoulder and looked back, and saw the President as he had both hands at his neck...he made no utterance, no cry. I saw no blood, no anything. It was just sort of nothing, the expression on his face, and he just sort of slumped down. Then very soon there was the second shot that hit [my husband] John. As the first shot was hit, and I turned to look at the same time, I recall [my husband] saying, 'Oh, no, no, no'. Then there was a second shot, and it hit [him], and as he recoiled to the right, he said, 'My God they are going to kill us all.'"

And then, Nellie Connally testified, there was the third shot "and I felt...spent buckshot falling all over us and then, of course, I could see it was the matter...brain tissue or whatever, all over the car and both of us."

Specter, naturally, advised the Commission to pay no mind to Mrs. Connally. Her recollections were too vague and unreliable. So, for that matter, were those of the widow Jacqueline:

"Well, there must have been two...because the one that made me turn around was Governor Connally yelling. And it used to confuse me because first I remembered that there were three and I used to think my husband didn't make any sound when he was shot. And Governor Connally screamed like a stuck pig. And then I read the other day that it was not the same shot that hit them both. But I used to think that if I only had been looking to the right I would have seen the first shot hit him, then I could have pulled him down, and then the second *(sic)* shot would have gotten Governor Connally. But I heard Governor Connally yelling and that made me turn around, and as I turned to the right my husband was doing that. He was receiving a bullet..."

Perhaps Jackie was still in shock, but not the Connallys. Yet, like good soldiers, they would ultimately fall into line and pronounce the Warren Report correct: there had only been one assassin and that man was Lee Harvey Oswald. (Now, of course, Connally too is beginning to waffle.)

If Specter's quaint theory of aerodynamics had even the slightest degree of validity, then the most time that would have elapsed for the "magic bullet" to pass from Kennedy to Connally would have been two frames, not ten or more. The evidence is cinematic. So, for that matter, is the very distinct probability that there were two fatal headshots, not one.

The Commission saw the Zapruder film, and yet it would base its conclusion that the fatal headshot came from behind on FBI blow-ups of all the frames. As is evident in Volume 18 of the 26-volume Appendix, frames #314 and 315 are printed in *reverse*, making it appear as if there was no bullet from the front. An accident?

Sharp-eyed critics, notably West Coast researcher David Lifton, had a friend write a letter to FBI photo specialist Lyndal Shaneyfelt, asking for clarification. Shortly thereafter, a *personal* letter from J. Edgar Hoover arrived, acknowledging:

"...you are correct in the observation that [the frames] are transposed in Volume 18, as noted in your letter. This is a printing error and does not exist in the actual Commission Exhibit." Maybe not. But we only have Hoover's word for it, which based on what we know today, wasn't very good. And besides, the Commission decision *was* based on the reversed frames.

Another interesting photographic oddity concerns the controversial throat wound in the President. We already know about the verbal and artistic "surgery" that moved the back wound up by six inches, and the realignment of trajectories so that the bullet was shown to have entered JFK at a 17 rather than a 45-60 degree angle. This, too, apparently came after seeing Zapruder's film. Apparently, the Commission staff took the angle from the southeast corner window of the sixth floor of the Depository, to where the limousine was between Zapruder frames #210 and #224— completely disregarding the physical law that holds that the line between two fixed points is a constant. But then, the points were anything but fixed: the southeast corner of the Depository remained where it always had been, but according to Dealey Plaza groundskeeper Emmett Hudson, the Stemmons Freeway sign behind which Kennedy is said to have received the first shot was moved *right after the assassination,* and a year later, *removed entirely.* No small point, but again, one to which the Commission didn't address itself, ever.

History does not often give us a play-by-play picture of the killing of a head of state. Matthew Brady was not at Ford's Theatre the night Lincoln was shot, but Abraham Zapruder was on Dealey Plaza the moment Kennedy was. What follows, then, is a frame-by-frame description of those 22 seconds.

There's a snippet of a child digging soil on a

patio—perhaps Zapruder's grandchild? Stop. Now we see Marilyn Sitzman and two others getting ready for the parade. Zapruder adjusts for light reading. Abruptly, the sequence ends. *FRAMES 1 to 132:* We see three lead motorcycles turning from Houston onto Elm Street. But wait, what have we here? One of the three cyclists leaves the formation, either staying on Houston or swinging onto the Elm Street extension leading to the railroad yard and parking lot behind the Depository. We can't follow him. In any event, he goes off-screen to the left and doesn't reappear. Now, note the reaction of the second cop: as the first cycle leaves the motorcade, he appears dumbfounded, turns his head to the right, looks over his shoulder to see where his colleague is going. He visually trails him for about twenty feet of his own travel. Why did the cyclist leave? The Report didn't ask,

FRAMES #133 to 153:

The limousine is in front of the Depository, about to take its 137-foot and 6-inch ride into history. It is, according to the film speed, traveling an average of 11.67 mph, well under the prescribed Secret Service minimum. JFK is waving to the crowd, wiping a lock of windblown hair from his face. All else appears normal. The car keeps coming towards us.

FRAME #154:

JFK is looking to his left, his right arm resting on the car door.

FRAMES #155 to 156:

No longer exist. They are missing from the film. We are at the first splice, one that the Government and Time Inc. have publicly denied exists (by omitting any reference to these frames, ever). Which is why, in Volume 18 of the Report's Appendix, the Zapruder sequence *starts* not where

Zapruder began but at frame #171. Ask us no questions and we'll tell you no lies. Was there something on these two frames we shouldn't see? Did something happen to shatter JFK's tranquility? The sound of a shot, perhaps, a blank, a signal?

FRAMES #157 to 188:

All we know is what we see starting at #157. The President looks troubled. He appears to be responding to something in a split second—one ninth of a second or two frames—because now he looks sharply to his right and the oncoming Stemmons Freeway roadsign. Then he relaxes and begins to wave again, but slowly, warily. Something's clearly amiss.

FRAMES #189 to 205:

The President is hit. The relationship between his right hand and his face changes drastically. From the angle of the Zapruder camera, it appears that JFK's hand jumps forward, but in fact it's his upper torso that's pushed slightly to the rear. Could it be that this is where something enters his throat? It is not a frivolous question since it could just be that Zapruder's camera may have seen something no one else did: because, inexplicably, right after frame #189, the film loses a degree of sharpness that can only be explained by the photographer reacting unconsciously to *something*. And if this *was* the first shot, it could not have come from the Book Depository.

FRAMES #206 to 209:

JFK's arm continues to drop. His entire body is now obscured by the road sign. Only his head is still visible. But something else appears to be obscured. For at frame #207 there is an obvious horizontal line running through the entire width of the frame, just below the midway point.

FRAMES #210 to 212:

We pause. At #212 we see a similar line one-third of the way down the frame. Freezing it, we encounter something strange: on the top half of the frame, we see a tree on the right, but on the bottom half, the tree is *in the middle*. The freak is actually man-made, since #212 turns out to be a hybrid. Frames #208, #209, #210 and #211 have all been spliced out. Why?

Time Inc. explains that there had been an accident in its photographic department: a junior employee seems to have damaged the four frames while enlarging the film into 4x5 transparencies, and in splicing, he also damaged frames #207 and #212. A not terribly convincing story, for it's hard to believe that Time Inc., having paid so hefty a sum to Abraham Zapruder, would entrust such an historically valuable and costly film to a beginner.

But here's a puzzler: if frame #210 is missing, how could the Commission have said it was here that JFK received his first bullet? We will see it was a purely erroneous claim, highly disputable by the testimony of retired U.S. Air Force Major Phillip L. Willis.

Major Willis was a bystander who happened to take sixteen 35 mm. color slides of the assassination—six before, one during and nine afterwards. He has been selling twelve of them to the public since November 1963, the fifth in his commercial series being pivotal to our challenge to the Government's claim about Zapruder frame #210.

As Willis testified: "The shot caused me to squeeze the camera shutter and I got a picture of the President *as he was hit with the first shot....*" Willis was standing on the south curb of Elm

Street, directly across from the front door of the Depository. He was aiming northwest.

In Willis #5 we see, in the foreground, the two port-side motorcyclists and the Secret Service follow-up car, just behind the Lincoln. Clearly visible is the back of JFK's head and the top nine or ten inches of his back. We also see, in the background, the triple underpass, a wooden stockade fence and the retaining wall of the "grassy knoll". We also see the concrete pedestal, *and* Abraham Zapruder and Marilyn Sitzman. We can also make out the head and torso of a man on top of the retaining wall, and in front of the Stemmons Freeway sign, a man holding an open umbrella. We will return to both shortly.

Willis hadn't intended to squeeze the shutter. It was an involuntary reaction to the shot, and it was "so instantaneous, in fact that the crowd hadn't had the time to react."

Now, the Dallas Police, Secret Service, FBI and the Warren Commission all agree that neither Lee Harvey Oswald nor anyone else, for that matter, could have fired a shot at the limousine between frames #166 and #210 because the foliage of the oak tree would have blocked his line of sight—and fire. And that, therefore, the first crack he would have had at a visible target would have come at frame #210 at which point, from Zapruder's viewpoint, the limousine was obscured by the road sign.

But if we now closely examine Zapruder's footage, we see Major Willis—just as we see Abraham Zapruder in Willis #5. There's no road sign blocking their respective views.

(The Bell & Howell "Director" series camera, according to B&H officials, photographs informa-

144

tion not only in the normal "picture area" but *also* in the left-hand border area between the sprocket holes. When Zapruder had copies of his film made in Dallas, and when *Life* magazine had copies made in both Chicago and New York, this sprocket hole area was masked out. Nothing sinister here, just routine customer service. Only in the *original* print did this extraneous information survive. Examination at Time-Life, revealed that as Zapruder panned to the right, Willis disappeared to the left—into the sprocket hole area at frame #202. He remained there until somewhere between frames #210 and #212. By frame #213, he's gone from the film forever.)

The critical object that appears in both Zapruder and Willis is the *left shoulder and arm* of Secret Service agent Clint Hill. In the Willis photo, a straight line drawn between Zapruder's camera and the right-hand edge of the Stemmons Freeway sign, will extend onward to the center of Clint Hill's left arm, before heading into the lens of Willis' camera. Conversely, a line leaving Willis' camera will travel through Hill's left arm, pass the same road sign edge, and into Zapruder's lens.

And where does this startling confluence take place? Not in Zapruder #210 but *eight frames earlier*—in #202.

Which means that between the time the first shot was fired and the time the sound reached Phil Willis' ear, and the reaction time to press his shutter, we have quite a gap. Arbitrarily allowing for one second between gunshot and film exposure, this means that the first shot that caused Willis to press his shutter must have been fired somewhere around Zapruder frame #184. (A number of Warren Report critics are more generous and place it at

#189). Suddenly, it all makes sense: the President at #189 is *indeed* reacting to a shot, thus accounting for the second splice.

For if the image in the sprocket hole area of Zapruder's film would have shown Willis *lowering* his camera *before* frame #210—when the Commission said Oswald fired his first shot—then Willis took his famous photo *before* Oswald could possibly have gotten off that first round. On the other hand, *had* Oswald shot at #210, then Willis' photo could not have been taken before #228—nearly two seconds or 26 frames after it actually had been taken. The Commission couldn't have it both ways, but apparently tried to.

FRAMES #213 to 223:

Now our eyes catch something else, a strange object to the right of the roadway sign. At first indescribable, by frame #221 it is clearly an open umbrella. As JFK approaches, it starts to rise and twirl clockwise. Why should we care? Because it is the only open umbrella in Dealey Plaza, and this morning's grey, overcast weather has given way to brilliant sunshine and blustery winds, too windy for an open umbrella. (Afterwards, questioning of spectators by independent researchers indicated that the umbrella had been *closed* until the motorcade turned onto Elm, and then it opened. Photographs taken after the fusillade—while people were still clambering to safety—show the man closing his umbrella, glancing at the receding motorcade, and slowly, almost nonchalantly, walking up Elm towards the Depository. He has never been identified; the Commission never asked. There is conjecture that the twirling umbrella may have been some sort of signal).

FRAMES #224 to 236:

The President begins to re-appear from behind

the road sign. In #224, only his left arm is visible, completing the arc begun in #189. In #225, his face and torso become visible. His arms now rise in a protective motion towards his throat, and continue to rise to #227. At this frame, a shot strikes him in the back—the shot that would become the "neck" shot. We submit that this was not the first shot but the second, and that it came not from the Depository but possibly from the second or third floor of the Dal-Tex Building. If so, we have a third gunman to contend with.

FRAME #237:

Connally takes his first bullet. His cheeks visibly puff out as the shot knocks the wind out of him, fracturing his rib cage, fragments puncturing and collapsing his right lung. It enters his back at a 27 degree angle, at a 20 degree right to left axis: it could not have come from the Depository.

FRAMES #238 to 254:

Now Connally's right shoulder buckles, and his hair becomes disarranged. He lurches towards Nellie, who begins to pull him down—a life-saving move, it would turn out.

FRAME #255:

Another pivotal picture requiring another freeze on our part. It is precisely at this point that one of the single most important still photos was taken—not only of the President but of his "assassin".

James W. (Ike) Altgens was an Associated Press photographer. According to his own estimate, he was standing on the south curbside, 15 feet from the oncoming limousine. He even appears in the Zapruder film, his Nikkorex 35 mm. camera to eye, using a 105 mm. telephoto lens. His shutter clicks at a point (the film tells us) 3.6 seconds after the "back/neck" shot and 3.2 seconds before the fatal head shot(s). The photo, taken through the

Lincoln's windshield, shows Kennedy clenching his fist at his throat, Jackie's gloved hand holding his left arm just above the wrist. We make out Connally, himself just struck and about to career into Nellie's lap.

We also see three Secret Service agents, on the running board of the follow-up car, looking sharply to the rear. Police motorcyclist James Chaney, on starboard, is looking right into the passenger compartment. To the left we see the oak tree—and standing in the Depository doorway, a man, the most controversial subject in this entire scene.

He is wearing a T-shirt with a torn elastic neckband. Over it, a shirt that appears to be open to his midriff. He is in his early 20s, clean-shaven. He bears an uncanny likeness to Lee Harvey Oswald. *Indeed, he could have been and probably was Oswald!*

The FBI never called photographer Altgens to testify until the Warren Commission had been goaded into examining this picture by New York *Herald-Tribune* reporter Dom Bonafede on May 24, 1964, and the very next day, by columnist Maggie Daly in the Chicago *American*. They had both identified Oswald in the picture; why hadn't the Commission?

The FBI hadn't been entirely asleep: three months earlier, on February 29, Billy Nolan Lovelady, a co-worker of Oswald's, told the FBI that he'd been on the right side of the steps in the Depository doorway. Asked to point himself out in the Altgens photo, he fingered the man who looks like Oswald. Lovelady recalled on that day he'd been wearing a "red and white vertically striped shirt". *Tilt.* By no stretch of the imagination is the man in the doorway wearing a red and white vertically striped shirt, nor is he standing on the right side of the steps. He appears left of center on the steps. And so, the FBI didn't rush this data to the Commission, for obvious reasons.

While it is true that Oswald and Lovelady shared many similar facial features—leading to the confusion—the shirt discrepancies are too great. Other amateur films made that day, in color, show two men resembling each other facially, but only facially. Actually, Lovelady's memory failed him: he was wearing a broad red and blue plaid shirt, while Oswald's was an orange tweed-like affair—a pattern identical to the shirt worn by the man in the Altgens photograph. When arrested, Oswald wore a T-shirt with a broken elastic collar, *and* the same orange tweed shirt with missing buttons (accounting for the open front in the Altgens photo).

While the cheeks, noses, hairlines and eyes of the two could, in truth, belong to either, one (Oswald) was clean-shaven, the other (Lovelady) had a growth of beard. This is evident from seeing three other amateur films, two in color, one in black and white. "Crucial as this indentification is" to the heart of the case, observes researcher Harold Weisberg, "in all ten million words (the Report) does not print any of these...photographs."

No wonder: had it done so, the verdict would never have stood up. Lee Harvey Oswald could not have stood in the doorway on the first floor while he was on the sixth floor killing the President with a rifle. As Weisberg puts it, pictures may not lie, but "they can be *made* to lie by ignoring them."

FRAMES #256 to 312:

Kennedy now begins to lean forward. Connally, in agony, is shown still clutching his

Stetson in his right hand. Obviously, his wrist has not yet been fractured by Specter's magic bullet. *FRAMES #313 to 344:*

A shot hit Kennedy from behind, by all appearances, in the right temple. At this point, the head seems to explode in a starburst of blood, skull fragments and brain matter. AP photographer Altgens was close enough to hear Jackie cry, "Oh, no!" He told the FBI later that he:

> "... was staring in utter disbelief at what [he] had just witnessed and was so aghast that [he] froze and did not snap the picture."

Altgens remains one of the best eyewitnesses. At the moment of impact:

> "there were flesh particles that flew out of the side of his head in my direction from where I was standing, so much so that it indicated to me that the shot came out of the left side of his head."

This would seem to contradict the Government's contention that the rear bullet took out the right side of the President's head.

Pictorial corroboration is offered also by another 8 mm. color home film, by Orville Nix, standing on the opposite side of Elm Street from where Zapruder was. It, too, shows Kennedy's head driven violently *backwards,* though not quite as graphically as Zapruder's film, in which JFK—his body held rigid by the backbrace—is hurled violently back and to the left with such force that it appears to be actually *lifting* him out of his seat.

The Nix film also shows us, at moment of impact, a man who appears to have been one of the gunmen. He can be seen *behind* and to the *left* of Zapruder and he appears to be aiming a rifle in

Kennedy's direction. In Nix's fourth sequence, he disappears, while all else—including spectators—remain frozen.

Now, it is basic Newtonian physics that when an object is struck by another object, the force of the moving object will transfer a degree of momentum to the stationary object.

In this instance, the moving object is a bullet traveling approximately 1,900 feet per second, the stationary object is JFK's head. The Zapruder film shows the presidential head moving forward, but only for one frame (#312-313) at a calculated rate of acceleration of 69.1 feet per second per second. But now, between #313-314, an immediate reversal of direction takes place. The backward acceleration is now measured at 100.3 feet per second per second. In all of the 18,704 pages of the Report and its appendices there is not *one* word about the obvious and undeniable backward motion of the President's head and torso. That's because they may not have been looking for it when they saw the film; and because in the still blow-ups, the FBI "accidentally" reversed those crucial frames.

This is what we see. We also see something else, notably that Jackie's left hand is holding JFK's left hand in her lap, her right hand now cradling the President's back—which would make it rather difficult (as Itek's photo analysts suggest) that she, and not the impact of a bullet, *pushed* JFK back. Even if her hands were elsewhere, she could not have done so at a speed one-fourth of that shown on the film, and certainly not as soon (1/8th of a second) after impact. Furthermore, Itek's John Wolf totally disregards the fact that Kennedy is thrown *sidewards* to his left, and spun counterclockwise. The kindest thing one can say about Itek's "explanation" is that it borders on deliberate misinformation.

Police motorcycle escort Bobby H. Hargis, closest to the car on the left, testified, "I was splattered by blood and brain and a kind of bloody water" in such vast quantities that "I thought at first I might have been hit." (Hargis is the cop shown in various pictures dismounting and running up the incline of the "grassy knoll", convinced that's where the shots came from.) His partner, officer B.J. Martin, riding five feet to the left and eight to the rear of the limousine, said he was showered "by blood stains...and other material that looked like pieces of flesh".

Parts of Kennedy's skull were also found behind and to the left of where the fatal shot(s) impacted. Deputy Constable Seymour Weitzman came across a chunk of skull at curbside 10 to 15 feet to the *left* of the limousine's path. The next day, a skull fragment was picked up in the grass on the *south* side of Elm, 25 feet from the killing zone, by college student Billy Harper. He eventually turned it over to Dr. A.B. Cairns, chief pathologist at Methodist Hospital. Later, Dr. Cairns told the FBI it "looked like it came from the occipital (rear) region of the skull". Forensic pathologists have difficulty explaining how a rear shot could drive a chunk from the occipital region 25 feet to the rear; they have no difficulty with such an event resulting from a right-front tangential wound (see Chapter II).

FRAMES #345 to 406:

Now we see Jackie climb out of her bloodstained seat and onto the trunk of the limousine. Until she testified, it was assumed she was trying to crawl and run away; now, of course, we know she was in a state of shock, trying to retrieve a piece of her husband's brain that had landed on the trunk. Clint Hill, at #367, climbs aboard, ready to force Jackie back. He testified:

"...she was...reaching for something. I thought I saw something come off the back, too...I do know the next day we found the portion of the President's head in the street."

FRAMES #407 to 447:

Zapruder, also in shock, keeps on filming. At #407, his B&H camera picks up a strange object in the foliage of the shrubbery to his right. We see it for the first time at #412: the distinct outline of a man's head. At #413, Zapruder stops panning for one frame, and the head, ears, and what could be the stock and barrel of a rifle become vividly clear, only to fade as Zapruder resumes panning towards the triple underpass.

FRAMES #448 to 486:

In his final frames, Zapruder also picks up the stockade fence. It is possible to discern the outline of at least one person who might, conceivably, have been a member of the hit team. At #486, he releases his finger from the camera.

We are left with two issues raised by the film. One is that the Report claims Specter's super-bullet penetrated Connally's rib cage and on its way to his thigh, shattered his wrist. But the film shows us that at the time of the fatal *head*shots, well after Connally has been wounded, he is still holding his Stetson, 4.2 seconds after the Commission says he ought to have let go. A blow-up of the entire sequence starting at, say, #210 reveals that before #313, his wrist has not yet been assaulted. And at the time of the Kennedy headshots, we see *no* trace of blood on the exposed white cuff of Connally's shirt. It is therefore not illogical to suggest that his wrist may have been fractured by a fragment of the first headshot, or indeed, by the spent bullet itself.

The second issue concerns the shot(s) that missed. The Report insists there was only one miss, but that doesn't jibe at all with the findings of at least *three* different bullet marks on the surrounding terrain. Not all could have been fragments.

One bystander, James T. Tague, was standing on or near Main Street—twice as far from the Depository as the limousine. He was struck by a concrete chip that had been blasted off the curbstone. It cut his left cheek, requiring outpatient care at Parkland Hospital. If, as the Commission says, this was the second shot, then expert rifleman Oswald missed the limousine by 21 feet to the right and 33 feet overhead, the bullet traveling 260 feet instead of 90. There also were no copper traces found on the curbstone, thus suggesting the Tague bullet came from somewhere else, and from someone other than Oswald.

Then there was a linear bullet mark in the concrete right next to a manhole cover on the south curb of Elm in the killing zone. This indelible scar was located that same afternoon by a Dallas policeman. The only thing is that the angle of impact lines up not with the Book Depository or the Dal-Tex Building but with the Dallas Records Building (jail), right next to the Police headquarters.

Another mark, the third "miss", is a long scar on the north sidewalk of Elm. Its origin seems less clearly defined than the other two. It could have come either from the southwestern corner of

Dealey Plaza or the *western* corner of the Book Depository. If this is so, then the testimony of the one eyewitness who *actually* saw a gunman in the Depository would be confirmed. His name was Arnold Rowland, who told the Commission that minutes before the motorcade had turned onto Elm, he'd pointed the gunman out to his wife, describing him as a Secret Service agent with rifle. By the time his wife looked to where Rowland had pointed, the man had backed away into the shadows of the sixth floor. There was no Secret Service contingent in the Book Depository. The Commission totally twisted Rowland's testimony: moving the gunman he saw to the opposite end of the building.

Looking back, then, the Zapruder film offers abundant evidence of the classic military ambush: a triage of fire, with the slowly moving target hemmed in on all sides. The gunmen couldn't have missed.

How many there were remains a matter of conjecture. We know one thing: it couldn't have been a lone assassin, perched where the Commission had put him. Had he been there, he would not have waited for the limousine to make its turn. He would have fired as it came towards him on Houston; indeed, at the point the limousine turned, at about 8 m.p.h., this mythical lone assassin could have *dropped* the Mannlicher-Carcano on Kennedy's head and crushed his skull.

We do not doubt that there were gunmen in the Depository. They had their instructions: hold your fire until the car has turned into Elm, from which there would be no escape.

Was one of the gunmen Oswald? Based on the

Altgens photo and the testimony of some of his co-workers (who put him on the first floor at 12:15 p.m., the exact moment some "eyewitnesses" on Dealey Plaza declared they saw the "assassin" on the sixth floor), we'd say, *no. Someone* was on the sixth floor, and *a* Mannlicher-Carcano was fired. But there's nothing in terms of evidence physical, or cinematic, to implicate Oswald.

The paucity of the evidence is so overwhelming that even staff lawyer Wesley J. Liebeler, who should have known better, lapsed into freshman law school gibberish when he memoed Rankin: "The best evidence that Oswald could fire as fast as he did and hit the target is that he did so". It's almost as good a *non sequitur* as Walter Cronkite's explanation on the CBS Warren Report retrospective of June 1967:

> "It seems reasonable to say that an expert could fire that rifle in five seconds. It seems equally reasonable to say that Oswald, under normal circumstances, would take longer. But these were not normal circumstances. Oswald was shooting at a *President*."

A better final word on the shooting is that of French ballistics expert Renaud de la Taille. Writing in *Science et Vie,* de la Taille calls the Mannlicher-Carcano "the least precise of military rifles". To have hit Kennedy, given his mediocre marksmanship and the poor condition of his sniperscope, Oswald should

> "...therefore have pulled the trigger .13 seconds before President Kennedy's head reached the center of the scope. It amounts to a feat such as could be realized only by a crack shot with years of training behind him...when one considers that military firing at mobile targets requires four-fold machine

gun mountings putting out tens of missiles a second, the firing being directed by automatic correctors...one will better assess Oswald's miracle."

The President Goes South

"Dallas is a sort of Humble Oil Company road map of Albert Camus' Existentialist hell. Only here we can see set down, block by block, the details of its landmarks: here the hero, John F. Kennedy, is dead in the center of his parade and here the prisoner, Lee Oswald, is dead in the center of his custodians."

—Murray Kempton

The next-to-last words John F. Kennedy heard over the deafening noise of the tumultuous street reception came from Nellie Connally. "You can't say Dallas doesn't love you!" And he was still conscious when Connally, struck by *his* bullet, cried, "My God! They're going to kill us all!"

Kennedy really didn't want to go to Texas. He had to go. Party unity demanded it; the 1964 election may have depended on it. The trip, conceived as early as June, was to be an attempt to pacify the warring tribes of Connally and those of his rival, Senator Ralph Yarborough. Privately, JFK wished a plague on both factions. But without some sort of truce, Kennedy could not count on the state's twenty-five electoral votes, even *with* Johnson on the ticket. Back in 1960, they'd barely managed to carry Texas with a plurality of 46,233.

He was clearly looking forward to getting out of

what he called "nut country" after that night's gala spread at the LBJ Ranch. He was scheduled to spend the weekend at "Wexford", the new $100,000 retreat in Virginia's hunt country. Cabot Lodge was due for a Sunday breakfast update on post-Diem Vietnam. On Saturday, he expected to see his old friend Bill Attwood, the former *Look* magazine editor and U.S. Ambassador to Guinea. Attwood had recently joined the U.S. Mission to the United Nations under Adlai Stevenson as an advisor on African affairs. He'd been approached, at Castro's behest, by the Guinean Ambassador to Cuba with the proposition that Washington and Havana start talking again. Castro bridled at Moscow's bit and had instructed his aide, Dr. Rene Vallejo, to let Washington know he wanted "to talk personally to us about improving relations and was pleased to find out we were willing to listen," Attwood recalls. So, unknown to Secretary of State Dean Rusk, JFK told Attwood to move speedily towards effecting a reconciliation. Now the publisher of the Long Island paper *Newsday*, Bill Attwood says a breakthrough was "imminent" when Kennedy was shot.

Yet, on the very *day* Kennedy was killed— according to the Church Committee's report on foreign assassinations—the CIA was equipping a "dissident official" within the Castro government with a ballpoint pen containing a poison hypodermic needle. While this would suggest that the Langley hierarchy was not informed about the Dallas "plot"—why kill Castro when Kennedy would not live out the day?—it also reinforces the belief that the Agency would have stopped at nothing to prevent the reconciliation.

On November 21, JFK flew to Houston to dedicate the new Aero-Space Medical Health

Center at Brooks Air Force Base. That night, there was a testimonial dinner for Congressman Albert Thomas. The Presidential party then flew into Ft. Worth to spend the night. Johnson had flown in to Dallas ahead to speak at the bottlers' convention.

On the morning of the 22, when Kennedy returned to room 850 of the Hotel Texas in Ft. Worth after speaking at a breakfast meeting of the Chamber of Commerce, Kenny O'Donnell showed him a copy of that morning's Dallas *News*. There was an ad, sardonically headlined "Welcome Mr. Kennedy to Dallas". It was a scurrilous piece of trash that ticked off twelve "counts of treason" for which the President was told he must answer. Kennedy was not amused, but tried to shrug it off:

> "Look, if anybody really wants to shoot the
> President, it is not a very difficult job. All one
> has to do is get on a high building someday
> with a telescopic rifle and there is nothing
> anybody can do to defend against such an
> attempt."

On November 7, the White House had sent agent Winston G. Lawson down to Dallas to meet with resident agent Forrest V. Sorrels and check out security and the lay of the land. They had preferred to arrange Kennedy's speech in the low-ceilinged Women's Club, closer in town, but Connally wanted the Trade Mart, not because he expected a record turn-out but because at the Trade Mart, the dais would be a two-level affair. He and JFK would be on top; Yarborough and his lieutenants below.

On the 18th, Lawson returned, this time to ride the proposed motorcade route. Security would be difficult. He guessed there probably were more than 20,000 windows along the length of the run from Love Field to where they would swing onto

Stemmons Freeway to the Mart, and the Dallas Police Department simply couldn't cover them all. The next day, the 19th, the Dallas papers published the route map: the caravan would go all the way down Main Street, *bisect Dealey Plaza*, and jump the slight divider past the triple underpass and swing onto the Stemmons Freeway ramp. Apparently, the fatal Main-to-Houston-to-Elm zigzag was a last-minute improvisation, made to accommodate either the voters or the assassins. No one yet has explained who made the switch, why, and on whose authorization.

Dallas Police Chief Curry, who would ride in the pilot car, had informed Lawson that his people's supervision would stop at Houston and Main because there wouldn't be much crowd traffic after that. Sheriff Bill Decker, it was later rumored, had told his deputies not to exert themselves for this parade. Worst of all was the laxity of the U.S. Secret Service; at least the one positive thing to have come out of the Warren Report were its recommendations on improving presidential security: JFK's legacy to Gerry Ford.

It shouldn't have happened, at least not that way. Not with the assassination blueprint, that famous Miami tape, that described the plans to kill Kennedy. Chief Headley had sent it up to the Protective Research unit. What went wrong?

Just about everything. Take the motorcade itself. Since its founding in 1860, the Secret Service had never allowed the President and the Vice President to be in close proximity in the same city and in the same procession—with the exception, perhaps, of clasping each other on the back on the podium of the renominating convention. Why this time, and in politically schizophrenic Dallas of all places?

The Secret Service procedural manual further states that even in "safe" cities, motorcades in which the presidential limousine has the protective bubbletop removed must go at least 44 mph, and/or move through a *"cordon sanitaire"*—a route so well covered that all windows are sealed and police sharpshooters are stationed on rooftops. In Dallas that day, the motorcade traveled at about 12 mph and when it made the fatal zig-zag it slowed down to 8 mph.

The sequence of the cars was also at variance with planned procedure. The presidential limousine was to have been seventh in line, but actually ended up right behind the lead car, a 1963 Ford carrying Chief Curry and other local officials, and in front of the 1959 Cadillac convertible bearing the Secret Service detail. What is highly curious is this: usually, the press vehicle precedes the presidential limousine so that its occupants can photograph the President. At Love Field, where the cars were assembled, the press car was numbered "six"—the limousine being tagged "seven." In actuality, the press car ended up in the tail end of the motorcade—fourteenth. As a result, none of the photographers in the press car recorded the assassination at the moment it happened—photographic documentation that would have been of considerable evidential importance. Was this an accidental mix-up?

Retired Air Force intelligence officer L. Fletcher Prouty, who dealt in presidential security during the FDR, Truman and Eisenhower years, maintains, "No one has to direct an assassination—it happens. The active role is played secretly by *permitting* it to happen." Kennedy, he feels, was murdered "by the breakdown of the protective system that should have made an assassination impossible. Once insiders knew that he would not be protected, it was easy to pick the day and the place."

Who *were* these insiders? Prouty has his hunches, as do we all, but proof is impossible to get. He does say, though, that "those responsible for luring Kennedy to Dallas were not even in on the plan itself." They didn't have to be. "All the conspirators had to do was to let the right 'mechanics' know...."

What seems so incomprehensible, after the Miami tape tip-off, was that the Warren Report says the Secret Service's Protective Research section claimed to have had "no listing for any individual deemed to be a potential danger to the President". (In 1967, Miami newspaper reporter Bill Barry asked the Secret Service about this discrepancy, and the reply he got was, "I can't comment, and you can't quote me on my no comment." The FBI was equally Sphinx-like to Barry's question: "We had nothing to do with the tape." Asked if he even *knew* about the tape, that is, had the Secret Service told the FBI?, the agent answered, "I wouldn't be able to answer your question.")

Given the treatment accorded UN Ambassador Adlai E. Stevenson the month before, when he had been figuratively driven out of town by an enraged, spitting mob, it would have been prudent—suggests Colonel Prouty—to have called in outside help. If the local cops were incapable of maintaining law and order, there was always the crack 112th U.S. Army Intelligence Unit. Its commanding officer, Col. Maximillian Reich, had offered his unit's services to the Secret Service, but he was told they weren't needed.

Quite possibly, Kennedy himself had something

to do with this curious *laissez-faire* attitude. He bridled at being surrounded by bodyguards, those "Ivy League charlatans" who kept him from pressing the flesh. "The President feels politics and protection don't mix," JFK aide O'Donnell once told Gerald A. Behn, head of the Secret Service's White House detail.

Until Kennedy, all presidential limousines had agents riding on the running boards. But SS 100 X, the 1961 custom-built Lincoln Continental, came with retractable running boards, actually dashboard-controlled hydraulic side-steps. They were not one of Henry Ford's better ideas: people who pressed too close to the running car ran the risk of having their legs cut off below the knee. So they were never used, and the agents rode behind in a follow-up car.

That morning, they were less than alert. The night before, nine of the twenty-eight agents assigned to the President had stayed out late, drinking too much at a Ft. Worth dive called The Cellar. At the time of the shooting, Senator Yarborough recalled, "their reactions were sluggish". Only afterwards it would turn out that no one had ever troubled themselves to actually go into the Depository to check out its potentiality as a hazard, and even more shocking, out of a nation of nearly 200 million, the Secret Service had only 400 people on file as "potential assassins".

Not that Oswald would have been one of them. We know his dossier wasn't one of the 400, although we can't be sure that the Dallas cops didn't have their own little Oswald folder stashed away somewhere. And as reporter Bill Barry found out, the FBI and Secret Service weren't talking much to each other about presidential security.

(Today, with its budget increased from $5

million to $95 million, the Secret Service has gone from file folders to computers, from 400 to 47,000 names—none of them, incidentally, women, until Fromme and Moore came along in 1975.)

It has been suggested, over the years, that Lee Harvey Oswald got his job at the Texas School Book Depository *just* so that he could kill John F. Kennedy. This seems doubtful. He got his job on October 15—more than a month before the White House announced Kennedy would be visiting Dallas. Furthermore, as Marina herself told the FBI during her first night of "protective custody"—before she learned to do the Government's bidding—her husband hadn't even heard of JFK coming to Dallas when he'd visited her and the children in Irving the night before. And shortly after 9 a.m. on the 22nd, according to co-worker James Jarman Jr., he and Oswald were looking out of the sixth-floor window and saw people beginning to cluster at the corner of Elm and Houston. Oswald, according to Jarman, asked what the occasion was, since it was only that morning that the papers indicated the motorcade would be coming by the Book Depository, and Oswald—it was generally known—did not read the papers. Jarman told him and, as he later told the Commission, "Oswald said, 'Oh, I see', and walked away."

If Oswald didn't know, it's plain that other people *did*. People in the position to plant enough evidence linking the killing to Oswald in the Book Depository, people who knew about the last-minute change in the route of the motorcade, and with enough time to create back-up evidence. The gun that was found on the sixth floor *had* been fired, although there is no way to prove it had been fired there, or by Oswald. Three spent shells *were* found, by the Dallas Police, although here again, it cannot be proven they actually held the bullets that hit the two men below; two of the four cartridge cases (the fourth, with bullet, was found in the gun's chamber) bore marks characteristic of the rifle that was found, one did not and had a dented lip. It could not have held a projectile that day.

Still, two ballistically matched fragments were found that night in the presidential limousine, and one whole bullet—Commission Exhibit 399—was retrieved more or less intact at the hospital.

Dr. Josiah Thompson of Haverford College, one of the most down-to-earth critics of the Report and a former *Life* magazine consultant on the assassination inquiry, maintains:

> "Clearly, Oswald's rifle was used. Whether it was fired by Oswald himself is still open to question, but the contention that it was the *only* weapon fired at the President becomes increasingly unacceptable as the facts accumulate."

We will see why as we go along. But in order to do so, it becomes necessary to look back, to see where Oswald came from and what brought him and John F. Kennedy together on that November day.

The "Assassin" Goes East

"Obviously, the Passport Office believes travel abroad to be not a right that is exercised at the discretion of the citizens but a privilege to be exercised at the discretion of the State Department."
—Prof. Henry Steele Commager

Like the man he was accused of killing, Oswald didn't want to come to Texas; he'd been sent back home by the Government, ostensibly in disgrace. He was a defector who had changed his mind. Or so we were told afterwards.

Lee Harvey Oswald was born on October 18, 1939, in New Orleans, two months after the death of his father, Robert E. Lee Oswald, the second of Marguerite Claverie Pic Oswald Ekdahl's three husbands. At age three, he joined his eight-year-old brother Robert, and ten-year-old half-brother John Edward Pic, in an orphanage because the widow Oswald could not provide. He came out the next year and in 1945, got a stepfather, Dallas businessman Edwin A. Ekdahl.

That marriage lasted three stormy years and obviously affected the boy. In spite of a high IQ (118) he was an "average" student, and in 1952, after Marguerite, Robert and he moved to New York so that they could be closer to John Pic, stationed there with the Coast Guard, he lapsed into truancy. His anti-social behavior has been used by the Warren Commission to build its case for the "lone nut", but there are Nobel Prize winners walking around these days whose childhood was a great deal more traumatic than

Oswald's. In any event, two years later, the Oswalds moved back south, to Marguerite's hometown of New Orleans. At age 16, Oswald dropped out of school and tried to enlist in the U.S. Marine Corps.

For the next ten months, Oswald took a variety of menial jobs, biding his time until, on October 24, 1956—eight days after his 17th birthday—the Marines accepted him. It was to be a turning point in his life.

After boot training at Camp Pendleton, outside of San Diego, he was shipped to the Naval Air Technology Training Center in Jacksonville, Fla., where began the amazing transformation of "Ozzie Rabbit" into bookworn Oswald. He began studying the Russian language, learned it well enough to subscribe to Soviet periodicals; he became a history buff, soon proving to be a worthy political debating partner for his commanding officer, a graduate of the Gerogetown University Foreign Service School. Along the line, he received his security clearance, for he was now becoming an experienced radar technician, having been sent to Biloxi for specialized training.

In August 1957, he shipped out for the Orient, arriving in Japan on September 12. His assignment: USMC Air Control Squadron #1 (MACS-1) at Atsugi, a highly secret staging area for U-2 reconnaissance aircraft sent aloft over China and North Korea, twenty miles west of Tokyo. That was the year of the famous Quemoy-Matsu Crisis, when the Red Chinese threatened to invade two offshore islands held by the Nationalists. Eisenhower sent in the Seventh Fleet, and MACS-1 sent Oswald to Taiwan, then to Cubi Point, another U-2 base in the Philippines. In December 1958, he was reassigned stateside to El Toro, for advanced radar intelligence training and foreign languages. No one objected to his receiving Soviet newspapers and political journals. The Warren Report even tells us "a careful check of local records...disclosed no derogatory data."

Now, pay attention. In March 1959, a full nine months before he was scheduled for discharge, the erstwhile high school drop-out decided to go to college. Not just any college, say, like Tulane or the University of Texas, but to the Albert Schweitzer College in far-off Churwalden, Switzerland. He wanted to "study philosophy". Oswald was accepted by the school for the 1960 spring term. Seemingly impatient to get out, Oswald on August 17 applied for a "hardship" dependency discharge; it seems that eight months before, according to his forms, mother Marguerite had suffered an "industrial accident" back in Ft. Worth and now could not support herself. The monthly allotment payments Oswald sent apparently were insufficient.

If the request was irregular—he failed to produce supporting medical evidence for the claim—so was the way it was handled. His discharge was approved in a record eleven days, no questions asked. On September 11, he was mustered out.

It is clear that somebody up there liked him—the Office of Naval Intelligence, perhaps; or, they might have seen something in him that had escaped the Freudian eye of Dr. Hartogs. For, seven days before he got out, Oswald applied to the State Department for a passport. On these forms, he gave his civilian occupation as "shipping export agent", but the purpose of securing the passport was "to attend the Albert Schweitzer

This is the Altgens photograph. Both Kennedy and Connally have been hit. Note JFK's hands at his throat, Jackie's gloved hand at his left wrist. Nellie Connally has begun to pull the Governor into her lap. The focal point is the man in the doorway who fits the description of Oswald.

This blow-up of the man in the doorway shows him wearing the same tweed-patterned overshirt and the same T-shirt with worn elastic that Oswald wore at the time of his arrest .

This Polaroid photo was taken by spectator Mary Moorman at the moment the two headshots impacted. (See Z-313)

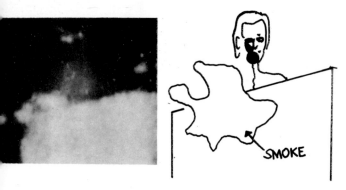

A blow-up of the same photo (left) shows the indistinct face of the man seen in Z-413. The same blow-up is highlighted (right).

SMOKE

The top photo is a print of Z-413, showing what could be the
back of an assassin's head. Below is a wider-angle view of the
same scene, taken by the FBI in Feb. 1964, showing the retaining wall behind which the putative gunman took cover. The
overlay shows the Zapruder camera's field of vision.

Z-157

Z-212

Z-210 Mysteriously spliced out are six vital frames from the Zapruder film, yet the Warren Commission glossed over them. The first splice, at Z-157, deletes JFK, as yet unhit, reacting suddenly to something that appears to catch his attention, and turning his head 90 degrees from left to right. The second splice, at Z-212 (note split tree trunk) appears to have been made to shore up the "single bullet theory". Among the missing frames is Z-210, the first point at which Oswald could have fired.

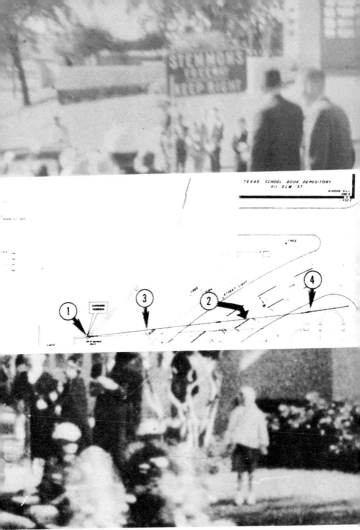

The top photo, by retired USAF Major Phil Willis, was taken a split-second *after* the first shot struck JFK. The middle diagram, by the FBI, lines up both Willis (at #4) and Zapruder (at #1). Note the road sign (#3) and Secret Service agent Clint Hill (#2). The bottom photo, Z-202, shows Phil Willis at the precise moment he took the photo. At this point, Oswald could not yet have fired.

The controversial Warren Commission photo exhibits CE-133A and CE-133B are anatomical fakes "found" by Dallas police hours after the assassination. Oswald, shown the top photo while in custody, branded it a composite. The bottom photo shows a different head-to-body size ratio and both show many shadow discrepancies.

These blow-ups of Oswald's head in CE-133A and B dramatize the transparency of the "evidence." In the bottom photo, Oswald's head is cocked slightly to his left, yet the shadow directly under his nose (see top close-up) moves—not in relation to the light source but to the angle of his head. Also, when the heads are super-imposed, feature by feature, the man in the bottom photo is approximately 4 inches taller than the man at the top.

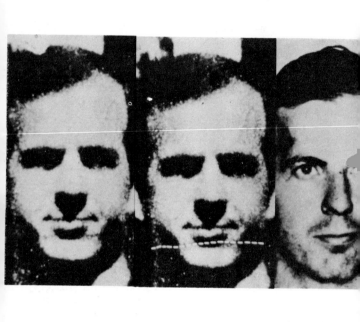

College in Switzerland and"—please note—"the University of Turku in Finland."

Though Oswald by now spoke Russian, he knew no French, German or Finnish, a decided handicap for any freshman at those colleges. But his passport came though one day before his discharge.

On September 14, he visited the "ailing" Marguerite in Ft. Worth. Three days later, with a four-month touring visa in hand, he booked passage to Europe on the Lykes Bros. freighter, the *S.S. Marion Lykes*. The price of the ticket was $220.75, nearly $18 more than the Warren Report said was in his only known bank account. (The Commission also said he financed his trip with $1,500 in savings, but did not specify where he'd put these savings. Under his mattress, perhaps, since its investigators could locate no other bank accounts or even a safe deposit box. Oswald had a reputation for frugality, but how much could he have set aside from the $3,452.20 net that he'd received over the past three years?)

When the *S.S. Marion Lykes* sailed on September 21, Oswald was one of four passengers aboard. It docked at LeHavre on October 8, and the next day he was in London. And here we encounter another oddity.

Though informing United Kingdom customs officials that he would be staying in England a full week before flying to Switzerland and college, he deplaned the very next day for *Finland*. But there's a discrepancy here. The Warren Report says he left "that same day", the 9th. But hotel records produced by the CIA show Oswald having checked into the Torni Hotel in Helsinki on the 10th; his passport bore the U.K. stamp "embarked 10 Oct

1959." Why quibble? Because there was no *commercial* flight for Finland out of London on the 10th, that's why. The only way Oswald could have flown into Helsinki on the 10th would have been by military air, a "black" (intelligence) flight. Obviously the Warren Commission couldn't admit to that: it ignored its own Appendix and flew Oswald out a day earlier.

He remained in Finland five days and never went anywhere near the University of Turku. Instead, on October 14, he went to the Soviet Consulate and secured a six-day visitor's visa. He left Helsinki the next day by train, crossing the Finnish-Russian border at Vainikkala and arriving in Moscow on the 16th. That same day, he told his Intourist guide (and KGB informant) that he wanted to defect and become a Soviet citizen.

The Russians must not have believed him. They turned him down, and on the 21st, his visa running out, ordered him to leave the country by eight that night. That afternoon, at the Hotel Berlin (where, this time, he'd registered as "a student", Oswald slashed his wrists. The Soviets, now worried, rushed him to a hospital. After being patched up and put under psychiatric observation, the Warren Report says, he was released on the 28th, and three days later, it goes on, Oswald appeared at the American Embassy. There, he threw his passport on the receptionist's desk, along with a handwritten statement in which he "dissolved" his U.S. citizenship.

He was taken into Second Secretary and Senior Consular official Richard E. Snyder, who apparently tried to talk Oswald out of defecting—but, one gets the feeling, not very hard. Snyder, the Report intimates, was stalling for time until he had gotten a cable off to Washington and received back some clarification. Apparently there was a considerable spurt in defectors that year, Russians coming this way, we the other way. The Report insists the date of Oswald's appearance and the cable's departure were both October 31st.

Yet, what have we now? A Naval Message marked Confidential and dated November 3—Commission Exhibit 917, in volume X, page 75—from the Embassy's naval aide to the Commander of Naval Operations:

> ATTENTION INVITED TO AMEMB MOSCOW DISPATCHES 234 DTD 2 NOVEMBER AND 224 DTD 26 OCTOBER CONCERNING THE RENUNCIATION OF US CITIZENSHIP AND REQUEST FOR SOVIET CITIZENSHIP BY LEE HARVEY OSWALD FORMER MARINE AND [blank] OSWALD STATED HE WAS RADAR OPERATOR IN MARCORPS AND HAS OFFERED TO FURNISH SOVIETS INFO HE POSSESSES ON US RADAR

The Office of Naval Intelligence is asked to circulate this TWX to the FBI, State Department, CIA and Commander of the Marine Corps.

What's interesting here are the following: in the fifth line, something—amounting to forty-three spaces—has been blanked out. Oswald was a Marine and—and what? If not an agent or some sort of undercover operator, why have deleted it? Also, note the reference to October 26. Oswald was still at Botkinskaya Hospital on the 26th. Were the Russians talking to the Americans about their unexpected patient, or did the Warren Commission bollix up the retelling of the story? Just when did Oswald show up at the Embassy? Did he at all?

But to resume: Oswald ignored Snyder's suggestion to come back in a day or two. Instead, two days later, he sent an "angry letter" to Snyder, threatening to furnish the Russians with sensitive military data unless the Americans permitted him to renounce his citizenship. This is very strange. Some sort of charade is going on here. For whose benefit is it being played?

We soon find out.

Apparently, through a bureaucratic error—of course—the renunciation didn't go through. The Warren Report observes dryly, "Oswald never formally complied with the legal steps necessary to renounce his American citizenship," failing to add that (a) he was never informed of these steps and (b) there was no earthly reason for complying had he been informed. (The day before the ONI cable arrived, its people in Washington had already checked USMC files and, not surprisingly, found "no derogatory information" in them. ONI then advised the other intelligence agencies "no action against him [is] contemplated in this matter.")

After the assassination, one of Oswald's superior officers in MACS-9 at El Toro, Lt. John E. Donovan, testified:

> "He had access to the location of all bases in the West Coast area, all radio frequencies for all squadrons, all tactical call signs, and the relative strength of all squadrons, number and type of aircraft in a squadron, who was the commanding officer, the authentication code of entering and exiting the...Air Defense Identification Zone. He knew the range of our radar. He knew the range of our radio. And he knew the range of the surrounding units' radio and radar."

Early in 1960, when it was sure Oswald had crossed over, Donovan recalled, "We had to spend several thousand man-hours changing everything and verifying the destruction of codes."

As some suggest, it was a modest price to pay for getting a man into the enemy camp. For such a heinous crime as betraying his country's military secrets, perhaps exposing Disneyland to nuclear attack, his country gave Oswald an *undesirable*—not a dishonorable—discharge from the USMC Reserve. When Oswald finally got wind of this harsh sentence, two years later, he shot off an "application of review" that might have been drafted by a Pentagon lawyer (and for all we know, it might well have been). With consummate gall, Oswald sought nullification of the undesirable discharge while requesting a recommendation for *reenlistment*. In Minsk?

> "In accordance with par. 15 (e) (5) I request that the Board consider my sincere desire to use my former training at the aviation fundamentals school, Jacksonville, Fla., and radar operators school, Biloxi, Miss., as well as the special knowledge I have accumulated through my experience *since my release from active duty* in the Naval Reserve." (ital. Oswald's)

If Oswald was sending a cryptic message to someone at ONI about his work in the Soviet Union, it wasn't acted upon. We will see why it may not have been.

Back in November 1959, though, while Washington was pondering what to do about Oswald, or giving all outward appearances of doing so, he was holing up in the Hotel Metropole, in Moscow, strangely unhassled by the KGB which, only weeks earlier, had been so eager to rush him out of the country. There is no accounting for six weeks in the life of the would-be defector, although records exist of several press interviews given by Oswald in his hotel room to correspondent Aline

Mosby of UPI and to Patricia McMillan Johnson, a stringer for the North American Newspaper Alliance and occasional translator of Soviet law journals for the Embassy. That's the way NANA officials describe her in 1975; a number of assassination researchers feel she had closer ties to the CIA.

What went on during those six weeks may only be guessed at. Presumably, Oswald was spilling all sorts of information on West Coast radar and other tidbits that suddenly made him interesting to Soviet intelligence. Because, on January 4, 1960, while declining to accord him citizenship, the Russians did give him Identification Document for Stateless Persons #311479 and permission to stay in Russia on a year-to-year renewable basis. At the same time, they bundled him out of Moscow, and on January 13, got him a lathe operator's job at the Byelorussian Radio & Television Factory in Minsk, 450 miles away.

For pocket money, they gave him 5,000 rubles (or $500), sweetening his 900 rubles-a-month salary with an overage of 700 rubles, in effect giving him a take-home pay larger than the plant manager's.

But why?

Los Angeles TV helicopter traffic/weather reporter Francis Gary Powers may have the answer: Oswald was sent in to keep the Cold War going. In his 1970 memoirs *(Operation Overflight)* the former $30,000-per-year U-2 pilot wrote that it couldn't have been a lucky SAM missile that brought him down from a height of 65,000 feet over Sverdlovsk, 1,200 miles inside the Soviet Union.

Powers had been shot down on May 1st, 1960. Six days later, Premier Nikita S. Khrushchev announced an American plane had been shot down over Russion territory—and the State Department immediately confirmed that a NASA "weather research plane" flying out of Turkey had been missing since May 1, when the pilot— identified as a civilian working for Lockheed Aircraft—reported oxygen trouble. The plane had accidentally drifted across the border. Khrushchev responded to this lie by informing the Supreme Soviet (and the world) that the Russians had captured both the plane and the pilot, neither of which destructed. On May 9, Eisenhower bit the bullet and admitted the official lie, assumed personal responsibility, and implied the U.S. would continue its overflights.

It would appear Ike had been sandbagged by the CIA, which may have wanted Powers to be shot down in order to create the kind of international incident that would give Khrushchev justification to break up the mid-May summit meeting between himself, Eisenhower, Charles de Gaulle of France and Harold Macmillan of England. Which, of course, is just what happened. *Detente* at the time was desired neither by the CIA nor the Joint Chiefs.

What intrigues former CIA pilot Powers (who later was exchanged for the Soviet spy Colonel Rudolf Abel) was how the Soviets knew enough about the U-2 to bring it down, when (a) there had been no U-2 overflights from April 1958 through April 1960 and (b) its development by Lockheed and development by the United States had been such a deep secret. *Someone* Powers feels, must have told them about its radar vulnerability.

Quite possibly, that someone was Oswald, although it would' be somewhat far-fetched to suggest the *entire* reason for his "defection" was to bring Powers down. Quite frankly, the Soviets didn't trust Oswald, even if his radar information proved correct. For one, there had been too many "defections"—four the year before Oswald crossed over, two since, and always by way of Finland. For another, there was really no way of testing out Oswald's data until five months after he'd been granted provisional asylum.

According to a *Soviet* defector to the West— KGB Lt. Col. Yuri Ivanovich Nosenko—the Russians worried about Oswald being a "mole", an agent insinuated into Soviet society by the CIA for future activation. They were not ready to eject him, nor were they willing to let him roam at will. This, at least, explains putting him in cold storage in Minsk, where he might be watched while making sure he would not be turned into a double agent. This fear, incidentally, surfaced after the assassination, and may explain why Nosenko— who defected a convenient three months later in Switzerland—was never quite trusted by the Americans. Nosenko passed himself off as a "disarmament expert" attending a Geneva conference, and only after showing U.S. authorities his Oswald file did he admit having been the official in charge of American tourists. Nosenko insisted Oswald had never told the Russians anything, and his input provided the Warren Commission with all the pastoral data it sought to picture Oswald as an innocent grown disillusioned with Communism while in Russia. Privately, American intelligence didn't buy Nosenko; one official told the *New York Times* in October 1975: "no doubt about it. Nosenko was a phony. Nosenko was a notorious deception—he really screwed up everything." Oh?

Not for the Russians, who must have sent Nosenko to the West in order to put to rest CIA and FBI fears that the "assassin" was a Soviet operative.

But the Soviet skepticism would go far to explain why Oswald, a little over a year later, made his first moves to come back out—and why the Americans were expecting him. Indeed, everything at our end would seem to point to an official anxiousness to get him out. The U.S. Embassy had even kept his passport in Moscow, waiting for Oswald to appear in person and claim it.

And Oswald knew it. In 1963, appearing on a New Orleans radio talk show that was engineered to "expose" the pro-Castro agitator as an American turncoat, Oswald admitted that when he was in Russia he was "under, uh, the protection of the, uh...American government."

Intriguingly, the Soviet authorities did nothing to hinder his exit, and even allowed him to take with him his Russian-born wife and Russian-born daughter. Good riddance, perhaps?

The official version read differently. Before he met and married his nineteen-year-old pharmacist, Marina Nikolayevna Prusakova, in March of 1961, Oswald had soured on the worker's paradise. Two months earlier, a year after arriving in the Soviet Union and after the Russians had renewed his option to stay for another year, Oswald had written Snyder. But, says the Government, Snyder was worried that perhaps the Oswald he knew was not the Oswald who'd written; Snyder therefore insisted Oswald appear at the Embassy in person if he wanted his passport back. Clearly the result of J. Edgar Hoover's June 1960 memo, fearing that with Oswald's birth certificate and other documents in hand, the Russians could easily ship out an Oswald impostor.

State Department testimony given in the Warren Report Appendix clearly shows it wanted Oswald out of the U.S.S.R. Preferably alone. They didn't like this Marina business at all; it was not in the plans. Worse, Marina's uncle Ilya, with whom she had been living in Minsk, was a security functionary with the Ministry of Interior. Could not Oswald be persuaded to come out alone and send for her later? Snyder tried but Oswald wouldn't budge. This deviation could well have led to his being cut loose by his "control" upon arriving in the U.S. It's worth a thought.

And so, a few months after their marriage, in June 1961, the Oswalds—she pregnant with their first child—appeared before Snyder to pass muster. In August, Snyder contacted Oswald in Minsk and advised him all systems were go; that it had been decided in Washington that he'd never really *legally* defected since he hadn't filled in the proper forms.

That December, the Russians sanctioned the exodus. But then came a hitch. Someone apparently had forgotten to plug in the Immigration & Naturalization Service. They didn't like this Oswald story at all; they were suspicious, and they balked. Impossible, they said, for Oswald not to have blabbed to the Russians. Of course, INS knew nothing about the man except that he'd been a sixteen-year-old high school drop-out who'd joined the Marines and then defected. Who would vouch for him, get him a job? How do we know, asked Immigration, that Marina wouldn't become a welfare burden?

Soon, however, after a bit of gentle persuasion

by both the State Department and the CIA, the Immigration people relented, but insisted that protocol be followed. Finally, in the spring of 1962, the Oswalds were ready to leave Russia. Before doing so, Oswald asked Snyder if he would be "prosecuted for treason" upon his return. With a straight face, Snyder assured him—"informally", of course—that this would be unlikely. After all, since Oswald had sworn he hadn't told the Russians anything about radar, on what possible grounds could he be charged with treason?

Snyder got Oswald to sign a promissory note for $435.71 in travel expenses, handed him a 30-day one-way visa and on June 1, put the three Oswalds on a train heading West. They crossed the Soviet border at Brest June 2 and according to the Report, left Rotterdam aboard the *S.S. Maasdam* two days later. But the Report does not seem to account, again, for a time warp, namely the two or three days the Oswalds spent in Amsterdam (possibly being debriefed) nor does it explain how it was that *only* Marina's passport showed a stamp denoting a crossing from East Germany to West Germany at Helmstedt. Perhaps Oswald didn't require such a bureaucratic nicety.

Two things the efficient Mr. Snyder overlooked, perhaps quite intentionally, was [a] the stipulation under U.S. law that such State Department loans are made only to people "whose loyalty to the United States Government [is] beyond question, and (b) the obligation to instruct the Passport Office to "flag" the Oswald file or put a Look-Out Card in it, a routine step embassies and consulates take to prevent stranded tourists from defaulting on their loans.

Now, back in 1962, if an absent-minded college professor so much as stepped across the Bavarian border to have lunch in a Czechoslovakian pub, or attended an academic seminar in Budapest, he could expect to undergo a thorough "de-briefing" upon his return to the West. But in the case of defector Oswald, who pried himself all the way into the original Borscht Belt and stayed for supper and then some, all established systems suddenly went tilt.

The *S.S. Maasdam* docked at Hoboken, N.J. on June 13. The Oswalds had $63 to their name as they debarked. Greeting them was no phalanx of beady-eyed intelligence officers or FBI agents, but a lone figure: Spas T. Raikin, representing himself as an official of The Travelers' Aid Society. He thoughtfully shepherded the Oswalds through Immigration and Customs, took them to Manhattan and got them a room at a Times Square hotel, and asked if there was anything else he might do.

It is worth noting here that while Raikin may indeed have been employed by Travelers' Aid, he was (and perhaps still is) also an official of The American Friends of the Anti-Bolshevik Nations Inc., one of a number of CIA-financed supranationalist, anti-Soviet emigre organizations. It occasionally works in concert with The Tolstoy Foundation, of which more in a moment.

Obviously, Oswald didn't expect to find himself stranded in New York. Raikin apparently put him in touch with one of the city welfare agencies, who took pity on the stragglers. Oswald's story was that he had been a Marine stationed at the U.S. Embassy in Moscow, and had renounced his citizenship after having been threatened with courts-martial for having married a Russian girl. They lived in Minsk, and Oswald, quickly disillusioned, spent two years battling Soviet bureaucracy to get an exit visa for himself, wife and child (who then was four months old), and that he was now dead-broke after having paid for the tickets out of his meager savings.

Through the Dallas office of the Social Security Administration of HEW, which at the time was funding a program that provided "temporary assistance to United States citizens and their dependents who have returned from a foreign country and are without available resources," the New York City officials arranged to have Oswald's brother Robert wire up $200 flight money. Oswald at first refused to accept his brother's largesse, insisting the Government pick up the tab. But he finally gave in, and on June 14, the Oswalds flew into Ft. Worth.

There, the Department of Health, Education & Welfare was ready to assist some more. According to an FBI memorandum of November 27, 1963, HEW in Washington wrote the Dallas Regional Office, "instructing that arrangements be made by the Dallas representatives of HEW for the family following arrival in Texas." The instructions were dated June 22. It said, "Oswald apparently went directly overseas following his discharge from the U.S. Marine Corps and eventually studied as a veteran under the GI Bill in Switzerland."

Obviously, the people who had controlled Oswald's movements up to then hadn't taken HEW into their confidence. Switzerland, *indeed.*

From Russia with Love...And Squalor

> "He was quite a mysterious fella, and he did have, uh, connections that bore examination. The extent of the influence of these connections on him, I think, history will deal with much more than we are able to now...."
>
> —Lyndon B. Johnson to
> Walter Cronkite, April 1969

Somebody Up There still liked him, that was obvious. Precisely one year to the day after he had come home to Texas in seeming ignominy, Lee Harvey Oswald walked into the State Department office in New Orleans and applied for a passport. Twenty-four hours later, he got it. And in September that year, he once more left the United States, this time for Mexico. He had made no secret of his plans to re-defect to the Soviet Union, going by way of Cuba. And the CIA watched him, photographed him, tapped his phone. Only now, the plans went awry: neither the Russians, nor the Cubans, would take the bait.

His passport file had mysteriously been left unflagged. Routinely, the FBI, CIA, ONI and a half a dozen other intelligence agencies request the Passport Office to flag, or place Look-Out Cards, in the files of those citizens whose activities they regard as questionable, whose travels abroad might prove to be "embarrassing". But in Oswald's case, nobody asked.

Why? Here was a person who, as Sylvia Meagher points out, "had affirmed his allegiance to the Soviet Union, proudly declared himself to be a Marxist, and even offered classified radar data to the Soviet authorities." But when asked, after the assassination, what accounted for its astonishing lack of interest, the FBI told the Commission:

"The facts relating to Oswald's activities...did not warrant such action. Our investigation...disclosed no evidence that Oswald was acting under the instructions or on behalf of any foreign government or instrumentality thereof."

In reapplying for his passport, Oswald had been painfully truthful, just as he had been in the summer of 1961 when he traveled up from Minsk to meet with Embassy official Richard E. Snyder. He told the New Orleans people his previous passport had been cancelled by the State Department, and in Moscow two years earlier, in filling out his application for the passport renewal, he'd filled in all the right blanks correctly. In the part of the form where it asked if the subject had acted for or against the best interests of the United States, Oswald checked off the latter. In post-assassination testimony to the Commission, it was revealed that he oughtn't to have done so, that a clerical or typographical error had been made. But it didn't really matter, anyway, since it also turned out that *that* particular form, or carbon thereof, never did get sent to Washington by the Embassy, because Oswald had filled in *two* applications. At whose behest, the Embassy people didn't say, but one may surmise that one form went into the public record, the other into some "eyes only" folder.

Once the CIA teletyped the State Department that Oswald had been seen entering the Soviet Embassy in Mexico City, knowing what it did about Oswald, the State Department did nothing.

An official of the Passport Office told an incredulous assistant counsel of the Warren Commission that no thought was given at this point—October 22, 1963, one month before the assassination—to revoking Oswald's passport. Carroll Hamilton Seeley, Jr. testified:

> "I did nothing...other than to note the fact that I had read the telegram....There was no particular passport significance to the fact that a man shows up down at the Soviet Embassy in Mexico City...."

If, at this point, there is still any doubt in the reader's mind that the last thing anyone wanted was to curtail Oswald's meanderings, consider the following telling bit of testimony from Harvard Professor Abram Chayes, then the State Department's legal advisor, describing why such heroic efforts had been made on the behalf of the Oswalds back in 1961-2:

> "...we were very anxious to get him back...we had him on our hands then...he was very directly our responsibility, so that anything he did or that went wrong during that period, he was under our protection and we were necessarily involved."

So now, in June 1962, he *was* back, but nobody knew quite what to do with him. It seemed that, having pulled him out of Mother Russia's ambivalent embrace, the Government simply cut him loose, to fend for himself.

Nobody had bothered to debrief him. But then, on June 26, the FBI wanted to see him. He had a two-hour interview in the Ft. Worth field office, and the agents who spoke with him found him "arrogant and unwilling" to discuss his defection, as if to say, "what business is this of yours?" The FBI report described him also as "tense and drawn

The blow-up (above) of Z-312 shows the exact position and angle of JFK's head at the moment of the first headshot. The diagram (below), known by the Warren Commission to be in error, shows how the President's head would have to have been angled to receive a wound from the 6th floor of the Depository.

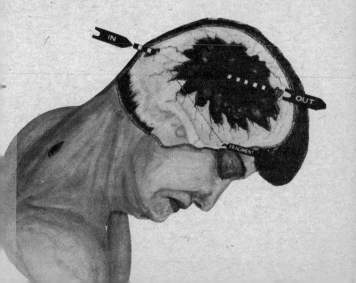

CERTIFICATE OF DEATH
NAVMED W (REV. 4-58) FRONT

See NAVMED DEPT. for instructions regarding number of copies and subscription.

Form filing at station:
The White House, Washington, D.C.

President John Fitzgerald Kennedy

4. STATUS
President of the United States

2 years
11 Months

7. FILE OR SERVICE | 8. RANK/RATE | 9. CORPS | 10. BRANCH OF SERVICE | 11. PLACE OF BIRTH (City and State or Country)
NA | NA | NA | NA | Brookline, Massachusetts

12. DATE OF BIRTH (Month, day and year)
May 29, 1917

13. AGE (Years, months) (Days, if under 1 year)
46 years 6 months

Catholic

15. COLOR OF EYES
Blue

16. COLOR OF HAIR
Auburn

17. COMPLEXION
Ruddy

18. HEIGHT
72"

19. WEIGHT
172

20. MARKS AND SCARS (Based on health record)

4" scar 2nd, 3rd and 4th lumbar spine
4" scar upper left leg, well healed

22. NEXT OF KIN OR FRIEND (Relation, name and address)
Mrs. John Fitzgerald Kennedy, The White House, Washington, D.C.

23. ADMITTED TO SICK LIST (day) (If on active duty, last duty station before current admission to sick list)
The White House, Washington, D.C.

24. DATE ADMITTED TO SICK LIST (Month, day, year)
November 22, 1963

25. PLACE OF DEATH
Parkland Memorial Hospital, Dallas, Texas

26. TIME OF DEATH (Month, day, year, hour)
November 22, 1963 1:00 p.m.

27.
I. DISEASE OR CONDITION DIRECTLY LEAD-ING TO DEATH. (This does not mean the mode of dying, e.g. heart failure, asthenia, etc. It means the disease, injury or complication which caused death.)

(a) Gunshot wound, skull

APPROXIMATE INTERVAL BETWEEN ONSET AND DEATH

ANTECEDENT CAUSES. (Morbid conditions, if any giving rise to above cause (a), stating the underlying cause last)

DUE TO (b)

30 minutes

DUE TO (c)

II. OTHER SIGNIFICANT CONDITIONS. (Conditions contributing to death but not related to the disease or condition causing death.)

The official death certificate by JFK's personal physician, Admiral George G. Burkley, confirms that the President was struck not in the neck but "in the posterior back at about the level of the third thoracic vertebra." This is 5¾ inches below where the Commission put the wound.

29. NAME

John Fitzgerald Kennedy

30. SUMMARY OF FACTS RELATING TO DEATH

President John Fitzgerald Kennedy, while riding in the motorcade in Dallas, Texas, on November 22, 1963, and at approximately 12:30 p.m., was struck in the head by an assassin's bullet and a second wound occurred in the posterior back at about the level of the third thoracic vertebra. The wound was shattering in type causing a fragmentation of the skull and evulsion of three particles of the skull at time of the impact, with resulting maceration of the right hemisphere of the brain. The President was rushed to Parkland Memorial Hospital, and was immediately under the care of a team of physicians at the hospital under the direction of a neurosurgeon, Kemp Clark. I arrived at the hospital approximately five minutes after the President and immediately went to the emergency room. It was evident that the wound was of such severity that it was bound to be fatal. Breathing was noted at the time of arrival at the hospital by several members of the Secret Service. Emergency measures were employed immediately including intravenous fluid and blood. The President was pronounced dead at 1:00 p.m. by Dr. Clark and was verified by me.

31. DISPOSITION OF REMAINS

To the White House, Washington, D.C.

32.

DATE SIGNED November 23, 1963 SIGNATURE

George Gregory Burkley RADM (MC) USN
Physician to the President (Rank)

33.

APPROVED: COURT OF INQUIRY OR BOARD OF INVESTIGATION _____ (WILL OR WILL NOT) _____ BE HELD.

DATE SIGNED _____ SIGNATURE _____

(Commanding Officer) (Rank)

COPY

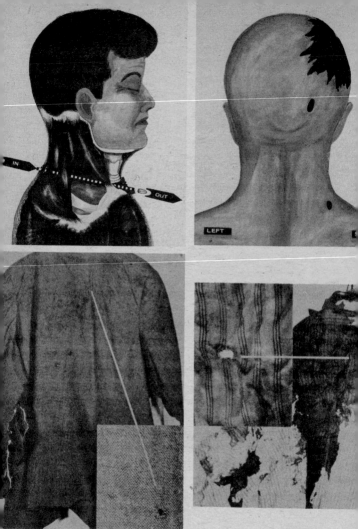

VERBAL PLASTIC SURGERY: The top drawings, by a Government artist who had seen neither JFK's body nor the autopsy photos, show the back bullet entering his neck—5¾ inches higher than the official death certificate or the original autopsy diagrams depicted, and contrary to FBI and Secret Service eyewitness testimony. Below, the bloody shirt and suit jacket show the true point of entry of the back bullet. The lie was needed to explain the throat "exit" wound.

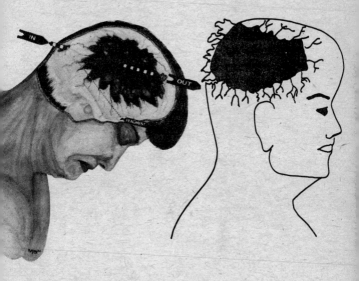

The Warren Commission version of JFK's head wounds (left) shows the point of entry four inches below the point seen from photos by Atty. Gen. Ramsey Clark's medical panel in 1967. It also depicts the frontal "exit" wound facing forward. But all witnesses on Nov. 22 in Parkland Hospital described the massive head wound as exiting to the rear (right).

AUTOPSY DESCRIPTIVE SHEET   NMS PATH-8 (1-63)

AUTOPSY

NMS # A 3 2 2 3 2 2 DATE 11-22-63 HR. STARTED_____ HR.COMPLETED_____

NAME: _____ RANK/RATE _____

DATE/HOUR EXPIRED: _____ WARD _____ DIAGNOSIS _____

PHYSICAL DESCRIPTION: RACE: _____   Obtain following on babies only:
                                   Color
Height_____in. Weight_____lb. Hair_____   Crown-rump _____ in.
                                             Crown-heel _____ in.
Color eyes _____ Pupils:Rt_____mm, Lb.____mm   Circumference:
                                             Head_____in. Chest_____in.
WEIGHTS: (Grams, unless otherwise specified)   Abd._____in.

LUNG, RT. ~~320~~ 320   KIDNEY, RT. 1385   ADRENALS, RT. _____

LUNG, LT. ~~290~~ 290   KIDNEY, LT. 140   ADRENALS, LT. _____

BRAIN _____   LIVER 650   PANCREAS _____

SPLEEN 90   HEART 350   THYROID _____

THYMUS _____   TESTIS _____   OVARY _____

HEART MEASUREMENTS: A 7.5 cm. P 7 cm. T 12 cm. M 10 cm.
                    LVM 1.5 _____ cm. RVM .4 _____ cm.

NOTES:

Pathologist _____

The original "autopsy descriptive sheet" made by Comdr. Humes and verified by Adm. Burkley confirms the entrance wound in the back, not the neck, as did the death certificate. This document also puts the throat wound higher than the back wound, further destroying the "single bullet theory."

Evidence of at least 3 shots that missed their mark is found on the curbs and sidewalk of Dealey Plaza. None of them could have been fired from the sixth floor of the Depository. The scar on the south curb of Main St. (left) is known as the "Tague hit"; that on the south curb of Elm St. (center) must have been fired from the Records Building; and that on the sidewalk by the north curb of Elm St. (right) must have come from the western end of the Depository.

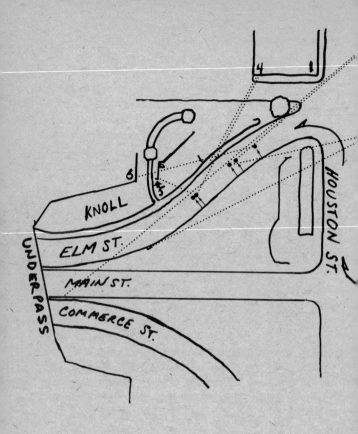

This map of the Elm St. killing zone shows the approximate position of the Presidential limousine during the sequence of shots. The Warren Commission insisted all shots (dotted lines) came from the 6th floor of the Book Depository (1) when, in fact, both eyewitness testimony and physical evidence indicate other points of origin. To the authors, it is most likely that the Kennedy party was trapped in a classic military ambush—with cross-fire coming from the Dal-Tex building (2), the County Records Building (3), the *south-western* corner of the Book Depository (4), from behind Abraham Zapruder on the "grassy knoll" (5) and from behind the wooden stockade fence fronting the parking lot (6).

up," and "inclined to be just a little insolent."

Just a little. Because on August 16 the FBI was back. This time, however, the Mountain came to Mohammed. The FBI drove to Oswald's one-bedroom house on Mercedes Street, and conducted their second interview in a somewhat unorthodox manner: in the back seat of their car. This time, the FBI report found Oswald to have "displayed a less belligerent attitude." He agreed "to inform the FBI of any attempt to enlist him in intelligence activities."

Shortly after this meeting, Oswald wrote letters to *both* the Communist Party of the U.S.A. and the Socialist Workers Party (not exactly the best of fellow travelers) asking about membership requirements. He took out a newspaper subscription to the CPUSA's *Worker,* and a month or so later, took out the now-famous Dallas post office box 2915.

But we're getting ahead of ourselves. For it would appear that his benevolent friends in high places had not quite forgotten him, after all.

Shortly after their arrival in Ft. Worth, the young couple and their infant daughter were literally swept up by a group of elite, well-bred, highly educated and superbly connected Russian emigres who had long made their mark and established roots in the Ft. Worth-Dallas world of petrochemicals, aerospace and venture capitalism. Mostly well to the right of center, many of them had come to Texas after 1948, largely under the combined aegis of the rabidly anti-Communist Russian Orthodox Church in America, and The Tolstoy Foundation. The Foundation, a refugee resettlement group founded in 1939 by Leo Tolstoy's daughter Alexandra, originally helped Russian refugees flee Eastern Europe. After the war, it turned its attention to the survivors of the Hungarian uprising and to refugees fleeing Tibet and Mongolia. Most recently, it has turned to Vietnamese, Laotian and Cambodian refugees. In every phase of its operations, the common denominator has been anti-Communism, giving rise to the report that the foundation is now heavily supported by "discreet" CIA funding. Unquestionably, it has done a good job screening out of the refugee and expatriate groups potential left-wing malcontents and stragglers of dubious peerage.

By this definition of purpose alone, its people—notably Dallas director Paul Raigorodsky—ought to have had nothing to do with the defector Oswald. Quite the opposite, they embraced the Oswalds, particularly Marina and the baby, showering money, furniture, toys, clothes, food, party invitations—a White Russian version of the Welcome Wagon, which asked nothing in return.

Curious about this rush to adopt—here were sophisticated people well up in the higher socio-economic strata of the community, baby-sitting for what one of them called "a semi-educated hillbilly" and his withdrawn wife—the Commission asked why? It was told that the Oswalds held a certain attraction because they could bring back fresh news from the Soviet Union. Given what insights Oswald might have acquired on the lathe bench in Minsk, an airmail subscription to *Pravda, Izvestia* or *Trud* might have proved more productive, cheaper—and believable than that kind of *ex post facto* cover story.

For Oswald didn't reciprocate this collective kindness one bit. In fact, he resented their smothering presence and constant intrusions, and often let them know what they could do with their generosity. He would also turn on Marina, who was lapping it up, and rapidly acquiring an insatiable appetite for material things. Not surprisingly, the marriage started turning sour.

In July, after the FBI called him down, one of the Russians arranged for Oswald to become a sheet-metal worker with the Louv-R-Pak division of the Leslie Welding Company in Ft. Worth. He quit abruptly in October, not telling anyone (not even Marina) and began looking for a job in Dallas. Taking a room at the Dallas YMCA, he opened his postal box and through the Texas Employment Commission found an interesting job as a photoprint trainee with Jaggars-Chiles-Stovall, a graphics arts concern—the relevance of which would appear later in his short life. With Oswald appearing to have walked out, the Russians took in Marina and the child; but then there was a reconciliation, and he found them an apartment in Dallas. But by now, he'd managed to alienate just about all of the Russians except for a curious couple, George S. and Jeanne de Mohrenschildt. He, a much-married Russian-born petroleum engineer and geologist had an intriguing background in foreign espionage; she, his fourth wife, was a successful society dress designer. The Commission would be fascinated to learn that the de Mohrenschildts had taken a "hiking trip" through Central America and had popped up in Guatemala City just when the Bay of Pigs brigade was ready to take off. One thing about the de Mohrenschildts: they—like Marina—would tell the Commission everything it needed to know about Lee Harvey Oswald's instability.

The de Mohrenschildts were instrumental in bringing the Oswalds together, in February 1963, with Ruth Hyde Paine—and it was Paine who would arrange for Lee Harvey Oswald's job interview with the superintendent of the Texas School Book Depository later that year.

In most of the voluminous literature produced since the assassination, Mrs. Paine is generally depicted as The Good Samaritan who, because her own marriage was failing, would move heaven and earth to save Lee and Marina's. In truth, it would appear that Mrs. Paine had developed an emotional attachment to the hapless Marina, and that in the ensuing romance between the two women, Oswald would be frozen out. The demonologists go even further, and suspect Paine of having served as a CIA conduit, for some deep purpose yet to be revealed.

Mrs. Paine taught Russian to the employees of the Mobil Research Lab and other Dallas technocrats with a "need to know" the latest in Communist technology of the kind found only in Russian or satellite scientific and engineering journals. A Quaker convert and left-wing activist in the 1950's during her college days at Antioch, Mrs. Paine had just separated from her husband at the time she met the Oswalds. Her husband, Michael E. Paine, was an engineer at Bell Helicopter, and a descendant of the poet Ralph Waldo Emerson and Robert Treat Paine, one of the original fifty-six signers of the Declaration of Independence.

In late April 1963, Oswald's employment was terminated by the photo studio. The Warren Report says he was fired, but there now appears to be some question of that. It was just around that point in time—to use a Watergate phrase—that the Government of the United States began having difficulty controlling its anti-Castro wards, particularly in Florida and Louisiana. And just about then that Lee Harvey Oswald announced to Marina and Ruth that he wanted to go back to New

Orleans and try his luck there. His excuse was that he missed the ambience of the Crescent City, although how much ambience he had taken in as a poor teenager appears questionable. To be sure, he had not exhausted all of the employment possibilities in the lush Ft. Worth-Dallas growth area; there must have been some other compelling reason to go to New Orleans. There was.

Marina, of course, chose to see it—or, at least, *tell* it differently when the Commission questioned her about this period in Lee's life. She said she'd urged Oswald to go, to get out of town so that he would not again try to shoot people like Nixon and General Walker. (The general had been fired upon by an unknown sniper April 10, and to this date, the case has not been officially solved, although the prevailing wisdom since 1963 has been that it was Lee Harvey Oswald who had shot, and missed. It was only after Oswald had been murdered, after he could no longer be confronted with the "evidence", that the Dallas Police concocted the Walker "link", even though the ballistics didn't match. They got willing assistance from Marina. (Case in point: when the attempt first broke in the Dallas papers in April, the spent bullet was identified as a 30.06 calibre projectile—clearly not acceptable by a Mannlicher-Carcano 7.65. Rather than attempt a test to "prove" a connection, the police begged off, saying valid comparisons could not be made since the Walker bullet had been mutilated. Verbally, certainly.) Marina also concocted a story that Oswald had shot at Nixon on his trip to Dallas in the spring. One thing was wrong, however: Nixon had never made that trip.

Marina's testimony, which one assassination critic describes as "the scorpion's lash", may not have been all that maliciously intended. She was merely trying to save her own skin and to keep from being deported. What had happened was that, in filling out her Immigration and Naturalization applications at the American Embassy in Moscow, she'd lied. In the part where the INS asked if the subject had ever had any ties to a government organization, Marina had written "nyet". In fact, she'd been a member of the Komsomol, the Soviet Youth Organization, until her marriage. When the lie was ultimately discovered by the INS, the FBI was notified—and the FBI apparently let both Lee Harvey and Marina Oswald know.

After the assassination, no matter what else may have transpired between the two, Oswald told agent Hosty in no uncertain terms to "stop accosting my wife" in language similar to that which the FBI says Oswald used in the now-destroyed letter to Hosty of November 12. Hosty, we now know, visited Marina twice that month, on the 1st and the 5th. It is quite conceivable he might have spoken to her about the small matter of perjury.

But why? To keep "informant" Oswald in line? It could just well be that the immigration lie was the kind of Damocles' Sword the FBI held over Oswald's head—or so a number of assassination researchers have recently suggested.

There is some support for this contention. Right after Kennedy's assassination, when the Secret Service held Marina in "protective custody" outside of Dallas, the FBI would come by and nudge Marina a bit. And she didn't like it. As she later testified to the Commission:

"I think that the FBI agents knew I was afraid, that after everything that had happened I could not remain to live in this country, and they somewhat exploited that for their own purpose, in a very polite form, so that you could not say anything after that. ...[But] they cannot be accused of anything. They approached it in a very clever, contrived way."

Brother-in-law Robert Oswald was more direct. The FBI agents, he testified, had implied:

"that if she did not cooperate...in so many words, that they would perhaps deport her."

She cooperated, all right, to a point of wretched excess. Not just with the FBI but, more lethally, with the Warren Commission. Her stories, unfortunately, were just too contradictory, too inconsistent, her recall too perfect, that before long, the staff was unanimous in its feeling that she was not merely lying to protect herself but also to exorcise the ghost of Oswald past. Even David Belin was angered to the point of wanting to give Marina a polygraph exam. But Earl Warren, that kind, courtly man, wanted so desperately to believe the comely widow that the staff began referring to the questioning sessions as "time for Snow White and the Seven Dwarfs".

Ultimately, the Report put her down. "The credibility of Marina Oswald's story is subject to some question." To say the very least. But if the Commission didn't buy her spurious story, the gullible American public did. The Dallas *Morning News* paid her $68,000 for it, and *Life* kicked in $5,000 for photos that would ultimately be found to have been fakes; individuals sent in cash gifts totaling $70,000, a gun collector parted with nearly $12,000 for Oswald's alleged guns, and even the Government itself came through with a $17,729 judgment for Oswald's confiscated possessions. A year after the assassination, Marina Oswald was worth $250,000. In 1965, she married an electronics engineer, Kenneth Jess Porter, invested the loot in a bar that failed—the marriage almost did, too— and at last report, she was selling infant clothing in a suburban Dallas shopping center.

Yet, as to the validity of the supposition that Hosty and Oswald knew each other, belief must be suspended until such a time as the FBI opens up all of its files to inspection.

One thing is clear, and that is that Hosty never leveled with his own superiors—or with anyone else, for that matter. A June 3, 1964 FBI memorandum in the Warren Report asserts that:

> "Special agent Hosty has furnished an affidavit stating that at no time prior to the assassination of President Kennedy had he ever seen or talked to Oswald. In addition, Hosty stated that he had never made any attempt to develop him as an informant or source of information."

An artful rebuttal, to be sure, as it says nothing about some other agent not having signed up Oswald in 1962—such as Special Agent John W. Fain.

Yet, it doesn't explain how it was that Hosty's name, telephone number and automobile license plate came to be found in Oswald's address directory that was among his possessions at the Paine residence, when Oswald had been living in Dallas since mid-October; or why this particular entry had been deleted from the summary given to the Commission by the FBI on December 23; or why it would take the FBI until February 11 to own up to its arbitrary removal.

Down in Dallas, the local FBI field office undertook its own little cover-up the minute FBI bureau chief Shanklin heard of Oswald's arrest by the police. The afternoon of the arrest, Chief Curry had told the press that the FBI knew about Oswald being in Dallas before the assassination, that he assumed they had a file on him. Livid, Shanklin telephoned Curry and demanded an immediate retraction. Curry balked, although as a personal favor to the FBI bureau chief, he agreed to tell the press that "to my personal knowledge", he did not know of the Oswald rumor. "But," Curry recalled in 1975, "that's as far as I was willing to go for Shanklin. I would not and did not retract my original statement."

And when agent Hosty "reminded" Shanklin that he had been handling the Oswald case, Shanklin panicked lest the cops get wind of the FBI's prior interest in Oswald. Curry now thinks Shanklin was primarily concerned with the reputation of the FBI; others think he was plainly frightened by what Hoover might say when told that an FBI informant had just killed the President of the United States.

He immediately sent Hosty over to police headquarters to sit in on the Oswald interrogation. Meanwhile, he telephoned another FBI agent who was already over at headquarters, and—according to homicide captain J. Will Fritz, who eavesdropped on an extension—told the agent:

> "I want [Hosty] in that investigation right now because he knows those people he has been talking to...."

Oh?

Captain Fritz must have suspected, at this point, that there was more to Oswald than anyone had suspected. And confirmation wasn't long in coming.

The minute Hosty entered the interrogation

room, Oswald, calm and collected up to then, jumped up from his chair and, again depending on Fritz's testimony to the Commission, "beat on the desk and went into a kind of tantrum. He told Hosty, 'I know you. You accosted my wife on two occasions.' He was getting pretty irritable...I asked him what he meant by 'accosting'. I thought maybe he meant some physical abuse or something, and he said, 'Well, he threatened her.' And he said, 'He practically told her she would have to go back to Russia.' "

One must accept Captain Fritz's testimony with some reluctance, as it was Fritz who had made sure that no record or tape or transcript would come out of Oswald's interrogation. And, as we shall see, Captain Fritz also has much to account for.

Later in 1964, the Dallas *Morning News* broke with a story that Hosty had told a friend on the force, Lt. Jack Revill, that the Bureau had known all about Oswald. This, of course, caused enormous grief in the office of the Director, forcing Hoover, on April 27, to write Earl Warren a letter, hand-delivered by courier:

> "Special Agent Hosty unequivocally denies ever having made the statement [that the subject Oswald was capable of committing the assassination of President Kennedy]."

It is clear there had been more—much more—between Hosty and Oswald than either had let on. Oswald was dead, and before long, Hosty would be demoted and transferred to the Kansas City office.

The Cuban Connection

"If my son was an agent of the United
States, this should be known."
                              —Marguerite Oswald

If Lee Harvey Oswald knew little about graceful
high-ceilinged rooms, the Vieux Carré or four-star
dinners at Antoine's, just what was it that drew
him to New Orleans?

It's a question that the Warren Commission
never quite got around to asking, though they
seemed to spare us no detail in reconstructing his
activities during the five months he spent there.

Perhaps he wasn't drawn there at all, but, as on
earlier travels, was sent under orders. This time, to
pretend to be a pro-Castro sympathizer as a cover
for anti-Castro activities—to perhaps infiltrate
some of the more extreme right-wing groups and
report back to the FBI? If so, he was about to
undertake a most hazardous game, that of the
double agent. For as history shows, double agents
invariably become the victims of the double cross.
And if the groups which Oswald is suspected of
having infiltrated and informed upon saw through
his cover, a great deal begins to make sense.

For as medievalist Dr. Peter Dale Scott of
Berkeley points out, "In the event that one
organization uncovers the duplicity and takes
revenge, the second organization is unlikely to
respond for fear of blowing its cover."

Consider, then, this theoretical possibility: the
anti-Castro Cubans, like the Soviets in 1960,
recognize the arrival in their midst of an idealogue
of dubious credentials. They instinctively do not
trust him. But unlike the Soviets, who first

played him, then put him on ice, and eventually let him go, the hot-blooded Cubans see a better use for the infiltrator. With their plot to assassinate John F. Kennedy near completion, they and their fellow conspirators—a handful of CIA operatives, right-wing cops, "hit men" provided by the Syndicate—proceed to implicate the unwitting double agent. *Unwitting*, because the agent has gotten wind of the plot and has tried to tip off his "control". But his "control", for reasons unknown, ignores the alert.

The assassination goes off as scheduled; the agent realizes he will be implicated, and flees the assassination site. He picks up a revolver and goes to meet his "control" in a nearby darkened movie house. But the policemen who are in the cabal are aware of the *modus operandi*, and have arranged a secondary killing, a Judas goat. In this way, if they cannot pin the "crime of the century" on the double agent, then at least they can brand him a "cop killer" and eliminate him in that fashion.

But again, the double agent outwits his enemies. He does not "resist" arrest, does not get shot on the spot, and thus buys himself time. The plotters, fearful of eventual exposure, arrange for the agent's execution. And afterwards, with planted evidence abounding, they deploy the agent's left-wing pretensions to establish his guilt for all time. What they did not expect is for the Government to step in and certify this triple cross with the Warren Report.

If this sounds far-fetched, what is one to make of the Warren Report? To fully comprehend this byzantine theory—and, again, it must be stressed this can only be a theory as it is now too late to establish proof—one must grasp the essential historical background that brought us to this point.

Under the Treaty of Paris of 1898 that ended the Spanish-American War, Spain "relinquished" the island of Cuba to the United States "in trust" for its polyglot inhabitants. There followed sixty years of American domination over the island's political and economic affairs, that would end on January 1, 1959, with the overthrow by Dr. Fidel Castro of dictator Fulgencio Batista y Zaldivar. Before the year was out, Castro would be turning Cuba into a Communist satellite. *Fortune* magazine, in September 1959, estimated that during the first nine months, nationalization of U.S. industries had run into the many billions.

On March 17, 1960, largely at the urging of Vice President Nixon, Eisenhower authorized contingency planning for "Operation Pluto", a large-scale guerrilla war that would do to Castro what he, in turn, had done to Batista. The war was to be sponsored and financed by the U.S. but implemented entirely by Cubans who had fled to the U.S. The objective would be nothing less than toppling the insurgent Castro and returning Cuba to its place in the American investment picture. Nixon, in *My Six Crises,* wrote, "the covert training of Cuban exiles by the CIA was due, in substantial part, at least, to my efforts". His military liaison was Maj. Gen. Robert Cushman, USMC, later to become *President* Nixon's deputy CIA Director and a pivotal figure in the Watergate case.

That July, Congress cut the already frayed ties between the two countries by reallocating the hefty Cuban sugar import quotas to other sugar-producing nations. In retaliation, Castro seized another billion dollars of U.S. capital investments. So far, though, he had done nothing to upset the equilibrium of the remaining U.S. industry—vice. But when he did move on the Syndicate, according to columnist Jack Anderson, the loss turned out to be "a financial body blow that hit the underworld as hard as the 1929 stock market rocked Wall Street."

Though Kennedy's intimates would later swear he hadn't heard of "Pluto" until two weeks after his election, there's now sufficient evidence to suggest that he knew better. That same month, July, saw CIA Director Allen Dulles fly up to Hyannisport to brief the candidate on all outstanding intelligence matters—a precaution Eisenhower initiated to make sure that in the heat of campaign oratory, the country's security would not be accidentally compromised.

Picture, therefore, the reaction at the White House when, on October 6, Kennedy called for the liberation of Cuba by Cubans. Nixon was stunned, and trapped: he could obviously not accuse Kennedy of having breached security without tipping off Castro. So, during the fourth TV debate, he attacked Kennedy outright, accusing him of making "the most shocking, reckless and immoral proposal by a presidential candidate in our history."

Early in February, President Kennedy instructed Dulles to proceed with the *contingency* planning, but to hold up implementation. But, as JFK's intellectual-in-residence, Arthur M. Schlesinger Jr., recalled (in *A Thousand Days*): "Kennedy did not yet realize how contingency planning could generate its own momentum and create its own reality."

One reality, of course, was that not all Cubans

wanting to "liberate" Cuba were necessarily freedom fighters. Many were hard-line *Batistianos,* goons of the deposed dictator; many others were disenfranchised *Mafiosi.* No matter, in the CIA's eyes, they were all anti-Communists.

Another reality was the men who were being secretly trained by the CIA down in Guatemala and Nicaragua were straining at their leashes; they had expected to go in as early as December 1959. Furthermore, with newsmen like the *New York Times'* Tad Szulc having gotten wind of the jungle camps, it was becoming increasingly difficult to keep the plan secret. The neutral Organization of American States had not been notified of the plan. Last: Guatemalan President Idigoras Fuentes gave the White House an ultimatum to get the Cubans out by April.

What had begun as a limited guerrilla war plan had by now grown into a miniature Normandy, calling for clandestine American naval and air support—and the proposed assassination of Castro. By January 29, Kennedy still had not committed himself, and was vacillating between diplomatic isolation by the OAS and an outright military attack. By March 1, he'd been brought around to the latter. However, to preserve "deniability", there would be no U.S. air cover. The Cubans were free to do their own bombing; the U.S. would supply the planes, but would disguise them as Castro aircraft.

On April 14, the planes went in, bombed three airfields, claimed to have destroyed Castro's air armada of twenty-five obsolete planes, but actually knocked out only five. More ridiculous: they completely overlooked four T-33 jet trainers parked off one field.

On April 17, Brigade #2506, consisting of 1,400

men, hit the beach at Playa Giron in the Bay of Pigs. Only 135 were professionals, the rest were summer soldiers. Three days later, by the time the T-33 jets had raked the beaches and the Soviet SAV-100 tanks had driven the men into the Zapata marshes, the expeditionary force had all but been decimated. And Castro, plainly *un*-assassinated (JFK had also vetoed that part of the plan) was in firmer control than ever.

The CIA and Joint Chiefs of Staff had totally misread the reality of Castro's Cuba: the people did not rally with the invaders; there was no Fifth Column as none had been organized, and Castro was no *papier-mache* hysteric. He had lived up to his billing as *El Lider*—the leader.

Back in the White House, the Kennedy brothers were stunned. As Taylor Branch and George Crile III point out in their book on the Bay of Pigs aftermath, Jack Kennedy:

"...struggled to comprehend how so total a disaster could have been produced by so many people who were supposed to know what they were doing, who had wrecked governments other than Castro's without mishap or detection. They had promised him a secret success but delivered a public fiasco."

Worse for the image-conscious Kennedys, the world laughed at the mighty United States, its credibility now in shreds, its humiliation total. Nikita S. Khrushchev of the Soviet Union saw the United States as a paper tiger, and in far-off North Vietnam, Ho Chi Minh took note.

Actually, if the truth be known, Castro did not see it as a victory of Communism over Capitalism, but as a defeat of Multinationalism. In April 1961, Castro was still estranged from the Kremlin: what he wanted was a socialist state free of both U.S.

and Russian domination. Now, with his popularity among the uncommitted and Third World nations at an all-time high, the Government of the United States knew this could not be the end. (Left-wing political writer Robert Scheer points out that "Castro had to be killed precisely *because* he was popular. If he had been more like the dismal, uncharismatic leaders of Eastern Europe, the CIA would have loved him." Nobody in the Third World ever wanted to imitate Gomulka of Poland).

In public, therefore, Kennedy ate crow, admitting full responsibility for the disaster ("victory has a hundred fathers and defeat is an orphan"), vowing to splinter the CIA "into a thousand pieces and scattering it to the winds." He convened a Presidential Commission to investigate the CIA, ostensibly to bring it to heel, and after a decent interval, fired Dulles and his chief architects, bringing in as new CIA head West Coast businessman John McCone.

Privately, however, the Kennedy brothers put into action that famed Boston-Irish rule of "Don't get mad, get even." They laid plans for a $200 million "secret war" against Cuba.

Ultimately, the CIA would be fielding weekly commando attacks by teams of Cubans and Americans against coastal military compounds and harbor facilities. Demolition experts were sent in to blow up power stations, sugar mills and oil refineries. The U.S. Navy and Coast Guard went as escorts to Cuban pirates that intercepted grain shipments, and *this* time, the Kennedy brothers would not be so principled about proposals to take out Castro.

"Castro's assassination," said Defense Secretary Robert McNamara at one point, "is the only productive way of dealing with Cuba." And to handle this chore, the Administration turned to the Syndicate—figuring, as Tad Szulc has pointed out, "that the murder would then be pinned on the Mafia, which had lost its shirt with Castro's takeover."

Actually, the Mafia had been brought into the Cuban situation before Kennedy became President. In the waning months of the Eisenhower Administration, CIA Deputy Director of Plans ("Dirty Tricks") Richard M. Bissell, one of those fired by Kennedy in September 1961, had his Director of the Office of Security, Colonel Sheffield Edwards, contact Washington D.C. business consultant Robert A. Maheu, later to become the overseer of Howard Hughes' Las Vegas interests.

Maheu, an ex-FBI agent had become a $500-a-month CIA operative in 1954, while running his company in Washington D.C. In the fall of 1959, Maheu met with Los Angeles hoodlum Johnny Roselli (a/k/a Filippo Sacco) to outline an assassination program. He then brought Roselli together with Sam (Momo) Giancana, an associate of Meyer Lansky in various Havana casinos. The two set up shop at the Fontainebleau Hotel in Miami Beach, and began building a team of scouts and hitmen.

Giancana, according to *Time* magazine, put up $90,000 of the Mob's money to supplement the $100,000 that the CIA had allocated. With this money, Giancana's Chicago aide, ex-cop Richard Cain, began recruiting Spanish-speaking toughs to go in with the invasion. All this, of course, had been unknown to the White House of John F. Kennedy.

But when, in the aftermath of the Bay of Pigs, Robert Kennedy and McNamara thought of bringing the Mafia in, they didn't have far to look:

the Mob was already committed and already had a number of aborted tries behind them. It is still a matter of dispute whether John F. Kennedy *ever* personally sanctioned the up to twenty-four attempts on Castro's life. Schlesinger, for one, doesn't think so. "Nothing would have doomed the prisoners [from the invasion force] more certainly than an American attempt to kill Castro." No matter: Castro *thought* Kennedy knew of those attempts. So, apparently, did J. Edgar Hoover, who in May 1961 warned the Attorney General that this "dirty business" might easily backfire on the President.

What is interesting is that at a certain point, the CIA lost control of the Mob, which kept on trying to kill the Castro brothers without bothering to coordinate it with the CIA. David A. Phillips, ex-CIA Director of Latin American Operations, recently said that on several occasions, when his people got wind of an assassination plot beyond their control, he would tip off the Swiss Embassy to warn Castro. "I'd be surprised, though, if Castro knew it was the CIA that spared his life."

The only real effect of these attempts on Castro's life was to drive him deeper into the Soviet camp. Recently, it was learned that in August 1961, at an OAS economic conference at Punta de Este, Uruguay, a French journalist for *Le Figaro* arranged for JFK speechwriter Richard N. Goodwin to meet with Ernesto "Che" Guevara, Castro's chief theoretician. They spoke for three hours, Guevara arguing *still* for "peaceful coexistence", and offering to make broad concessions to the U.S. if it would only halt these incessant guerrilla attacks that were only getting started at the time. Goodwin promised to get back to Guevara with Kennedy's response; he never did, thus providing the Cubans with justification to ask Khrushchev for retaliatory long-range missiles.

Meanwhile, over the late spring and early summer months of 1961, the survivors kept straggling back to Florida, feeling both betrayed and abandoned by Kennedy. More than 1,100 of their comrades had been captured, many—notably the *Bastistianos*—put on show trials and publicly executed. Not until after the October 1962 missile crisis would the prisoners come home, and then only after Castro again humiliated the Kennedys by exacting a $53 million ransom in drugs, medicine and cash.

In their raging impotence, the veterans began turning on each other, and had it not been for the "secret war" that was then being organized, Miami might have experienced a Chicago-like gang war of Cuban against Cuban.

The only common denominator among the refugees was an unbridled hatred of Fidel Castro. There was nothing to tie them together into a community of exiles. And, as Schlesinger recalls, "every time two or three refugees gathered together a new *union* or *movimiento* was likely to emerge."

Back in 1960, the Eisenhower Administration had tried to bring these hopelessly fractionalized groups together under one umbrella—the *Frente Revolucionario Democratico,* or Cuban Revolutionary Front (CRF).

Three of the group leaders represented pre-Batista Cuba, two post-Batista. The former wanted restoration under the old, colonial order, with American business calling the shots; the latter had been ardent Castro supporters until he began his sharp lurch toward Communism. One of them was Manuel Artime, the CIA's "Golden Boy" who would ultimately be chosen as brigade leader for the $12-million fiasco. Kennedy wanted more balance to the CRF and thus invited in moderate left-winger Manolo Ray, another ex-Castroite, whose splinter group (*Movimiento Revolucionario del Pueblo*) Artime derisively called "Fidelismo sin Fidel"—Castroism without Castro. The upshot of this forced merger was the *Consejo Revolucionario de Cuba*—the Cuban Revolutionary Council— under whose banner the invasion was launched.

As front man, Kennedy selected Dr. Jose Miro Cardona, former law professor at the University of Havana who had served Castro as his first Prime Minister and then as U.S. Ambassador. The CRC was actually a veil behind which the CIA ran things. And after the Bay of Pigs failure, the CRC began crumbling and splitting into a myriad of small cells, typical of which was the *Directorial Revolucionaria Estudiantil*—the Cuban Student Directorate.

It is at this juncture that Lee Harvey Oswald re-enters the picture, since it was the DRE that most worried the FBI. Its founder was a former Havana lawyer named Carlos Bringuier, who had fled Cuba after the Bay of Pigs, settled in New Orleans, and tried for awhile to play along with Dr. Cardona's CRC as a delegate. But Bringuier wanted action, and Cardona preferred temporizing. So on his own hook, Bringuier at some point started cuddling up with right-wingers of many persuasions—cops and *capos*—to build his own little army of guerrillas in a network spanning the south, from New Orleans to Miami by way of Dallas.

With his brother-in-law, Rolando Pelaez, Bringuier's front was a New Orleans haberdashery called the Casa Boca. His funding came from many sources—Mafioso Marcello, an American right-wing group called The Crusade to Free Cuba Committee, and coffee tycoon William Reily.

It could therefore be hardly an accident that when Oswald, on April 25, bussed into New Orleans, he would look for a job and find one as a $1.50-an-hour greaser and oiler of coffee-roasting equipment at the William B. Reily Company.

After the famous "eyeball-to-eyeball" exchange of that previous October, during which Khrushchev blinked and agreed to remove his long-range missiles from Cuba, Kennedy demanded that the U.S. be allowed onto the island to inspect the abandoned bases. Castro, not surprisingly, refused. Khrushchev apparently then came up with a compromise solution: he would allow the U.S. to fly its U-2's over the island with the foreknowledge that the aircraft would not be shot down by the "defensive" surface-to-air rockets that were still in place and under total Soviet control. The price Khrushchev asked was an immediate cessation of Kennedy's "secret war". The administration really had no choice, and so it went along.

After effecting the prisoner release in December, Kennedy ordered a massive crackdown by all federal agencies on the myriad paramilitary activities. Out of nowhere, and with little fore-warning, crack teams of FBI, Secret Service, Treasury and Justice Department agents swooped down on hundreds of clandestine anti-Castro training camps in Florida, Texas and Louisiana. The splinter groups had obviously been well-infiltrated as the Government knew precisely where to strike next, and with deadly accuracy. Ammunition depots, thoughtfully accumulated by the underworld and right-wing Army people, were blown up; night-raiding parties operating out of No-Name Key off Florida were cut off by the Coast Guard.

The Kennedy Administration let it be known far and wide that it was now "taking every step necessary" to call off the Cuban adventure. For the second time in two years, the Cubans felt betrayed. But this time, they were not going to roll over and accommodate the *Yanquis*.

The raiders now shifted their bases of operations from the Louisiana bayous and Florida keys to the U.S. Virgin Islands and Puerto Rico, but now the State Department stepped into the fray. Because on March 15, 1963, things really got out of hand. Two Soviet freighters, docked in Havana, were attacked and almost sunk. The raiders had come from either Puerto Rico or St. Croix. The State Deparmtent was not going to risk another U.S.-U.S.S.R. eyeball-to-eyeball confrontation, because this time, Kennedy would have to blink.

The Cubans were seething. In Miami, gangs of toughs wielding chains attacked tourists, and in New York City, a group even fired a bazooka at the United Nations Building. Hate mail, such as the now-famous broadside calling for Kennedy's assassination, was further exacerbating the situation. It had become obvious to a number of high government people—including Hoover of the FBI—that the CIA had lost control of its clients, and even some of its own people, the American trainers.

On April 15, the last voice of moderation stopped talking. Dr. Cardona resigned from what was left of the Cuban Revolutionary Council.

It was just about then that a letter from Lee Harvey Oswald reached the offices of the Fair Play for Cuba Committee in New York, seeking membership information and literature. FPCC obliged.

On April 21, four days before Oswald packed his bag and left for New Orleans, FBI agent James P. Hosty Jr.—the man who claims never to have seen Oswald until the day of the assassination—received information to the effect that Oswald had been in touch with FPCC in New York. His source, he would note in an inter-office report dated September 10, 1963, more than two months before the assassination, was "Dallas confidential informant T-2".

Hosty would later claim this information had reached him from the FBI's field office in Manhattan, but the FBI's own inventory of the Oswald file produced no such notification. Was T-2 actually Oswald alerting his "control" via the FBI network?

At the same time, the Dallas Police department also put something in a new file. Up until April 24, on several occasions, a "white unidentified male" was seen passing out pro-Castro literature at "the intersection of Main and Ervay Streets" in Dallas. To paraphrase one of the Senators at the Watergate tribunal, "what did the Dallas police know, and when did they know it?"

Once employed at the Reily coffee company, Oswald would occasionally sneak out during his lunch break to pass out FPCC literature. He had established, over FPCC's protest, a "local chapter". Its total membership came to one—Lee Harvey Oswald. He listed as its address 544 Camp Street, which also happened to be the address of Cardona's now moribund Cuban Revolutionary

Council. And it was also the address of a private eye named Guy W. Bannister, who was to figure prominently in the Garrison investigation five years later. In 1954, Bannister had organized the "Anti-Communist League of the Caribbean", a CIA front that played a substantial part in the overthrow of Guatemalan left-wing strongman Colonel Jacobo Arbenz Guzman.

On August 5, Oswald visited Bringuier's Casa Boca. He told Bringuier that he was a trained ex-Marine raring to fight against Castro, but the Cuban was suspicious. Five days earlier, the FBI had raided an illegal ammunition dump at a Syndicate man's home outside New Orleans, and he'd heard the FBI was trying to infiltrate the DRE. He showed Oswald the door. Oswald returned the next day and again was told to go away. Three days later, August 9, Oswald paraded in front of the store, this time wearing a "Viva Fidel!" placard around his neck. Bringuier and some of his men rushed out, ready to start a street fight. "OK, Carlos," Oswald said calmly, crossing his arms behind him, "if you want to hit me, hit me." Bringuier declined the provocation just as the police arrived. They were hustled off to jail for "disturbing the peace."

But instead of asking to see a lawyer, Oswald asked for the FBI—a rather unusual response, and request. Meanwhile, he surrendered his wallet to Lt. Francis L. Martello. In it, Martello found all sorts of notes in Russian and English, his Soviet ID, the names and addresses of the AP and UPI correspondents in Moscow—the very last things a former defector would carry around with him unless he'd wanted word to get around of his checkered background. He also carried FPCC cards, one of them signed by "chapter head" A.J. Hidell. (Marina would later claim she'd forged the signature on Oswald's orders.)

Obligingly, the cops called the FBI and the local field office sent over special agent John Lester Quigley. The interview lasted ninety minutes. We have no record of what they talked about. We do know Quigley told the Warren Commission that Oswald had bragged about his FPCC chapter, claiming it had been set up in 1959, that it consisted of thirty-five members, etc. He also told the Commission that Oswald had described the leader, A.J. Hidell, and that Oswald spoke about wanting to re-defect to the U.S.S.R.

The next day, someone put up $10 bail, and Oswald walked out. Quigley filed his report, which presumably went out over the field network, with a copy ending up in Dallas. If anyone was worried about his plans to re-defect, no one said or did anything. Strange.

Not really, though. What agent Quigley may not have known is that Oswald was chummy with one of his colleagues, FBI agent Warren C. DeBruys. According to one of Bringuier's compatriots, a right-wing Cuban barkeep, Orest Pena, who was also an FBI informant (on *pro*-Castro activities), he'd served Oswald in his Habana Bar & Lounge on Decatur Street while accompanied by none other than agent DeBruys. But he never told that to the Warren Commission. As Pena recalled in 1975, back in 1964 DeBruys had warned him that "if you ever talk about me [to the Warren Commission] I'll get your ass." (DeBruys, now head of the FBI's San Juan office, denies knowing, meeting or talking with Oswald—but really, what else can we expect DeBruys to say?)

Six days after his overnight stay in the New

Orleans jail, Oswald engineered another bit of street theatre. This time he hired some locals at the Louisiana State Employment Office to help pass out FPCC leaflets in front of the International Trade Mart. (The Garrison investigators would make much of the fact that the former ITM director was Clay L. Shaw, but if Shaw and Oswald knew each other—Shaw having been fingered as a CIA agent—the secret died with Shaw in August 1974.)

Oswald had tipped off the news desks at WDSU-TV and WWL-TV apparently to insure some visibility on the 6 p.m. news that night. He was not disappointed: Oswald, the ex-Marine defector, now pro-Castro agitator, was seen in thousands of TV homes that evening.

On August 21, Oswald was invited to appear on a local radio show, "Latin Listening Post", by moderator William Stuckey. He was joined by Bringuier and by Edward Butler, an official of the Information Council of the Americas, a right-wing, anti-Communist group. It sounded like a set-up, with Oswald being forced to admit his unsavory past as a defector and traitor, a Marxist and Castro-sympathizer. Butler had all the information at his fingertips: earlier, he had contacted some friends on the House Un-American Activities Committee, who'd managed to put together a dossier on Oswald. Then Butler had alerted other right-wing Cuban groups to beware of the young agitator. (A few years later, researcher Weisberg would discover that Butler's INCA had "packaged" the telling August 21 "debate" as an LP record, with "dynamic commentary" provided by the right-wing fundamentalist, the Reverend Billy James Hargis. It would be part of the post-assassination defamation campaign.)

(Butler, incidentally, still seems to have respect

for Oswald. "He was no dummy," Butler said in 1975. "He was an articulate, capable propagandist. I never underestimated his intelligence.")

Quite possibly, Oswald had wanted things to break this way. With his reputation as a pro-Castroite now assured, he'd also become known in New Orleans as something of a harmless nut, not to be taken too seriously. Just as possibly, Oswald miscalculated: his very dubious background would make him an ideal "patsy"—something he might have realized the night he was arrested.

Meanwhile, Marina and the baby had joined him in New Orleans. It was a mistake; after a month, she wrote Ruth Paine an anguished letter, telling of the corrosive battles with Lee. Ruth wrote back, now finally professing her love for the Russian girl, and imprudently suggesting she quit New Orleans, and Oswald, and move in with her. Marina wrote, stalling. Finally, when the Reily coffee company fired Oswald for "inefficiency and inattention" (or perhaps for his pamphleteering), and with Oswald "ranting and raving" (Marina's words) about wanting to return to Russia, Marina—now seven months pregnant— had had it. Mrs. Paine drove to New Orleans to fetch Marina and the baby, and Oswald, strangely, showed little remorse.

On September 17, Oswald went to the Mexican Consulate and picked up a fifteen-day Tourist Card under his own name. A week later, he took a bus to Houston, and from there to Mexico City, arriving there on the 27th. At this juncture, things become exceedingly complicated in the peripatetic life of Lee Harvey Oswald.

On the night of September 26, while Oswald was supposedly en route to Mexico, a twenty-six-year-old Cuban emigree, Mrs. Sylvia Odio, received three visitors in her Dallas apartment. They were two Cubans named "Angelo" and "Leopoldo", and an American introduced to her as "Leon Oswald". All three claimed to have just arrived from New Orleans, that they were members of JURE—the *Junta Revolucionaria*—the *left*-wing splinter group formed by Manolo Ray after walking out of Cardona's CRC. They seemed to know a great deal about Mrs. Odio and her anti-Castro millionaire parents, who were at that moment rotting in jail on the Isle of Pines.

(Mrs. Odio, who had contacted the FBI with her story after seeing the captured Oswald on TV the night of the assassination, was interviewed on December 18, 1963, and subsequently went before the Warren Commission to repeat her story.)

The excuse for the visit, Mrs. Odio continued, was that the men wanted her to do some translation. In fact, though, they'd come to "promote" the man called Oswald. "Leopoldo" told her:

"You know, our idea is to introduce him to the underground in Cuba because he is great. He is kind of nuts. He told us we don't have any guts, 'you Cubans, because President Kennedy would have been assassinated after the Bay of Pigs,' and some Cubans should have done that, because he was the one that was holding the freedom of Cuba actually."

"Leopoldo" further told Odio that "Oswald" had said "it is so easy to do it". The next day, "Leopoldo" again called Odio, again touted his friend "Oswald", again said he was "the kind of man that could do anything like getting underground in Cuba, like killing Castro," and again described him as "an expert shotman."

The Commission plainly disbelieved Mrs. Odio, especially after she'd failed to identify as "Oswald" the man shown on TV news still passing out pro-Castro literature in New Orleans. Then, the Commission staff trundled out photos of three men *it* said had admitted visiting Mrs. Odio in Dallas: Loran Eugene Hall, Lawrence J. Howard and William H. Seymour, the latter bearing a striking resemblance to the real Oswald. But Mrs. Odio failed to recognize the trio. The Commission dismissed Mrs. Odio as "unbalanced" and discredited her story; they never considered, apparently, that Mrs. Odio *may* have been part of a larger skein—a set-up by the right-wing Cubans to get her to call the authorities on November 22 to arrest Oswald, in the event he eluded the dragnet.

What's interesting is that Loran Hall, also known as Lorenzo Eugenio Pascillo, a native of West Covina, Calif., was a soldier of fortune who had fought with Castro in the Sierre Maestre in 1958; that after falling out of favor with the new regime, Hall was jailed along with one of the Trafficante brothers, until both were repatriated to the U.S. in 1962. He then became involved with the anti-Castro guerrillas. Larry Howard likewise was one of the CIA cadre in the "secret war", as was Seymour. Why they would pass themselves off as members of the left-wing JURE is something else that the Commission didn't delve into, even if Odio was "fantasizing".

Still, a few Commission staffers weren't convinced the woman was crazy: there were too many details that matched facts Odio couldn't have possibly known if she were just a refugee odd-ball craving attention. But with Rankin pushing for a deadline to close the investigation, the staff was told to lay off, to forget Odio. A pity. As critic Weisberg says, "Why was the Commission so unperturbed that anyone would *want* to counterfeit such an unimportant man as Oswald *then* was?"

That fall, there would be other incidents involving "double Oswalds". Most have been thoroughly written up by now—the "incident" at the Dallas Sports Drome rifle range where a man loudly identifying himself as "Lee Oswald" made a perfect nuisance of himself by firing at other people's targets and scoring bull's eye after bull's eye; the "Oswald" who took a used car for a test-drive at 70 m.p.h. on the Stemmons Freeway and then told the salesman that he was about to come into a lot of money and if that wasn't good enough to get him credit, he'd go back to the Soviet Union "where they know how to treat workers like men", etc.

But one incident has not been fully reported. Appearing in late November, 1975 on a CBS News "inquiry" into the assassination, former convicted pro-Castro gunrunner Robert Ray McKeown, a friend of Jack Ruby's, claimed to have been visited two weeks before the assassination by Lee Harvey Oswald. He described this Oswald to CBS News correspondent Dan Rather as "a little guy . . . small blond-headed fellow," and his companion as "a tall Latin with a mustache" named "Hernandez". They'd first approached him to buy "lots of arms like bazookas and machine guns," and when he turned them down McKeown said, Oswald offered to pay $1,000 each for four "powerful Savage automatics with telescopic sights."

Again, they appear to be part of a mosaic-in-the-making—but strangely, they are somewhat sloppy diversions. Thus, McKeown described "Oswald" as blond when he was dark-haired, and acting as an agent for others when the verdict is that Oswald was a loner. Then there's the fact that both the FBI and the CIA would have known that the real Lee Harvey Oswald didn't know how to drive a car; the Cubans might not have known.

Some critics, of course, make much of the fact that few of the Oswald documents—ID cards, passport applications, unemployment benefit records—provide any consistent physical characteristics. Thus, on his USMC enlistment papers, Oswald is shown to be 5'8", while his discharge papers make him 5'11". Photographs taken in Minsk show him to stand two inches higher than Marina (who was 5'3" and didn't wear heels), while in death, his autopsy record describes him as 5'9". Some have even postulated that the CIA employed two Oswalds, one who played a domestic role, the other who was sent into Russia, but these are games anyone can play—even the Commission did when Rankin and Boggs puzzled about the vastly different styles of writing between the Oswald of Minsk and the Oswald of Dallas and New Orleans. But this theory falls apart on the autopsy table in Dallas: the wrists of the Oswald killed by Ruby clearly showed the scars of his Moscow suicide attempt.

Regardless of the temptation to suggest that Lee Harvey Oswald never did go to Mexico, that it was all a feint involving a "second Oswald," the evidence is fairly overwhelming that he did, indeed, make the trip. The demonologists make much of the fact that the photo the CIA sent up to Langley of "Oswald" entering the Soviet Embassy was obviously not Oswald. Former Latin American CIA specialist David Phillips concurs, pointing out that while the CIA did make phone taps and observed him entering the Cuban Embassy, they can only surmise Oswald visited the Soviets. "No photo of Oswald was ever made," he recalled in 1975. "We still don't know who that man in the photo was. We marked the photo as that of an 'unidentified white male', period."

Moreover, there are bus records and the hotel registry to prove Oswald was in Mexico City, and there are affidavits signed by both Cuban and Russian embassy officials to that effect—and they would hardly do the bidding of people trying to frame Lee Harvey Oswald.

So we know fairly well that Oswald arrived in Mexico City on the 17th, having made the leg from Houston via the Flecha Roja Bus Line; that he checked into a $1.28-a-day room at the Hotel del Comercio, and that on the same day hied himself to the Cuban Embassy to demand a transit visa to Havana. For his *bona fides,* he whipped out his New Orleans press clippings and waved the FPCC literature, but the Cubans weren't buying. Instead, they told him to go to the Soviets and first get from them a Russian entrance visa. But the Russians, too, turned him down, whereupon he stormed back to the Cubans and created an unpleasant scene.

The suggestion has been made that at this juncture, Oswald may really have freaked out and blown his "cover", and that when the FBI got wind of this aberrant behavior, it decided then and there he'd become unreliable, not someone to take seriously, even as an informer. That might explain Hosty's indifference to Oswald's threatening letter shortly before the assassination. But what still needs to be explained by someone in Washington is why, when the CIA asked the Office of Naval Intelligence for a photo of Oswald to check against the one taken of the "unidentified white male" visitor to the Soviet Embassy, ONI declined to provide one.

The Mexican junket a fiasco, Oswald came back

to the United States on or about October 4. He went straight to Irving to try for a reconciliation with Marina, was rebuffed, but was then helped by Ruth Paine to find a job as a $1.25-an-hour shipping clerk at the Texas School Book Depository.

We know that on October 10, his second daughter was born; that he visited Marina on most weekends, always at his initiative, never at her request; that Marina never even tried contacting him, except once. And that was on November 18—four days before the assassination—when, according to her testimony before the Commission, she learned he'd taken his room in Dallas under the pseudonym of O.H. Lee. For some strange reason, that discovery resulted in a furious telephone argument. It couldn't have been the first time Marina discovered her husband had disguised himself.

Three days later, on November 21, Oswald hitched a ride back to Irving with co-worker (and neighbor) Buell Wesley Frazier. According to Frazier, Oswald said he had to go home to pick up some curtain rods, but that may have been Oswald's own cover story so that he would not have to tell this 19-year-old boy that his real mission was to try to make up with his angry wife.

Alas, he failed there too. Marina snubbed him, froze him, declined to have any physical contact with him. And so, the Warren Commission—most notably simplistic-minded Gerald R. Ford—came to its slam-bang conclusion: rebuffed by Marina, frustrated sexually and professionally, Lee Harvey Oswald the next morning went to the garage where he'd hidden his Mannlicher-Carcano 6.5 mm. rifle, drove with Frazier back to the Depository, and at 12:30 p.m. on November 22, kept his appointment with destiny.

How poetic. How absurd.

THE FRIENDS OF
JACK LEON RUBY

> "...the evidence does not establish a significant link between [Jack] Ruby and organized crime...[we] found no evidence of any suspicious relationship between Ruby and any police officer."
> —The Warren Report

If there are still questions concerning Oswald's involvement with the forces of foreign and domestic intelligence, there should be none about Jack Leon Ruby's involvement with the forces of crime and rascality.

In dealing with Ruby, the Commission was all too aware of the rash of rumors that cropped up after Oswald was shot down in cold blood before the horrified eyes of an army of reporters, policemen and millions of TV viewers. Ruby must have been acting on behalf of the cabal that killed the President; he had silenced the accused assassin.

For all its massive efforts to depict Ruby's act as one conducted in a "moment of madness", unrelated to anything except his unstable personality, his hunger for instant fame, whatever, the Commission failed miserably. It did nothing to dispel the lingering doubts that there was more, much more, to this so-called irrational, solitary act.

Ruby was "not just a 'good ole boy' who ran a whorehouse," observes Penn Jones, a gritty little populist Texas newspaper editor who has spent more than twelve years looking into the assassination and its aftermath. Nor was he merely "a small peanut" in the Dallas underworld, as former Dallas County Sheriff Steve Guthrie once maintained.

Jack Ruby was a violent, coarse, foul-mouthed man, given to (as the Warren Report put it) "sudden and extreme displays of temper and violence." Dallas newsman Gary Cartwright, who knew him, puts it less delicately. He was, writes Cartwright,

> "...a mean-tempered prude who loved children and hated ethnic jokes. He didn't drink or smoke. He was violently opposed to drugs, though he maintained his own high energy level by popping Preludin—an upper— and it was rumored that he operated a personal clearing house for mob drug runners. He was involved in shady financial schemes and the IRS was on his back...sex shocked and disturbed him."

Standing 5'9" and weighing 175 pounds, Ruby "had the carriage of a bantam cock and the energy of a steam engine," making believe he was a V.I.P. when in fact, Cartwright points out, he was a forlorn, pathetic creature who couldn't even make history—"he only stepped in front of it." Ironically,

> "When he emerged from obscurity into that inextricable freeze-frame that joins all of our minds to Dallas, Jack Ruby, a bald-headed little man who wanted above all to make it big, had his back to the camera."

Former defense counsel Tonahill still thinks of

his late client as "a Damon Runyon character, a total inconsistency," a compulsive glad-hander with aspirations far greater than his ability to achieve. Had the Warren Commission and the FBI really exerted themselves, they might have found more in his background than "Guys and Dolls."

At his dingy, walk-up strip-joint, the Carousel Club at Commerce and Akard—"a fuckin' classy joint," as Ruby liked to call it—the proprietor habitually brutalized the hired help and the customers with equal abandon. But few ever bothered to press assault-and-battery charges: they knew they would get no sympathy from the Dallas Police department. Ruby was on a first-name basis with at least 700 of the city's 1,200-man force, plying them with booze, food, and women. Also with information they could use to meet their quotas of arrests.

Former Dallas Assistant D.A. Bill Alexander laughs scornfully at all those published reports that Ruby was a police buff. "That's horseshit," says Alexander, "he didn't think anymore of a policeman than he did a pissant. It was just good business. The Vice Squad kept plus and minus charts on the joints because the licenses came up for renewal each year. The Vice Squad can kill a joint if they get in the wrong mood...."

And so Ruby violated the midnight curfew with impunity, escaped convictions on liquor-law violations and other civic ordinances. He had an arrest record, mostly for such "minor infractions" as carrying a concealed weapon or simple assault. He never so much as served an hour's time.

We know that the Oswald transfer to the County Jail had been scheduled for precisely 10 a.m. and that therefore it should have been only logical that given Ruby's antics during the preceding day and a half—of being at the center of the action—he ought to have been at Police Headquarters at 10 a.m. But he wasn't. He didn't show up until 11:20 a.m. and three minutes later, Oswald was dying from Ruby's gunshot. It is immaterial that the reason for the one-hour-and-twenty-minute delay was that Captain Fritz wanted one more try at extracting a confession from Oswald; what is material is that Ruby *knew* the transfer had been delayed and furthermore knew *precisely* the moment at which Oswald would be brought downstairs. Why the Commission didn't look into this anomaly is worse than puzzling, for there was no shortage of unexplained curious coincidences to go into.

Consider the testimony of Scripps-Howard newsman Seth Kantor. He saw and spoke with Ruby at Parkland Hospital at 1:30 p.m. C.S.T. on November 22—a half-hour after Kennedy had been pronounced dead. So did a second witness, Mrs. Wilma Tice. Yet, the Commission refused to believe them; they preferred to believe Ruby, who "emphatically" and "vehemently" denied having been at Parkland. Why such passion? Many critics still believe it was Ruby who had "planted" CE 399, the Specter "magic bullet" that just happened to roll out from under a stretcher and helped clinch the posthumous case against Oswald.

And in the early hours of Sunday morning—at about 2:15 a.m.—both the local office of the FBI and the Sheriff's Office were called by an anonymous party claiming to speak on behalf of a "Committee of 100". The man said they would "kill the man that killed the President" the next morning. The fact that the unidentified caller did not call the police, in whose custody Oswald was at the moment, and who would have perhaps recognized the voice, leads many to believe it was Ruby calling. (Ironically, the call spurred the Sheriff's Deputy on duty to contact Chief Curry to arrange for Oswald's transfer that night; had Curry been reachable, it's conceivable Oswald might have lived to stand trial.)

Aside from the question of what sort of institutional madness would have prompted the Dallas law-enforcement officials to stage a transfer for maximum press coverage the next day—the only possible reason for such a delay in moving Oswald to a safer jail—there's the more important question of why the Commission chose not to come to grips with the gut issue. Namely, whether the caller was Ruby or not, the threat should have raised in the Commission's collective mind the issue of premeditation. It should have, but didn't, for the same reason the Commission did not entertain for a second the possibility that there may have been more than one assassin. Ruby, they insisted, acted on the spur of the moment.

Then there is the question of why Ruby, a man given to violence, a man with a police record for carrying a concealed weapon, should have been allowed to roam free through police headquarters for two days, at one time wearing borrowed press credentials, until the opportunity came to kill Oswald.

It is interesting to remember that for all their denials, at least 36 of the 75 cops that accompanied Oswald on his last few steps into oblivion, knew Ruby on sight. And that afterwards, not one policeman would be able to tell the Commission how Ruby got into the garage.

Correction: one policeman could have, but he was one the Commission did not chose to call to testify. Curious. Very curious. His name was Lt.

George E. Butler, an old friend of Jack Ruby's, going back to 1947, whom we will meet later in this chapter. Butler was assigned to the Juvenile Bureau of the Criminal Investigation Department. The FBI interviewed him on December 9, 1963. He had little to tell them. But on his own, that same day, he arranged to be interviewed by two policemen who were checking out Ruby's background. He told them that (a) Oswald was really Ruby's illegitimate son, and (b) that Ruby had applied for a Mexican travel visa at around the same time that Oswald was in Mexico City. The first was obviously a sick joke, the second a possible red herring—but one to which the Commission didn't address itself, not even to ask how a cop assigned to CID juvenile affairs would know about Oswald's Mexican travels.

What makes Butler even more interesting was the testimony of Thayer Waldo, a reporter on the Ft. Worth *Star Telegram*. Waldo had known Butler as a prime contact in the Police department; he'd gotten a number of good leads from him in the past. But on that fateful Sunday morning, Butler didn't seem to be himself:

"...this almost stolid poise, or perhaps phlegmatic poise is a better word, that I had noticed all through even the most hectic times of the 22nd and the 23rd, appeared to have deserted him completely on the morning of the 24th. He was an extremely nervous man, so nervous that when I was standing asking him a question after I had entered the ramp and gotten down to the basement area, just moments before Oswald was brought down, he was standing profile to me and I noticed his lips trembling as he listened and waited for my answer. It was simply a physical characteristic. I had by then spent enough hours talking to this man so that it struck me as something totally out of character."

If the Commission was curious as to what had wrought this dramatic change in Lt. Butler, nobody asked. The answer, again, would have been Unthinkable.

Nor did the Commission ask to see Ruby's lawyer, Tom Howard, who had just happened to drop into the jail office seconds before his client was about to commit murder, just at the precise moment Lee Harvey Oswald was being brought off the jail elevator. He waved at a detective, and said, "That's all I wanted to see."

There's an enormous amount of work the Commission, seemingly deliberately, declined to do in looking into the life and times of Jacob Rubenstein of Chicago. And the reason goes back to the old threshold question of conspiracy. The Commission so compartmentalized its work-load that the subject of a possible Oswald-Ruby link would be dumped into the lap of only one of fourteen assistant counsels. The result was predictable. Recalls Warren Report critic Peter Dale Scott of Berkeley:

"After the Report was published and whenever I spoke to one of the lawyers, I'd invariably get responses like, 'I never dealt with that,' or 'I never saw any evidence which would support that theory.'"

So, in trying to cosmeticize Ruby for history, the Warren Commission never really looked for a commonality of interests between Ruby and Oswald—namely an interest in Cuba. We suspect that Oswald's interest was that of an *agent-provocateur*; we can only surmise that Ruby's was more commercially motivated since he was working for people whose overriding concern was to speed the day they could once more go back to Havana—the Syndicate.

The Warren Commission, relying greatly for its Ruby input on what the Dallas police told the FBI, insisted all along that his criminal links were, at most, tenuous. It did admit that "in his youth, Ruby was unquestionably familiar, if not friendly with some Chicago criminals." The Commission was simply too kind. "Throughout his life," the Warren Report notes, his criminal connections were "limited largely to professional gamblers," and "there is no credible evidence that Ruby himself gambled on other than a social basis."

Old Sportin' Life must have had quite a social life because at one point, before Ruby shot his way into the history books, he was said to have owed the Internal Revenue Service something like $40,000 in back taxes. But don't look for a reference to that in the Warren Report Appendix.

Born in Chicago in 1911, Ruby—like Oswald—was a chronic truant and school drop-out. As early as age five, he was found to be "incorrigible" by the Chicago Juvenile Court. Ten years later, the FBI learned, he was one of twelve boys (including boxer Barney Ross) running numbers for Al Capone's cousin, Frank ("The Enforcer") Nitti in Chicago's tough 24th Ward. The FBI painted a rosy picture: the boys "believed that these envelopes did not contain any messages or anything of value...[Capone] did this in order to make them think they were earning a dollar and in order to keep them from hanging around the street." A regular P.A.L. operation. Of course, these street-savvy lads also believed in the Tooth Fairy, or perhaps the FBI agent who wrote up this report did.

In his early twenties, Ruby headed West and began peddling newspapers door to door and race tip sheets at Santa Anita near Los Angeles and Bay Meadows in San Francisco. Returning to Chicago in 1937, Ruby joined his chum Leon Cooke and helped organize Local #20467 of the Scrap Iron & Junk (Waste) Handlers Union. In December 1939, secretary-treasurer Cooke was mortally shot by the union's president, John Martin. Cooke lingered until January; Martin was acquitted and not long after was ousted by Paul (Red) Dorfman, who would emerge in the public eye ten years later as a power behind the rise of James Riddle Hoffa of the Teamsters.

In Volume 22 of the Appendix, the Warren Commission indicated that "an extensive search of the [police] records did not reflect any reference to...Jack Ruby or Jack Rubenstein or to the murder of Leon Cook" (*sic*). Of course not: Jacob Rubenstein did not legally change his name to either "Jack" or to "Ruby" until eight years after the shooting of Cooke—whose surname came with an "e". And just how "extensive" the search was is questionable: a look in the newspaper morgue of the Chicago *Tribune* would have produced a story that had run in the issue of Dec. 9, 1939, indicating that police were questioning the newly named secretary-treasurer, Jacob Rubenstein. And a call to the State Attorney's office in Springfield, Ill., would have revealed that during Ruby's first year as the local's money man, the State of Illinois had seized the books and confiscated the charter of Local #20467 on grounds that it wasn't a union but "a fraud...a front for organized crime." And if someone had *really* tried, they'd have cross-checked some of the material that came out of the 1957 McClellan Hearings, notably the involvement of mobsters John ("Johnny Dio") Dioguardi and Anthony ("Tony Ducks") Corallo in the Waste Handlers Union. This lackadaisical research by the FBI seems rather untypical.

Crushed by Cooke's murder—Ruby subsequently adopted "Leon" as his middle name as a living memorial—and his labor career nipped in the bud, Ruby next went into the novelty business, selling punchboards, games of chance and after Pearl Harbor, patriotic busts of FDR and "Day of Infamy" wall plaques. Later, he drifted into selling automobile glass and in 1943, reclassified 1-A, Ruby was inducted into the Air Corps. Spending the rest of the war stateside, he got out in 1946, returned to the novelty business (this time with brothers Sam, Hyman and Earl), and started hobnobbing with the likes of mobsters Dave Yaras and Lenny Patrick.

That same year, Yaras and Patrick had been arrested, indicted but not convicted for the murder of one James E. Ragen. This is important because the Warren Report skirted the matter entirely until forced to look at it by the stream-of-consciousness testimony of Ruby's sister, Eva Granovsky (Grant). The FBI once more seemed to be all thumbs in its research.

Ragen had been a member of the Syndicate, and had succeeded the late Moses ("Moe") Annenberg—father of our former Ambassador to Great Britain Walter S. Annenberg—as head of "Continental Press", a private and quite illegal racing wire. The Chicago mob wanted in. In fact, they wanted the whole thing since Continental was competing with its wire, "Trans-American", operated by Jacob ("Greasy Thumb") Guzik. Since Ragen wouldn't sell out, he was murdered, allegedly by Dave Yaras & friends. But they beat the rap:

just when the trial was about to get underway, witnesses recanted or—recalls Ovid Demaris (in *Captive City*)—"died in a hail of bullets." It was all quite cozy in Chicago after the war: Yaras left for Miami where he would eventually organize a Teamsters local, and buy a piece of the Cuban action and Guzik's lawyer would get his due by becoming State Attorney and eventually Chief Judge of the Chicago Criminal Court, presumably on the qualification that it takes one to sentence one.

Jack Ruby, meanwhile, had not been standing by idly. Yaras had hired him to make nice-nice with the local police so none of his racing parlors would be busted, and in 1947, Ruby, too, cashed in his chips. He was one of some twenty people whom the Syndicate "transferred" to a new branch office—Dallas.

He sold his interest in the novelty business to his brothers for $14,000 and reinvested it in sister Eva's new Singapore Supper Club in Dallas. This not only gave him a place to hang his hat but it also served as a hang-out for his friend Paul Roland Jones, a known opium smuggler and occasional hit man.

Orginally, the mob looked at Dallas as a growth market for juke boxes and other coin machines, which supplemented other business activities such as running liquor into nearby "bottle" states. It was, in 1947, a penny-ante $18 million-a-year business. They could do better by bringing down the Trans-American wire. But for that they needed help. So Jones asked Ruby to set up a meeting with the newly elected Sheriff Guthrie. The bribe offer ran in the order of $150,000 a year, and the Sheriff thoughtfully had the conversation bugged and recorded. Later, the offer helped send Jones to prison on a narcotics charge. Ruby set up the meeting, but the man who bugged it was the same Lt. George E. Butler who would, sixteen years later, be suspected of having arranged Ruby's well-timed arrival for Oswald's execution. (Interviewed in jail by the FBI, Jones suggested that if they wanted to know who had put Ruby up to it, the man to see would be Dallas underboss Joe Civella. The FBI didn't.)

Butler and Ruby got to be close friends, and Butler would be instrumental in making Ruby an unofficial member of the Dallas police "establishment". In the years that followed, Ruby became jack of all trades, master of few: he bought, managed and sold one nightclub after another, peddled vitamin supplements and arthritis elixirs, marketed pizza crusts, managed a nightclub performer, and in 1959, became an exporter of jeeps to Cuba.

What suddenly got Ruby into the Cuban situation was his longstanding friendship with gambler Lewis J. McWillie, a former Ft. Worth underling for L.B. ("Benny the Cowboy") Binnion. By 1959, McWillie had long since moved up the organization and was now in Cuba working for the Lansky and Trafficante brothers as a casino manager. In August that year, McWillie invited his old friend Ruby for an eight-day "social visit," and sent him the tickets. Ruby went, according to the Report. What the Report doesn't say is that the next month, Ruby returned to Havana—for one day. According to the FBI report in the Appendix, he flew out of Miami on Pan Am Flight 415 on September 12 and returned the very next day on Flight 750. It could hardly have been much of a social visit; it was more like an important business meeting.

For by September 1959 it had become pretty evident to the Syndicate that its days in Cuba under the new Castro regime were numbered, and that it had better prepare for any contingency, including—if need be—to cozy up to the Government of the United States.

The Government and the Mob have been strange bedfellows for a long time, going back to 1942, when an official in the Office of Naval Intelligence telephoned New York lawyer Moses Polakoff, whose client—"Lucky" Luciano—was at the moment doing heavy time in the maximum security prison of Dannemora in upstate New York. Luciano did not have to ask what he could do for his country; his country told him. In exchange for mobilizing his goons to keep the wartime New York waterfront free from Axis sabotage, Mr. Luciano was transferred to the relatively "soft" Green Haven Prison and got the promise of a post-war review of his 30-50 year sentence.

In 1946, after an extraordinary parole session, approved by Governor Thomas E. Dewey (who, as a racketbusting D.A., had sent Luciano up), the whoremaster-general of the United States was deported to his native Italy for what the Bureau of Narcotics hoped would be early retirement. As we shall see, their hopes were naive.

The ONI-Luciano Compact of 1942 was recognized also by another intelligence agency, the wartime Office of Strategic Services, the forerunner of the CIA. OSS was established in 1941 by President Roosevelt as the wonderfully misnamed "Office of the Coordinator of Information"—the "coordinator" being retired Major General William J. ("Wild Bill") Donovan. What started out as a think-tank of college professors was quickly transformed into a lethal paramilitary fighting team (some of whose early members are still sitting in Langley, Va., puffing at their pipes while thinking up new strains of deadly poisons with which to wipe out entire nations). To the OSS, the deal with Luciano meant one could do business with organized crime, and so we did, first in Sicily during the invasion, then in Latin America. In fact, the Government never stopped doing business in the Americas with the Mob, as we've learned over the past two years.

(Last year, in his appearance before the Church CIA Committee, mobster Johnny Roselli so impressed the chairman with his excellent memory that Senator Church complimented the witness. "How do you do it? Do you take notes?" And with unconscious humor, Roselli replied, "no sir, only cash.")

A year after Luciano settled in Naples, he'd snuck back to the Western Hemisphere, this time re-establishing himself in Carlos Prio Socarras' Cuba. But when the Narcs got the word, the State Department exerted pressure on the Cubans, who then reluctantly shipped Luciano back to Italy. But before he left, "Lucky" deputized Miami-based gambling head Meyer Lansky as his proxy. Lansky, the acknowledged inventor of the "skim", actually waited until 1952 to move into Havana in force. It would take a $250,000 bribe to Socarras and the return from exile of strongman Batista, but the payoff was a $100-million-a-year business just in gambling and kinky sex. Luciano had turned Havana into the principal gateway for the Palermo-Marseilles heroin trade, many more untold hundreds of millions of dollars. One of Lansky's customers was the CIA, which used smack to keep some of its puppets on the string.

But in 1956, Lansky cooled on dope. Congress

had passed a tough Narcotics Control Act that was frankly crimping Lansky's style. It was at about this juncture that the Syndicate started investing in legitimate business, such as offshore Cuban oil exploration. Many of Lansky's mainland distributors went along; one didn't. Albert Anastasia protested too much, and in October 1957, at a Mafia summit meeting in Sicily, the "main office" voted for Lansky against Anastasia. A week or so later, Anastasia was shot to death in his barber-chair in New York's Hotel Park Sheraton. In 1958, the last year of Batista's reign, Havana rapidly began losing its importance as a narcotics port, and began gaining importance as the underworld's Zurich for laundering skim money from Las Vegas and other Mob-controlled enterprises such as Trans-American.

Lansky saw Castro's handwriting on the wall long before his crony Batista did. So, in 1958, he instructed his people in Cuba and on the mainland to start playing both sides of the street—Castro's as well as Batista's. With one hand, the Mob continued to buy its slot machines from Batista's brother-in-law, General Roberto Fernandez y Miranda; with the other, it supplied Castro's bearded guerrillas with needed arms and medical supplies.

Obviously, these could not be purchased on the open market. They'd have to be smuggled in from the mainland. Enter New Orleans multi-millionaire kingpin Carlos Marcello, Bobby Kennedy's nemesis. Marcello's network covered not just Louisiana but neighboring Texas, as well, owning a number of gambling establishments in the Dallas-Ft. Worth area, and funding such marginal operations as Ruby's Carousel.

And so, Ruby's involvement with Castro arms

smuggling began on or about May 30, 1958, when, according to an uncorroborated FBI report that surfaced six years later during the Ruby trial, a Kalamazoo woman named Mary Thompson said she'd been introduced by her brother-in-law, a Dallas cop, to a man she remembered only as "Jack". (The meeting took place in Islamadora, Fla. "Jack," she said, had moved from Chicago to Dallas, where he ran a club, and "he took me to his car, opened the trunk, and showed off guns he said were going to supply Castro.")

This largesse on the part of the Mob may explain Castro's benevolence upon seizing power; he'd gone after Anaconda, United Fruit and other giant U.S. industries, but he strictly left his hands off the Syndicate's properties, even deputizing some Americans to work in his government in patrolling gambling. At that early stage of his agrarian revolution, Castro could ill afford to lose the tourist trade.

Lansky had left Cuba with Batista and eventually moved his operations to Freeport in the Bahamas, still trying to run things by rote in Havana. But soon, he got Castro's message: the take was to stay in Cuba and not follow Lansky out of the country. Clearly, Castro would not play ball as Batista had; the *quid pro quo* was now on a different footing.

Early in 1959, Jack Ruby—according to one witness the Commission tried to discredit—"made preliminary inquiries, as a middleman, concerning the possible sale to Cuba of some surplus jeeps located in Shreveport...and asked about the possible release of prisoners from a Cuban prison." *Whose* prisoners is still unclear, but one can readily guess that they weren't Batista's. Ruby said he was acting "on behalf of a person in Las

Vegas" he declined to name. But the deal fell through since his contact—gunrunner Robert Ray McKeown—was by then on a five-year probationary sentence and no longer wanted to tangle with the Justice Department.

For such a "nebbish" or "small peanut," Ruby carried around some mighty potent names and phone numbers in his notebook, among them, high-ranking Teamster official Robert (Barney) Baker, and Milt Jaffe, a major investor in the Stardust Casino in Las Vegas, and partner of Tony Cornero Stralla, a former California bootlegger (and incidentally, a World War II OSS undercover operative in Latin America).

By the end of 1959, the Syndicate dropped Castro and adopted the anti-Castro exiles, and our man Ruby was in the thick of things. Consider the Warren Commission testimony of a former Ruby employee, Nancy Perrin Rich.

Nancy and Robert Lee Perrin were floaters. She'd been a vagrant, addict, prostitute, even police informer; he lived largely by his wits, selling his services as speedboat operator to the highest bidder. During the Spanish Civil War he'd worked for the Franco insurgents as gunrunner; now, he was working for the Cuban exiles, helping to transport refugees out of the island, through the U.S. Coast Guard barrier. The Dallas police had arranged for Nancy to get a job as a bartender at Jack Ruby's Carousel. Ruby liked to beat up his girls, and after repeated charges of assault and battery against Ruby were laughed out of the police station, Nancy Perrin quit Ruby.

The summer of 1962, she told the Commission, she and Robert attended a series of meetings in Dallas with some underworld types and a U.S. Army officer—since identified as a mysterious

Colonel L. Robert Castorr of Arlington, Va. (whom the Commission sought not to investigate). The Colonel and his friends wanted to make a deal with Perrin: while he was running refugees out of Cuba, would he run arms in? The military hardware had been "liberated" over a three-month period by the Colonel from a nearby Army base. The Perrins were taken to the back of the house, shown into a shack, and as Nancy Perrin recalled:

> "My God...it was an Army supply depot! There were guns, there was one BAR left over from World War II...20 or 30 cases of hand grenades...half a dozen landmines...."

They didn't like the set-up, and named an outrageously high price they hoped would price them out of consideration. But no, the Colonel made a telephone call, and during this or the next meeting—she was unclear—"I had the shock of my life. I am sitting there. A knock comes on the door and who walks in but my little friend Jack Ruby. And you could have knocked me over with a feather. He took one look at me, I took one look at him and we glared. We never spoke a word."

Ruby and the Colonel left the room. As they did, Perrin noticed "a rather extensive bulge in his...about where his breast pocket would be." And when the two came back in the room, all smiles, she noticed Ruby's bulge was gone: the money had been delivered. But the Perrins changed their minds, and left.

"I smelled an element that I did not want to have any part of," she told the Commission, and the staff lawyer asked, "...and that element was what?"

"Police characters, let's say," Nancy Perrin replied. If anyone would know, she'd know. Several weeks later, Robert Lee Perrin died suddenly under rather mysterious circumstances in New Orleans: he'd swallowed four ounces of arsenic. A suicide? Nancy Perrin didn't think so.

Why the Commission chose not to call Colonel Castorr, a known and acknowledged friend of retired Major General Edwin A. Walker, puzzles many researchers. So does the fact that—as Dr. Peter Dale Scott points out—"nowhere in the 10.7 million words of the Report or the 26 volumes does [Meyer] Lansky's name ever appear. While we know nothing that might link Lansky to the Dallas shootings, it is nevertheless undeniable that many of the snarled and apparently disparate threads from the assassination story lead into the dark surrounding Lansky's operations."

Certainly, they ought not to have glossed over the quaint relationship between Ruby and McWillie, when it was fairly common knowledge in Dallas in 1964 that Ruby was not his own man. Most inexcusable of all, though, is that knowing of Ruby's close involvement with more than half of Dallas' police force, they only bothered to talk to a few, and not even the ones with most to offer.

The most obvious reason is that the Commission—again skirting the important question of conspiracy—feared that whatever testimony such interviews would produce could rip the cover off one of Ruby's sidelines, pay-off man between cops and robbers. (The suggestion that Ruby, like Oswald, was an FBI informer only came up recently, in a declassified FBI memo from Hoover to Rankin dated June 9, 1964. Hoover wrote Rankin that between March 11 and October 2, 1959, during the jeep export phase of Ruby's commerical life, FBI agents met with Ruby no fewer than nine times, "in view of his position as a nightclub operator who might have knowledge of the criminal element in Dallas." Yet, *Times-Herald* reporter Hugh Aynesworth told Gary Cartwright of the *Texas Monthly* that the attempt was meaningless. The FBI, said Aynesworth,

> "wanted [Ruby] as an informer on drugs, gambling and organized crime, but everytime they contacted him, Ruby tried to get his competitors in trouble... and after awhile the FBI gave up on the idea."

The FBI could not give the Carousel any kind of immunity, but the cops could. But why the Bureau would seize that particular moment of time was not explained.)

The Commission certainly knew of Ruby's pay-off activities. According to testimony in Volume 23 of the Appendix, Ruby was the The Man to see in 1955 if you were a prostitute and wanted to work the new Statler-Hilton. And in 1956, in that same volume, we meet two undercover Narc informants, identified only as "Mr. and Mrs. James Breen". The "Breens" told the Los Angeles field office of the FBI that Jack Ruby of Dallas was the liaison for "a large narcotics set-up operating between Mexico, Texas and the East". In 1962, a nameless jailed numbers operator told the FBI that he had been "advised that in order to operate in Dallas it was necessary to have the clearance of Jack Ruby... [who] 'had the fix' with the county authorities."

Now, these tidbits did not come to the fore after Ruby had gained national notoriety, but *before*. And yet, here is the Warren Report, page 224, blandly insisting the staff had "found no evidence of any suspicious relationships between Ruby and any police officer." Or the Mob.

Dr. Scott has his pet theories of why the Commission would suddenly be afflicted with cataracts: the stuff was there, waiting for someone to gather it in, but the FBI balked right down the line, fearing what such revelations might do to the Mr. Clean image of the Director.

Hoover, we know, had a passionate interest in horse racing, something he shared with Ruby. One might sit in the grandstand while the other was pushing tip sheets downstairs. Nonetheless, it was a mutuality of interests, and they were bound to know some of the same people. Hoover hob-nobbed with Texas oil billionaire Clint Murchison, the owner of the Del Mar race track in Southern California (favored, incidentally, by Johnny Roselli). At the time, Murchison owned Holt, Rinehart & Winston, thus was Hoover's publisher as well, (to say nothing of Mark Lane's *Rush to Judgment*).

According to muckraker Fred J. Cook (in *The FBI Nobody Knows*), Hoover used to rationalize his attendance at Del Mar by reminding his critics—with a straight face, one hopes—that the track's charitable contribution to the Boys' Clubs of America "helps directly in making the nation sturdy, for Communist penetration is currently directed mainly at labor organizations and youth organizations." And besides, added Hoover, "from a law-enforcement standpoint, a well-conducted race track is a help to a community if only for the reason that the people at the track are finding an outlet for their emotions."

When visiting Del Mar, Hoover would invariably stay at Murchison's Del Charro hotel in La Jolla, up the coast from San Diego. His $100-a-day tab was always picked up by the Murchisons—clear through the time the FBI was investigating the Murchisons for their possible involvement in the Bobby Baker scandal. (Unsubstantiated reports place the total of Hoover's tab at $23,000 over the years. It wasn't just Elliot Ness who was Untouchable, that much seems clear in hindsight).

Hoover's chumminess didn't just begin and end at the track, but spilled over into all sorts of interesting precincts of business and society. The investigatory and law-enforcement mechanisms of the Bureau could only be activated, or stopped, at the Director's say-so, that much we can see from the way the Warren Report was put together. Typically, no sooner had the President been assassinated and his brother's power as Attorney General begun to wither, than the FBI stopped feeding Bobby Baker data to the Justice Department.

Kennedy knew, as did Hoover, that 27% of Baker's Serv-U Corporation was in the hands of certain Las Vegas people, including those involved in the overlapping empires of Lansky, Murchison and Hoffa. Says Peter Dale Scott:

"There is now sufficient evidence of an intricate web of interlocking gambling and law-enforcement interests in which Ruby had enmeshed himself since leaving Chicago for Dallas in 1947, to suggest that the full story of Ruby's associates would have been embarrassing. Not only to the Syndicate but also to various Dallas law-enforcement authorities—*and* J. Edgar Hoover and the FBI."

The only thing of which we may be fairly sure is that Hoover and Ruby never met. The same cannot be said for Ruby and Oswald: unlike Hoover, Oswald traveled in an orbit parallel to Ruby's. Oswald's older brother Robert insists the two knew each other, but was unable to offer the Commission any proof. Lee certainly didn't seem to recognize his executioner that Sunday morning.

What is quite possible, though, is that the two may have attended the same Dallas meetings of the right-wing Cubans. It can be no accident that Oswald carried in his notebook the name and address of General Walker, whose aide, Robert Allan Surrey, was a bridge-playing partner of FBI agent James P. Hosty, or that Ruby was serving as a money conduit between unnamed sources and the mysterious Colonel Castorr, who would often join Walker at those DRE meetings.

It's more than apparent that Ruby could tell one Cuban group from another. During that weekend of November 22, at one of D.A. Wade's press conferences, the District Attorney told the press that the alleged assassin was a member of the "Free Cuba Committee". Not so, came a voice from the back of the room, *Fair Play* for Cuba Committee." The voice was Jack Ruby's.

A WELL-PLANNED POLICE ACTION?

"Starting with Sunday afternoon, you could no longer find a policeman in town who said he knew Ruby..."
—Seth Kantor, Scripps-Howard

Jack Ruby entered the police garage at 11:20 a.m.. Less than a minute later, they brought Lee Harvey Oswald down, manacled to several detectives. He was, one reporter recalls, "a trussed-up, slowly-moving target." Ruby fired just one shot; Oswald instinctively tried to bring his handcuffed arms up but to no avail. The autopsy report noted he died at Parkland Hospital at 1:07 p.m. of a gunshot wound; he didn't. He had bled to death after a Dallas policeman applied artificial respiration to the grievously wounded prisoner. It hardly seemed accidental.

Officially, the Dallas Police wouldn't even own up to his murder. Researcher Sylvia Meagher discovered that on Oswald's jail card, someone had crossed out "DECEASED 11-24-63" and with utter gall inserted the notation "TRAN TO CO 11-24/11:20 a.m."—"transferred to the County Jail." Even the Warren Report couldn't bring itself to describing his death as murder; it keeps referring to something called an "abortive transfer".

How had Ruby gotten in? Had he been tipped off that the "abortive transfer" had been delayed by one hour and twenty minutes so as to time his arrival? If so, by whom? And, most important, was Ruby acting on his own behalf, or on instructions?

Within minutes of the shooting, speculation was rife that Ruby had been sent in by the assassination plotters to silence Oswald, and the Warren Commission duly applied itself to looking into that report. But since there *were* no plotters as far as the Commission was concerned, Ruby *must* have acted alone. The lone assassin and the lone avenger. Why not? If the American people would buy one, they'd buy the other. And to a remarkable degree, while they're no longer buying the first, they still cling to the belief that Ruby was crazy.

Like a fox, perhaps. A gambling fox. Ruby always liked to take chances, and whoever approached him that weekend offered him the longest oddds of all—after all was said, shot and done, Ruby would emerge the hero. He had all these friends at Police headquarters; surely, his friends would not see him burn in the electric chair. An even bigger risk faced those who had put Ruby up to it: that Oswald would talk. Oswald was supposed to have been silenced in the movie house, but he beat those odds. Now, if the transfer from the city jail to the more secure County Jail came off, there'd be little chance to keep him from eventually telling the authorities all he knew, or guessed.

And so, after the fatal shot had torn into Oswald's gut, Ruby put himself at the mercy of his friends. "You all know me," said he, "I'm Jack Ruby."

They all knew him, all right, but to the embarrassed city fathers, Ruby was a blot on the city's shield. They demanded and got a death sentence. But after the appellate machinery had been set in motion, Ruby, the gambler, won: his conviction was overturned and a new trial—outside of Dallas—was ordered. But Lady Luck had run out: during the autumn of 1966, Jack Ruby started running a high fever, feeling nauseous, spitting blood. His jailers said he was faking and denied him diagnosis and hospitalization. A blood clot killed him on January 3, 1967. The autopsy showed him riddled with cancer. Again, we are left to wonder whether their lack of concern was an oversight. For if what Ruby intimated to Earl Warren was true, if he knew more than he'd been willing to discuss within the confines of his ten-by-ten-foot cell, it would unquestionably have to come out sooner or later. The new trial would be held in Wichita Falls, outside of the jurisdiction of the Dallas Police. The odds against Ruby keeping his mouth shut then were too great. It explains much about the medical care he received in Dallas.

On that Sunday morning, security was especially tight after the telephone "threat" of the night before. An elaborate ruse had been set up. There were two ramps leading to the garage, one from Main Street, the other from Commerce Street. Parked on the Commerce Street ramp was a decoy armored truck; the cops figured all attention would be on that ramp. The Main Street ramp would be used for the unmarked police car by which Oswald would actually be whisked out. However, the car was not in position inside the garage. In addition to the two ramps, both heavily guarded, there were five doors leading from the abutting municipal buildings—the Records Building and the Police Headquarters. Apparently, all five were tightly secured with a guard at each.

Ruby later claimed to have come down the Main Street ramp; the Commission refuted this. Too many people had seen through the ruse of the armored truck and were watching the ramp. None saw Ruby coming down. He must have come in through one of the five doors, possibly waving his press badge. Ruby also insisted he'd been sending a Western Union telegram four minutes before he entered the garage, and that he went to the garage on an impulse. One hour and twenty minutes late? Ken Dowe, a reporter for station KBOX remembered that the day before, he had casually joked to Ruby, asking if he'd be at the transfer. Ruby replied, not at all jokingly, "You *know* I'll be there."

Putting it bluntly: both Oswald and Ruby were victims of a "police action," one that for Oswald, at least, may have begun months before.

It must be remembered that virtually the entire case marshalled against Oswald by the Warren

Commission was built not by the FBI but by the Dallas law-enforcement officials who produced most of the evidence—most of it, we now suspect, fabricated. Since it is unlikely that higher-ups such as Chief Curry would have involved themselves in so shoddy an operation, we can only assume that lower-ranking police officers were involved, people in such critical areas as print identification, ballistics, crime laboratory and records. All it would take would be a small handful of people. Their motivation would not have been monetary: they would have had to have been politically committed to such a scheme, and we may assume they were.

Policemen generally stand somewhere to the right of Louis XIV and Savonarola; in Dallas in 1963, there was no shortage of cops holding dual memberships in the Klan, the Minutemen of America and the John Birch Society. A number of them had a little business with the Mob on the side. Most were friends of Jack Ruby.

It is hard to believe that Ruby wasn't tipped off, harder still to believe Ruby just happened to drop in. As to the first, we have newsman Thayer Waldo's testimony about Lt. Butler's extremely nervous behavior seconds before Oswald was walked in, as if Butler expected something to happen—and it did. As to the second, all we have are the second-person recollections of a Dallas cop, now retired, who was told afterwards that Ruby had first gone upstairs to Police headquarters and then had been brought down via a *service* elevator, by Assistant Chief of Police Charles Batchelor. By the time that came out, in 1971, Batchelor was dead, and the report therefore had to remain just that, a report. Still, it cannot be denied that nothing that took place that weekend in Police Headquarters seemed to have much to do with "law and order".

Consider, therefore, the very distinct possibility that the Kennedy plotters, having made their decision to carry out their plan, would have to coordinate with certain law-enforcement officers in the city in which the killing was to take place—if only, as Col. L. Fletcher Prouty suggests, to loosen security enough to allow the killers to do their thing.

It is also possible that Oswald the patsy may have been an afterthought. That involving him came about only well after it had been decided to go for Kennedy somewhere in the South, perhaps as late as September. This, at least, would explain the whole episode with Mrs. Odio and the rash of "double-Oswald" appearances all over Dallas. While the official decision to visit Texas may not have been announced by the White House until early November, we recall that the decision had been made as early as June. Unquestionably, at some point well before agent Lawson's first inspection visit to Dallas, word must have reached either the Sheriff's office or police headquarters of the President's impending trip.

Worth remembering also is Klansman Milteer's taped conversation of November 9: "They will pick up somebody within hours afterwards—just to throw the public off." A coincidence? Hardly.

If providence gave them Oswald, thereby offering the plotters the opportunity to remove a suspected double agent-*provocateur*, the only problem would be the Feds. They could obviously not be brought in, and we may safely assume they weren't. They implicated themselves through their incredible laxity before the assassination, and afterwards, through their frantic scramble to disavow any suspected role in the crime. Those who may have been involved locally quickly recognized the advantage handed them, and so they effectively neutralized the Bureau's vaunted investigatory effectiveness by banking on its rigidity, its fear of having its incompetence exposed to its own hierarchy. As one former FBI agent recalls: "can't you just picture Hoover's reaction upon learning that one of his informers just killed the President?"

Let us therefore turn back the clock to 12:30 p.m. C.S.T., Friday, November 22, and see what happened, and what *didn't* happen. With Chief Curry now admitting that they really had nothing that would have put Oswald and the Mannlicher-Carcano on the sixth floor, we can safely eliminate a great portion of the Warren Commission's Report that deals with eyewitnesses—people like the 44-year-old hard-hat pipefitter, Howard L. Brennan, whom Representative Gerald R. Ford called "the most important eyewitness to appear before the Commission."

It was Brennan who told David Belin that he saw "Oswald" sitting sideways on the window sill (even though the sill was only one foot from the floor), standing and taking deliberate aim and firing (although to have done so "Oswald" would have had to shoot through double-pane window glass, and since he didn't, then the gunman would have had to have put his head between his knees in order to aim). Even more ludicrous was the Commission's straightfaced acceptance of Brennan's testimony that he saw (a) the fatal head shot fired, (b) the President's head explode, and (c) the gunman retracting the rifle—a feat that must have made Brennan's head spin faster than the speed of sound. Brennan later failed to pick Oswald out of the police line-up; he said that had he done so, his family would have suffered "Communist reprisals".

We cannot blame the Dallas Police for having invented Howard Brennan, but we can accuse them of deliberately creating the impression that Oswald had brought *the* gun to work with him that morning. According to 19-year-old Buell Wesley Frazier, Oswald's co-worker and Marina's neighbor in Irving, he had told him on the ride out to Irving the night before that he wanted to pick up some curtain rods for his room in the boarding house; that the next morning, Oswald carried back to Dallas a long paper bag in which, it was assumed by one and all, he had stashed the disassembled Mannlicher-Carcano. The Dallas Police thoughtfully provided the paper bag, claiming to have found it up on the sixth floor. The Warren Report shows us pictures of the bag; the Commission clearly bought the story, totally.

Yet in testimony, Frazier and his sister, who saw Frazier and Oswald off that morning, described the bag as being about two feet long, and that Oswald carried it by holding it from the top, as one would hold curtain rods, not hardware weighing a total of eight pounds.

The bag entered into evidence measured 38 inches, which would have made it long enough to contain the longest component of the disassembled Carcano, the barrel, which measured 34.8 inches. Commission Exhibit 142 was a home-made affair, made of wrapping paper and gummed tape. The Commission described it as "cogent evidence", because it had Oswald's right palmprint on the bottom, as it would have been left had he carried it by the butt. When Frazier and his sister insisted he carried it by the top, their recollections were airily dismissed as "mistaken".

If the bag was made on the premises, as charged, the man in charge of the mailroom, a 16-year veteran of the Depository, wasn't of any help: he didn't remember even seeing Oswald at or near his work station, and the man seemed to love his job so much he seldom left his post, not even for lunch; and no one ever remembered Oswald taking anything out of the building as bulky as a 38-inch-long bag which, incidentally, had no folds. Nor did the bag produced for the Commission have so much as a single oil stain. The scenario called for Oswald to have placed the gun in the bag the night before, when Marina was sleeping. The FBI described the gun as being "well-oiled".

It would seem, therefore, that the cops found a bag in the junk pile on the sixth floor and turned it over as evidence to the FBI since there was no other way of explaining how Oswald had brought in the gun, unobserved.

There are several post-scripts to the paper bag canard. One is that on Saturday morning, a free-lance photographer named Gene Daniels (covering the crime for the Black Star picture agency) happened to drop by Oswald's boarding house on North Beckley Street and there discovered the landlady and her husband in Oswald's room, hammering into the wall a set of curtain rods. He photographed the tableau for posterity. Obviously, there had been no curtain rods in Oswald's room up to then; now there were—and now, of course, Oswald's curtain rod story wouldn't hold up.

Two, young Frazier, of whom more will be said, didn't seem to come before the Commission emotionally unscarred. On Friday night, he was not merely brought in for questioning, as an ordinary witness might have been, but *arrested*. After dutifully telling the cops the curtain rod-bag story, he was released at 9 p.m., and driven back to Irving in a squad car. But midway there, the squad car was called back to Dallas, and Frazier was given a lie-detector test. Apparently, Oswald under questioning had vehemently denied the curtain rod story, but refused to take a polygraph examination until he was given legal representation. Captain J. Will Fritz, Head of Homicide, confused and perturbed by what seemed to be conflicting stories, put Frazier to the polygraph. The results were never published, and several years ago, an even stranger thing happened. Assassination researcher George O'Toole went down to Dallas with a Psychological Stress Evaluator and asked the cops that were there that night about the Frazier incident. They all denied that a lie-detector test was given, saying Fritz did not believe in polygraph examinations. The cops were still covering up in 1974; their own stress readings were high.

(Invented by several ex-CIA officials, doing business as Dektor Counterintelligence & Security Inc., Springfield, Va., the PSE appears to be an improvement over the polygraph. Where the polygraph measures four variables—pulse, blood pressure, respiration and perspiration—PSE measures the inaudible and subtle variations in voice modulation as far more accurate indices of stress and anxiety. A subject can control himself sufficiently to beat the polygraph; he cannot do the same with the PSE.)

Then there was the business of the nitrate examination. The firing of a rifle, certainly one requiring careful aiming as this one must have, invariably leaves traces of nitrate-containing gunpowder on the cheek of the person firing. Traditional law-enforcement investigatory procedure in all shootings calls for the application of a coat of warm wax to the accused's cheek, pulling off the powder residue and then bathing it in a solution of diphenylamine and sulphuric acid. Should the solution turn blue, there's a presence of nitrates. In the Oswald test, the solution did *not* turn blue.

Two of the most damning exhibits produced by the Dallas cops were photographs they said were found in Oswald's personal possessions stored in the garage back in Irving. They depict Oswald standing in a backyard, wearing a revolver, holding what could be the Mannlicher-Carcano in one hand, and in the other, a copy of *The Militant*, and the *Daily Worker*. One was shown to Oswald by the police at 6 p.m., Saturday, November 23. He immediately pronounced it a fake, a composite.

"That is not a picture of me; it is my face but my face has been superimposed...the rest of the picture is not me at all. I've never seen it at all."

Having worked for the Dallas photographic studio of Jaggars-Chiles-Stovall for more than five months, to say nothing of his military training in photographic analysis, Oswald would have been quick to spot a phony.

The Commission said Marina had told them she'd taken it. Oswald's brother Robert said *he'd* taken the shot with Oswald's Russian-made Imperial reflex camera. Obviously, one or both were lying—under pressure.

Oswald wasn't lying. Sharp-eyed critic Meagher spent months analyzing the picture. She points out that if Oswald was 5'9" and the rifle measured

267

40.2", and adding one inch to Oswald's height to account for his shoes, then the rifle would represent 57.4% of Oswald's 70" height. But the way it appeared on the February 21, 1964 cover of *Life* magazine, the gun accounts for 61% of his height. If the rifle is the Mannlicher-Carcano, the man's height would have to be three-fourths of an inch taller than shown.

Even more inconsistent were the shadows. The shadow of the body falls behind the man and to his right; that under the nose falls dead center—clearly inconsistent unless there were two suns on the day the photo was allegedly taken. *Allegedly*, because Marina claimed she'd taken the photo on March 31, 1963—a cloudy, sun*less*, rainy day (according to a check with the Dallas Weather Bureau)—and not the time of year for the bushes that appear behind Oswald to be blooming.

A closer examination of both photos reveal other oddities. In one photo, Oswald's head is straight but his body stance so askew that anyone else duplicating that position would topple over. Stranger still is that nose shadow: in the picture in which Oswald's head is shown erect, the shadow appears as a perfect V; in the picture in which his head is cocked, the shadow stays the same. And the strangest is what the critics now call "the world's first chin transplant". In the pictures, the chin of Oswald is squarish; in all other pictures of Oswald, the chin is narrow, clefted and pointed.

Naturally, the FBI couldn't entertain the frightful notion that the photos had been deliberately faked and planted, so it ordered photo expert Lyndal I. Shaneyfelt to duplicate the now-classic pose. In the FBI version the shadow of the body is consistent with the shadow of the Oswald photo—it falls precisely behind. But the face of the agent posing as Oswald has been blanked out. No comparisons can be made. Asked why by the Commission, Shaneyfelt replied:

"I blanked out the head because it was one of the employees of the FBI and I felt it was desirable to blank out the head because it was not pertinent."

Not pertinent? The entire point of the duplication was to check the body's shadow against that of the face.

What seems to be missing after Shaneyfelt's testimony is the bracketed notation [LAUGHTER]. There's something terribly strange about this damning photographic "evidence". The cops claimed to have found the photographs on Saturday, during a search of the Paine residence when no one was home—Mrs. Paine apparently had "gone shopping". Another thing: during their search, the cops didn't find the camera: the first the Commission saw of it was in February 1964, when Robert Oswald produced it. Perhaps there was no need to pick up the camera in November since the cops already had the print in hand before the assassination took place.

Sylvia Meagher also finds it somewhat odd that this doting father, this world traveler, never took any baby pictures, never shot any scenes in Russia, but "took" only incriminating photos. (Besides the backyard shots, the cops also produced a picture of the house of General Walker. The photo is generally uninteresting except for one thing. In the foreground is a car, but in the spot where the license plate should have appeared, there's a hole—punched into the print. Also punched out, presumably, was the year on the license plate, since anything but 1963 would have cleared Oswald of this added, posthumous charge.)

Also unexplained is how the blow-ups of the backyard photo produced by the police photo lab shows the offending newspaper to be *The Militant*. When *Life* and the *New York Times* blew up the negative, no printing was revealed. (But the *Life* staff played its game, too: it stripped *in* a gunscope to make the gun the certified "assassination weapon".)

If we accept, for a minute, that the Mannlicher-Carcano "found" in the Book Depository was, indeed, the property of A. Hidell (which may have been Oswald's FBI cover name), how did it get there? And if it didn't, when did it fire CE 399—the magic bullet? Of all the theories put forth, the only one that makes sense is O'Toole's.

He thinks young Buell Wesley Frazier may have been put up to getting it into police hands before the assassination. He, too, owned a gun—a British Enfield .303, and may have been recruited to do his patriotic duty.

> "Suppose that a policeman quietly approached an employee of the Book Depository and told him that Oswald was a Communist and a dangerous radical. Suppose he said Oswald owned a rifle and was suspected of using it in some crime, but the police could not obtain the weapon through formal, legal means. Suppose the officer asked the man to get the rifle for the police through some pretext in order to make ballistics tests. And suppose [he] agreed?"

It's an interesting supposition, more so in light of the pressure tactics applied by the cops to Frazier the night of the assassination, and the fact that since the assassination, Frazier has been positively elusive and will in no way discuss his role in the drama. And that when O'Toole finally did manage to get an interview with Frazier on tape (using a proxy) and ran the questions and answers through the PSE device, Frazier evidenced extraordinarily high levels of stress—far, far higher than those produced by running the tape of Oswald's midnight press conference ("I positively know nothing about this situation here") through the PSE.

Nowhere does the case against Oswald crumble more dramatically than in the recounting of his "flight" from the Book Depository, the alleged murder of Officer Tippit, and his arrest at the Texas Theatre.

The scenario starts with the shooting in Dealey Plaza. One minute and fourteen seconds after the *third* shot has been fired, Dallas Police Sergeant Marrion L. Baker, having jumped off his motorcycle, his gun drawn, sprints up to the second floor of the Book Depository and confronts Oswald, in the employees' lunchroom, calmly sipping a Coca Cola. School Book Depository superintendent Roy S. Truly, the man who had hired Oswald, runs up and assures Sgt. Baker that Oswald is OK, he belongs there. They depart.

Let's examine that in light of the Warren Report. According to the good book, Oswald has just fired his third shot, and ejected his third cartridge (three "spent" shells were found lying neatly in a row—too neatly). He wipes off his fingerprints, squeezes out from behind his home-made barricade of shipping boxes (so as not to be seen by anyone casually walking around on the sixth floor), and hides the Carcano so artfully that it will take until 1:20 p.m. for a Deputy Constable to find it. He then runs down four flights of stairs, dashes into the lunchroom, pops a coin into the machine, and gulps down enough Coke so that Sgt. Frazier can say it was half-finished. Elapsed time: *78 seconds!*

Clearly, the scene in the employees' lunchroom was Oswald's best, iron-clad alibi. Had he done all the things the Commission said he did upstairs, even in lightning time, and beaten Roger Bannister's record running down four flights, he'd have gotten there *after* Sgt. Baker.

Now, the Commission tells us, Oswald at 12:33 p.m. leaves the Depository. But does he run? No. Rather than flee east on Elm, away from the throng, he *walks* west, seven blocks out of his way to the corner of Murphy where, at 12:40 p.m., he boards a transit bus that is actually heading right past the Depository. Or would have headed that way. Because the traffic jam is so monumental that after two blocks, the bus is stuck, and Oswald asks for a transfer and leaves the bus. (Mark Lane, who represented Marguerite Oswald before the Commission, mused at this point in the telling that "the apocryphal murderer returns to the scene of the crime. Everyone knows that. But there's usually a more substantial time interval.")

Oswald walks three and a half blocks and hails a cab. So does an elderly woman. This desperate killer courteously allows the woman to take the cab and looks for another. He finds it, gets in, not in the back where he might hide his face, but up in front, with the driver. He shows no concern about being observed so closely. He instructs the cabbie to take him five blocks *past* his rooming house at 1026 North Beckley in the Oak Cliff section of Dallas—a clever, circuitous way. He gets out, and walks *back* to his boarding house. It is almost 1 p.m. He takes three minutes in which to put on a windbreaker and dashes out of the house. Twelve minutes later, the Commission says, Oswald arrives at the intersection of 10th and Patton Streets, where he is stopped by a patrol car. Officer J.D. Tippit, having heard a radio alarm for "white male, etc." appears suspicious. He beckons Oswald over, leans into the passenger side, rolls down the window and they speak. Tippit gets out of the car, prepared to walk around in front (his gun is not drawn) whereupon Oswald whips out a .38 calibre pistol and guns the cop down. Like that. He mutters something to the effect of "poor dumb son-of-a-bitch cop," empties his gun, scatters the shells in the bushes, leaves, cuts through side streets, drops his jacket, and eight blocks from the scene of his latest murder, sneaks into the Texas Theatre, a movie house, without bothering to buy a ticket. Alerted by a shoestore manager across the street, a small army of law-enforcement officials burst in. He's in the 10th row and after a scuffle, he's arrested and taken downtown to be booked.

Let's stop the reel and look again. For one the timing. Given the accounts of the busdriver and the cabbie (whose log shows the trip ran from 12:30-12:45 p.m.) it is highly improbable that Oswald could have arrived on foot at his boarding house at precisely 1 p.m. His landlady, Earlene Roberts, testified he got there "a little after one," and that he stayed for four minutes. Furthermore, while he was changing clothes, she saw a police car pull up to the curb directly in front of the house, honk the horn once or twice, and pull away. Earlene Roberts had poor vision: she could make out three numbers on the police cruiser, but could cite only two—a "1" and an "0". The Dallas police cruisers have two numbers only, and Officer Tippit's car was "10".

And when Oswald left, she said, he stood in

front of the house—at a bus-stop—for a route that happens to be heading in the direction opposite from where the Commission said Oswald was heading. Mrs. Roberts did not see Oswald get on the bus. Now, not more than eight minutes later, one full mile away, Officer Tippit met his maker. How did Oswald cover the distance?

There were something like twelve eyewitnesses to the "killing", the Report tells us. But eyewitnesses, we already know from Dealey Plaza, vary. The closest eyewitness identified the killer as having "black, wavy hair," which Oswald didn't. (The movie house cashier described him as "ruddy-looking", which Oswald wasn't). One eyewitness testified under oath that he passed by the scene in his car, saw the cop lying in the street, and "I looked at my watch and it said 1:10 p.m." Two other eyewitnesses put the time at 1:12 p.m. Star witness Domingo Benavides put it at 1:06 p.m. The alarm was called in on Tippit's radio at 1:16 p.m.

In recreating Oswald's foot travels from the rooming house, a trip that by its elastic timetable the Commission said took 13 minutes, the staff actually took 17 minutes and 45 seconds. By this figuring, Tippit must have been killed five minutes before Oswald got there to kill him.

None of the authorities, incidentally, could agree with one another about how many bullets were fired into Tippit. The Secret Service said two, Secret Service Inspector Tom Kelly said three, the emergency staff at the hospital removed four, and the Commission reported five. One of the bullets at the site didn't match its casing.

Also curious (and never explained) was the fact that the curbside window on Officer Tippit's car had not been rolled down, nor were any of Oswald's fingerprints found anywhere on the door. So much for eyewitnesses who "saw" Tippit roll down the car window, beckon and talk with the putative killer.

Domingo Benavides, acknowledged to have been closest to the killer, was never invited to the police line-up. He furthermore refused to identify Oswald after he'd seen his picture on TV. Rather than admit that their best witness could not be used against Oswald, the Commission declined to call him in, and merely took his deposition.

Mark Lane observes: "In an adversary trial, which this wasn't, Benavides might well have been an important witness for the defense." The witness the Commission did use, Helen Louise Markham, proved to be so totally unreliable, and so unstable a personality, that the staff lawyers came close to walking out on their Commissioners. They believed she had actually appeared on the scene *after* the shooting, picked up bits and pieces of information from other spectators, and blew herself up into a person of historical importance. She was in such a state of shock by the time she was brought down to the line-up, she felt unable to look at the characters paraded in front of her. But because the witnesses' testimony was so conflicting, the Commission arbitrarily insisted that hers be regarded as pivotal. She proved to be as valuable to the Commission as Brennan the pipefitter was—and to really underscore the tawdriness of the whole affair, she was invited to appear *with* the 36th President of the United States on a special USIA program on the assassination.

But who was Tippit, and what role did he play? In all the voluminous material written about the assassination, indeed, in the Report itself, there is little information about this policeman. All we're told is that at the time of his death, he'd put in ten years on the force, and had never been promoted. He held a weekend job at Austin's Barbeque, owned by a leading John Bircher, had a modest bank balance, was a devoted family man and churchgoer. But, strange to say, he had an unlisted phone number, and according to Allen Dulles, there were rumors about his involvement in some shady narcotics deals. He was a friend of Ruby's, according to Tippit's widow Gayle. And a growing number of assassination researchers are now beginning to think that either Tippit's murder was indeed coincidental—the murderer never having been caught, but the murder a suitable frame to hang on Oswald out of sheer frustration at having had a President shot down under their noses—or that he was a sacrificial lamb. Like Oswald, he could have been a set-up to make sure that if Oswald couldn't be gotten for regicide, then at least they'd get him for being a "cop-killer".

Certainly, there was something highly irregular about the way Oswald was arrested. The story that afternoon was that the alarm went out for someone of Oswald's physical description because superintendent Truly held a roll-call after the assassination and discovered only Oswald was missing. That's what the cops said. Only there was no roll-call that any employee could remember. What's more, of the 75 people in the Depository that noon, 48 were outside watching the parade, and afterwards, many drifted off, figuring there'd be no more business inside for the rest of the day.

The Commission said Oswald was initially fingered by shoestore manager Johnny Brewer, whose shop was a few doors down the street from the Texas Theatre. Brewer said he'd been listening to radio coverage of the post-assassination, heard the bulletin about a police officer being killed nearby, and as he heard the first sirens in the distance, happened to see a furtive-looking man skulking in the doorway. As the man walked off, Brewer followed him and said he saw him enter the movie house without buying a ticket. He alerted the ticket-taker who then called the cops. But why Oswald would want to draw such attention to himself by not buying a ticket when he had money on him was something no one sought to ask.

From all over the area came a posse of cops. More than fifteen men were involved—uniformed officers, plain-clothesmen, two police captains, an assistant D.A. and even an FBI man. They'd come for a cop-killer but not necessarily to arrest him. Some stood outside the exits, their guns drawn.

To Oswald, who may have gone to the Texas Theatre to meet his FBI contact—a most logical meeting place between informant and "control"— it must have been clear the cops had come to shoot first and ask questions later. The house lights flicked on. Officer M.N. McDonald didn't know just who it was he was supposed to be looking for, as he got set to work his way up from the front of the theatre. There were about fifteen people sitting in the orchestra. Then, as McDonald later recalled, a man—presumably shoestore manager Brewer— whispered that the suspect was in the center about three rows from the back. McDonald jumped off the stage, unholstered his revolver, and slowly headed towards the back. He kept staring at Oswald. But Oswald moved first; he stood up, shouted "this is it!" and knocked down McDonald who'd rushed the suspect. According to the cops, Oswald reached for his .38, whereupon McDonald claimed to have jammed his finger into the firing mechanism. As he was knocked down and pummeled, one policeman yelled, "kill the President, will you?" Oswald, in turn, yelled he was not resisting arrest, loud enough for all to hear. No being "shot while escaping arrest" for Lee Harvey Oswald. (As for the helpful informant who'd directed Officer McDonald to the man in the third row rear, he naturally walked out of the theatre— and out of the story. He'd played his role well.)

On a radio interview that afternoon, Sgt. (now Lt.) Gerald L. Hill seemed to know an awful lot about the prisoner—where he'd worked, his "excellent" Marine marksmanship, his defection to Russia, his Russian bride, everything anyone might possibly have put into a police dossier on Lee Harvey Oswald, except for one thing. According to the radio log in the police squad car, the prisoner's wallet revealed his name was *Oswald*, Lee Harvey Oswald. The Hidell alter ego was not known at the time of his arrest. There was nothing in the radio logs to indicate that the five cops who took Oswald downtown came across *any* identification card of A.J. Hidell. But later they changed their story, and claimed to have found both the Hidell and Oswald identifications.

The cops, of course, said they knew nothing about this man Oswald when they brought him in. Perhaps the Department didn't, but some people on the force did. Like Lt. Jack Revill, head of the Criminal Investigation Detail. That afternoon, he would berate FBI agent Jim Hosty for not having shared the FBI's dossier with him, when it's clear the Bureau knew all about him. Hosty protested that he was under orders not to share the information with the Dallas cops. But when Lt. Revill wrote up his report on Lee Harvey Oswald, he slipped up: he used the address of "605 Elsbeth Street, Dallas." Oswald never lived at 605 Elsbeth.

But he *had*, with Marina and baby June, lived at *602* Elsbeth Street—*until* April 24, when he moved to New Orleans.

Just how did Revill make such a "mistake"? Roy Truly at the Book Depository only knew Oswald's address to be c/o Ruth Hyde Paine in Irving, Texas, and Oswald himself, when arrested, only gave his North Beckley Street rooming house as his address. Clearly, someone in the Dallas police department had a marker on Lee Harvey Oswald going back to his earliest of Fair Play for Cuba Committee activities. (When pressed to explain by Commissioner Dulles, Lt. Revill merely said he'd gotten the Elsbeth Street address from "two other detectives". The Commission didn't probe further.)

Finally, there's the strange case of the late Roger Dean Craig. Craig was an up-and-coming Sheriff's Deputy. He claimed that 14 or 15 minutes after the shooting, he saw "a man running down [the grassy knoll] toward Elm Street" and get into a light-colored station wagon he subsequently described as a Nash Rambler with a built-on luggage rack in the rear. He mentioned it to Captain Fritz back in the Depository, just after the news of Oswald's capture for Tippit's murder came in on the police radio. Fritz told Craig it sounded like the man he'd described, and asked him to come down to the jail to identify Oswald.

Confronting Oswald, Fritz pointed to Craig and told Oswald, "this man saw you leave," and Oswald, quite agitated, told Fritz "I told you people I did." Fritz thereupon said, "calm down, son, we are just trying to find out what happened. What about that car?"

At this point, Oswald jumped up, and said, loudly, "that station wagon belongs to Mrs. Paine...don't try to tie her into this. She had nothing to do with it." And then, *sotto voce*, Oswald added, "everybody will know who I am now...."

Several things here are interesting. Captain Fritz asked Oswald about "the car", and Oswald spoke about "that station wagon". Next, this is the same Captain Fritz who, at no time during the entire twelve hours of interrogation, saw fit to take so much as a jotting on a scrap of paper, let alone a tape recording—or so he said. (Postal inspector Harry Holmes wasn't clued in properly: he told the Commission that at one point Oswald reminded Fritz "you took notes" when Fritz asked him to reiterate something Oswald had said earlier.) So perhaps he did take notes. And if he did, why are they being kept a secret?

Later, before the Commission, Fritz would deny the whole thing; in fact, he would even deny that he and Deputy Sheriff Craig had ever interviewed Oswald together—the denial based, perhaps, on the fact that shortly after Craig said this scene took place, Fritz had been called away for a very important, face-to-face meeting with Sheriff Bill Decker. One can't help but wonder what Decker told Fritz that couldn't have been said to him on a phone, but which required his physical presence. Because right afterwards, the non-stop interrogation began, of which no record was taken.

As for Craig, the Commission ignored his testimony. And in 1967, Craig—after agreeing to talk with Jim Garrison—was suddenly fired from the Sheriff's office. Thereafter, he began encountering a number of mysterious troubles, including an attempted shooting and a rather strange auto accident from which he never quite recovered. In May 1975, Craig was found with a rifle by his side. The coroner said it was suicide. There are some people who suspect foul play. He was the latest of many witnesses to the assassination to die an "unnatural death".

AD INFINITUM: "OPENNESS & CANDOR" IN THE WHITE HOUSE

"...it is a picture of someone narrow in vision, unable to see beyond today's gratifications to the larger consequences of his acts."
—Anthony Lewis on Gerald R. Ford

By a conservative guesstimate, the United States employs well over 155,000 men and women and spends in excess of $6.4 billion on what may be euphemistically called "intelligence activities".

Intelligence-gathering may now be Washington D.C.'s hottest growth industry, but at the same time, as we've seen over the past few years, it is also an industry that seems to have run amok.

The most talked-about component of this industry is the CIA. With its staff of 20,000, including more than 5,000 totally engaged in "clandestine activities", guessing its annual budget has become something of a folk art on the Georgetown cocktail party circuit. Defected spook Victor Marchetti, in his 1974 book, *The CIA and the Cult of Intelligence*, pegged it *then* at $750 million. In fact, it's considerably larger when you stop to include its many proprietary companies—airlines, banks, publications (some of which actually turn a profit) and its two most visible propaganda arms, Berlin's Radio Liberty and Munich's Radio Free Europe.

Yet, and this may surprise some people, the CIA figures midway down the intelligence totem pole in terms of size and spending power. Military intelligence—Army-Navy-Air Force—keeps over 106,000 people busy, spending about $4 billion a year; the code breakers and mail scanners of the National Security Agency account for another $1.2 billion of taxpayer money. And it appears that no self-respecting Cabinet member or Agency director can long endure in Washington without setting up his own spy shop. People generally know about the intelligence departments of the FBI, the Secret Service, the Internal Revenue Service, the Post Office, Treasury and Justice Departments; but what do they know about the spies who work for the U.S. Information Agency, the Securities & Exchange Commission, the Federal Communications Commission, the Nuclear Regulatory Commission (nee AEC), or for that matter, the Agency for International Development, the Departments of Commerce, Interior and Agriculture?

Now, it may well be that Lee Harvey Oswald was involved with more than one of them; certainly, his highly irregular departure from the U.S. Marine Corps must have come under the watchful eye of the Office of Naval Intelligence, for we know—from reading the Warren Report Appendix—that the cable traffic out of the U.S. Embassy in Moscow went not only to the State Department but also to the FBI, CIA and ONI, for *starters*.

And because these rumors would not go away, it was only natural that when President Ford decided to try and allay public suspicion about the

CIA's gross improprieties by establishing what is now known as "The Rockefeller Commission", the Government was forced to look into certain aspects of the Kennedy assassination.

But knowing of Ford's compromised position *vis-a-vis* the original Warren Commission inquiry, one would have thought that some of his White House advisors might have been a little more alert, if sensitive, to the idea of putting David W. Belin in charge.

To appoint Mr. Belin as Executive Director of The President's Commission on CIA Activities Within the United States meant that Belin would be asked to investigate his own performance as a counsel to the Warren Commission. The appointment was either unconsciously absurd, or consciously cynical.

For Belin's performance was not one either he or his country could have been proud of. Indeed, some of his co-workers on the Warren Commission now describe his antics as "shameful" and "unethical".

Case in point: in trying to put Oswald on the sixth floor of the Book Depository in time to shoot the President, Belin *knowingly* suborned perjured testimony from a totally unreliable witness, handyman Charles Givens.

Givens, who had a police record and was known to both the Dallas police and the FBI to be susceptible to bribery, was understood to have been willing to change his story for a price. Thus, he had first told the FBI the day after the assassination that he had last seen Oswald on the *first* floor of the Book Depository thirty-five minutes before the assassination. Later, he changed his story: he'd last seen Oswald on the *sixth* floor. Who'd gotten to Givens?

The FBI wanted to know. But Belin didn't. With

the FBI's original Givens statement before him, and knowing of the rumor that Givens had revised his testimony, Belin did not cross-examine the witness, did not even refer to his strange recantation, but simply put the second, suspect version into the official record. This would be the only "evidence" placing Oswald on the sixth floor.

And just to make sure no pesky critic would one day put one and two together, Belin made sure that the orginal FBI statement did not end up in the Appendix to the Warren Report; he had it routed directly into the classified files of the National Archives (where a sharp-eyed Sylvia Meagher would accidentally discover it in 1968).

Sly, slick and surreptitious, Belin would commit similar para-legal excesses throughout the ten-month-long "investigation" into the Dallas shootings. Yet, this lawyer would have the temerity, in 1973, to present his version of the Warren Report (*November 22, 1963: You Are The Jury*) in which he attacked his critics as "assassination sensationalists" and their "techniques of misrepresentation, fraudulent omission and smear."

Say what you will about Gerry Ford, but David Belin is not a stupid man. What makes him run? It puzzles many critics since, unlike others he served with on the Warren Commission, Belin never used his tenure as a stepping stone to a higher Government post. He simply returned to his law partnership of Herrick, Langdon, Belin, Harris, Langdon & Helmick, in Des Moines. No one disputes his brilliance: after all, he accumulated three college degrees at the University of Michigan in six years—the obligatory Bachelor of Arts, a Masters in Business Administration and a law degree. He was Phi Beta Kappa, one of the two "outstanding" seniors in law school, and associate editor of the Law Review.

Ambitious, to be sure, but a CIA agent, as some demonologists now suggest? Hardly. President Ford would not have been *that* foolish. Not with six of the eight Rockefeller Commissioners having intimate knowledge of, and past ties to, the CIA.

There's only one logical explanation for Belin's re-emergence, and that is that President Ford needed to make sure that the JFK part of the CIA investigation would be "controlled". And what better man to control it than the one assistant counsel to the Warren Commission who had not wavered one iota from his position of eleven years earlier?

For the White House had quickly grasped the enormous advantage given it by the "freak" element of the movement that charged that Waterbuggers E. Howard Hunt and Frank Sturgis were not only involved in the assassination as part of the CIA cabal, but were actually present at the shooting of Kennedy. The beleagured Ford must have seen this preposterous assertion as a marvelous diversion. No better man than Belin could be found to ridicule the claim; certainly, his entire demeanor during the Warren Commission investigation made him the ideal choice to so infuriate the critics that, sooner or later, they would blow their credibility and with it, that of the assassination /conspiracy movement.

Belin did not disappoint the President. He deftly turned the "Dealey Plaza tramps" story into a marvelous red herring. Though the witnesses who appeared before the Commission had unequivocally insisted that by no stretch of the imagination could the "tramps" in the photos be either Hunt or

Sturgis—their age, size, *gestalt* were all askew—the staff (a) ignored their testimony, (b) instead chose to act on comments made by some of the more extreme demonologists on TV *months* before by (c) deliberately twisting the given remarks to suggest that these responsible critics had identified the "tramps" as the Waterbuggers. Whereupon Belin coolly dispatched an accomodating FBI crew under photo expert Lyndal Shaneyfelt to Dealey Plaza to check out these "charges"—as if, twelve years later, anyone seriously expected to find some tell-tale evidence lying in the streets of Dallas.

Not as easily dismissable, however, was the Abraham Zapruder film. At the time the Warren Report came out, no one outside of the Commission and various Government circles, had seen the film. Time Inc., which owned it, sat on it. But since then, millions of Americans have seen the film, albeit poor, knock-off bootleg prints that still managed to convey the horror of the fatal headshots.

The interpretation of this film sequence would have to be destroyed if the film itself could not be. Because if the evidence of a frontal shot were left undisputed, then the promised "collapse" of the Warren Report would not have to await a full-scale Congressional inquiry. It would happen by itself.

For that reason, the film would have to be kept from the Eight Wise Men until Belin and his staff had a chance to go over the controversial parts that the critics said contradicted the official story of 1964. As it turned out, only one of the eight Commissioners were *ever* shown the film—a striking replay of the way things worked under the late Earl Warren.

On February 4, 1975, a month after the Rockefeller Commission set up business, co-author

Robert Groden came down to Washington to screen his print of the Zapruder and Orville Nix films. The screening was arranged in the office of Senior Counsel Robert B. Olson. Belin came in, sat down, and as Groden recalls, "looked terribly bored, obviously expecting to see the same super-poor quality bootleg print that had been shown around the country since 1967. But this was a second-generation copy of remarkable depth, clarity and color."

When the fatal headshot sequence appeared on the wall, Groden goes on, "Belin suddenly bolted upright in his chair. He seemed to be bouncing up and down, and then, when the President's head was shown snapping back, Belin jumped up, and with an accusatory finger at the wall, shouted 'neuro-spasm, neuro-spasm!'"

After the showing, Belin began talking about a letter he'd received from a doctor who felt the backward snap could have been the result of a neuromuscular reaction.

But in reaching for an unsolicited letter from an unidentified doctor, Belin seemed to be reaching far. He had no choice, really. This Commission could simply not entertain the possibility of a frontal headshot without admitting the existence of a second guman.

And so David Belin marshalled medical opinion to try and prove that what had actually occurred at that moment of impact was something called "de-cerebrate rigidity"—an instantaneous stiffening of the entire body, torso, head and legs, resulting from a seizure-like reaction to the brain's nerve centers being blown out.

One must give Belin some credit: it was a good, if desperate try. De-cerebrate rigidity is not an altogether rare medical phenomenom. Indeed, it often happens in gunshot cases, notably suicides. Belin summoned forth Dr. Alfred Olivier of the Army's Edgewood Arsenal—the same man who eleven years before had conducted the primary wound ballistics tests for the Warren Commission. Olivier's people had shot high-speed bullets into the heads of goats, and had recorded with high-speed photography convulsive stiffening within 1/25th of a second after impact. Belin's staff then got supportive testimony from such presumably objective medical experts as Detroit's Chief Medical Examiner Dr. Werner U. Spitz and Maryland neuropathologist Dr. Richard Lindenberg.

Not only could the seizure (or Belin's "neurospasm") have caused Kennedy's head to snap back, said the experts, but on top of that, there was always the very real possibility of the "jet effect". That is to say, when a high-speed bullet penetrates the air-tight chamber of the human skull, and explodes outward, the resultant sharp drop in air pressure tends to propel the head back in the direction of the point of entry.

There was only one trouble. To get the doctors to state all this in sworn testimony, Belin's staff could not afford to let them see the actual *motion*-picture footage of the event. For had they seen the Zapruder film, it is quite likely they would not have committed themselves to either the "jet effect" or "de-cerebrate rigidity". Kennedy's body does *not* stiffen. Quite the contrary, his head seems to loll backwards *independently* from his torso, and Kennedy is shown hurled back not quite as a human being but more like a *rag-doll* tossed against the back of the seat.

But as the famous essayist Matthew Arnold once wrote, "On the breast of that huge Mississippi of falsehood called history, a foambell more or less is of no consequence." Like his former colleague Arlen Specter, who made the autopsists describe the President's wounds on the basis of medical drawings produced by an artist who had had no access to the actual body or photographs thereof, David Belin opted to embellish one falsehood with another falsehood. What did it matter?

He would deploy the same guile in dealing with the possibility that in his final moments of recording the assassination, Zapruder may have captured the visage of one of several gunmen.

Earlier, in our detailed review of the Zapruder film, we mentioned an image of what appears to be the shape of a man's head during an 18-frame sequence towards the end of the film. This hatless head appears on the bottom line of the film, from the hairline up. The skin-tones of the neck at the hairline and the outline of the ear are quite discernible; they do not match the texture of the surrounding foliage.

Not only Groden says so. The Itek Corporation of Lexington, Mass.—ironically, a Rockefeller-founded optical research firm—found a similar disparity in that precise spot photographed by Zapruder when they analyzed, at *Life* magazine's request, the color slide shot from the opposite side of Elm Street by Maj. Phillip Willis, says Harold Weisberg.

Granted, the Commission staff members who viewed both exhibits could be "of the opinion that the images allegedly representing assassins [were] far too vague to be identifiable even as human beings." That was their privilege.

But what was not their privilege was to deliberately distort *what* they saw and for how *long* they saw it. For example, no one who has seen this particular sequence can fairly dispute that the shape—be it the head of a gunman or the Loch Ness monster—appears for a full eighteen frames and then goes off screen. But now read what the Rockefeller Report says:

> "...it was not believed reasonable to postulate that an assassin's head would come into view, and then disappear...in the space of about 1/4 of a second (the elapsed time between frames 411 and 415...)"

This was a blatant misrepresentation of established fact, and the staff knew it. It must have realized that whoever read Chapter 19 of the Rockefeller Report would do so without the benefit of seeing what the hell was being described. So the authors of the Report arbitrarily condensed 18 frames into four frames, figuring that even a beginner film student would see this is as far too narrow a time span for anything but a fleck of dust to appear on film and then disappear.

Their advocacy reportage would become even more deplorable in placing this "gunman". The Rockefeller Report puts the "gunman" where Belin wanted him to be, not where Zapruder's film showed him to be—54 feet from the camera.

Five feet in front of where Abraham Zapruder was standing there was a low tree. From the 4'2" high concrete structure on which he was standing, there extended, at a 90-degree right angle, a retaining wall heading perpendicular to Elm Street, before making a short, right angle back up the grassy knoll.

It was behind this cement "retaining wall" that Zapruder's Bell & Howell picked up the odd configuration. Zapruder, we recall, was recording at full telephoto, which meant he was working with a narrow field of view. Had he employed a wider-angle lens, it is quite possible the film would have picked up more of the retaining wall, and perhaps more of the controversial shape. But now that's a moot point.

Because what Belin's people did was again very much what the autopsists had done when they performed verbal/artistic surgery on JFK's back: they moved the gunman 45 feet toward the camera, pulling him out from his protective covering of the retaining wall, and placing him squarely behind the barren tree trunk directly in front of Zapruder's camera lens. The purpose of this becomes glaringly apparent in reading the following "conclusion":

> "An assassin would be unlikely to hide himself behind the barren trunk of a tree only a few inches in diameter, with only his head and shoulders behind the foliage, and with his whole person almost within an arm's length in front of a spectator taking movies of the motorcade. Neither would such an assassin go unseen and undiscovered, able to make his escape over open ground with a rifle in hand, again unseen by anyone among the numerous motorcade police, spectators and Secret Service personnel present...."

What a cruel, cynical hoax, knowingly committed to confuse and deceive the reader of the Report, even if such a reader would have a photograph in hand. By not mentioning the existence of the retaining wall, Belin's people simply wipe it off the map, and expose the "gunman" to be a mythical creature who couldn't exist, even in anyone's wildest imagination! The shape also appears in a still (Polaroid) photo taken by another spectator, Mary Moorman, and is also in the Nix film. Clearly, it was something that bore closer scrutiny.

In somewhat similar fashion, the staff makes short shrift of a possible second tangential gunman—the one Zapruder may have had in mind when he told the FBI the night of the assassination that he was sure the shot had come from over his right shoulder.

During the original Warren Commission hearings, much was made of testimony from people standing on top of the railroad bridge, who said they'd noticed a great deal of activity around the wooden stockade fence on the crest of the grassy knoll. Many eyewitnesses had even spoken of seeing "a puff of smoke" come from the cluster of vegetation around the fence. In all instances, their testimony was dismissed as "mistaken".

But here again, Nix picked up a strange shape that didn't seem to belong. The Nix camera, equipped with a poor quality lens, made it impossible to blow up the film sufficiently to produce any discernible facial characteristics; still, seconds after the shooting, before people are shown hurtling themselves to the ground and scurrying for safety, that shape drops out of the film.

Yet, here again the Rockefeller Report aborts the possibility of such an inquiry by stating:

> "With respect to the Nix film, the FBI reported that 'no figure of a human being could be found in the area' of another alleged rifleman, which was determined to be 'approximately nineteen feet to the right of where Mr. Zapruder was standing and clearly visible to him.'"

Said who? No one who testified to the Belin staff *ever* stated that the "second gunman" was visible to Zapruder. What they said repeatedly during the twenty-five hours or so of testimony was that *had*

Zapruder turned around (which he did not), he *might* have seen the second assassin crouching behind him (again, which he did not). Conjecture, thus, was compounded into stated belief—a characteristic Belin touch so evident from reading the Q&A's of the Warren Report testimonies taken by him.

And so it went, from the ridiculous to the inexcusable. For example, it had been firmly agreed upon in advance that no testimony given would be set into type until the witnesses had a chance to review their comments for typographical error and accuracy. The courtesy was not extended, the agreement was summarily broken. And exhibits, left on loan with the staff, were never returned; other exhibits, produced by the witnesses at considerable out-of-pocket expense, were never called for, and reimbursement withheld.

Groden recalls, "I had the distinct feeling that the exercise was keyed to provoke a walk-out. Their entire method of seeking testimony actually was designed to goad us into giving the kind of answers slick lawyers could immediately tear into. I really think they'd hoped we'd leave so they could call us 'non-cooperative witnesses'. But we didn't give them the satisfaction."

In retrospect, then, it was simply a reprise of the Warren Commission approach to seeking the "truth". Once again, vital witnesses were not called while the favor of non-vital, spaced-out witnesses was curried. Testimony was given behind closed doors. No cross-examination was allowed. The transcripts were slugged "Top Secret", although a review of the Rockefeller Report will show it to be nothing more than a rehash of the Warren Commission half-truths. And then, of course, the Rockefeller Commission disbanded, leaving no one in charge to deal with post-publication questions.

But this time, few seemed to ask. They didn't care. Virtually nobody in the country believed the Rockefeller Report. And it's clear Gerald R. Ford didn't either. He asked Senator Frank Church (D.-Idaho) to take up the CIA assassination probe, knowing that Belin's Report had failed to sway, failed to allay the worst fears of the electorate.

The feeling of the country was best summed up by Church's fellow committee member, Minnesota's Senator Walter F. Mondale, when he said,

"Pinning down responsibility for many of the actions we've uncovered so far has been like nailing Jell-O to a wall. Subordinates say they were told to do it; higher officers can't remember it."

If anything, the Rockefeller Report merely hardened the determination of the Congress to get into the assassination debate with a vengeance. And its failure to curtail Congress's curiosity had left the White House little room for maneuvering.

At year's end, in a somewhat foolish and desperate gambit to keep the cover-up in place, President Ford sent Senator Church a three-and-a-half page "personal" letter, in which he entreated the Idaho lawmaker to suppress his forthcoming Congressional report. The President invoked the rather pathetic argument that

"...public release...will do grievous damage to our country [and] would likely be exploited by foreign nations and groups hostile to the United States in a manner designed to do maximum damage to the reputation and foreign policy of the United States."

Furthermore—and laughable seeing as how the U.S. went around trying to kill or maim various heads of government—"it would seriously impair our ability to exercise a *positive* leading role in world affairs." (ital. ours)

While waving the flag, Ford also brandished a club by authorizing the Justice Department to go to court and see if it couldn't permanently embargo some 62 documents on or about CIA activities, some dating back to the Eisenhower Administration. According to Assistant Attorney General Richard L. Thornburgh, disclosure of these documents would "substantially harm" criminal investigation that the Department of Justice had undertaken after the publication of the Rockefeller Report. Mr. Thornburgh did not elucidate, other than to invoke that old canard that pretrial publicity would "constitute an unwarranted invasion of personal privacy of many individuals."

A clue to the White House's real motives was contained in the legal brief filed by CIA covert activities senior official Eloise Page. She maintained, "The disclosure of these documents would result in exceptionally grave damage to the national security because to officially *acknowledge* these plans would disrupt foreign relations vitally affecting national security...." (ital. ours)

So that was it. See no evil, speak no evil. It did seem a little late in the game, and seasoned Washington hands could only marvel at Ford's seeming naivete. Or was there more that not even the Church committee and its House counterpart (chaired by Rep. Otis G. Pike) knew about? Was it possible that while everyone's attention was focused on the plots against Cuba's Fidel Castro and the assassinated Rafael L. Trujillo of the Dominican Republic and Patrice Lumumba of the Congo, there were other, perhaps secondary, governmental targets nobody had yet heard about? And just where did the CIA's inward-directed activities stop? Why, for example, was it so insistent that eight dispatches—including one curiously dated November 22, 1963—not be made public *ever* as they "concern[ed] a sensitive covert operation"?

Senator Church was "astonished" at the President's outrageous request and indicated he would certainly not even consider it, not when "for months he has known of the Committee's intent to publish its findings."

What appears to be worrying the White House more than anything else is that from such a report the American public—not the foreign governments—would receive a detailed study of the anatomy of the various intelligence agencies over the past twenty years. The Kennedy murder, whether or not it came out of the intelligence Establishment, would only be a small part of this mosaic.

The Government of the United States plainly has few options left if it wishes to regain the confidence of an alienated electorate. To shilly-shally for another decade would almost insure a benign form of anarchy. To come to grips with the JFK assassination question may be the only way open to a restoration of credible dialogue.

A good way to start would be to take the issue off the lecture circuit, out of the college auditorium and off the street corner—and into the halls of Congress, where it may be studied under full power of subpeona. It will no longer do to convene yet another Presidential Commission: they no longer work, nor did they ever. Even Gerry Ford appreciates that.

The people should be made to understand, at the outset, that such a Congressional investigation might well end up inconclusively. Unlike the Watergate tribunal, a Kennedy "court of inquiry" may never produce a "smoking gun," much less the gunmen. For if, as we suspect, the actual hitmen were hirelings—contract "mechanics"— of either the mob or some other equally clandestine organization, we may be sure that they are today in no position to talk.

But there are others who can be made to talk, if not under the power of Congressional subpeona, then perhaps under grant of immunity. These are people who, all along, have known more than they have been willing to tell us. They are the people— "public servants"—who had a clear-cut, constitutional obligation to allay public doubt in the days, weeks and months following the assassination. Instead, they chose to ignore them, to inflame them. The brushfire has now grown beyond containment.

Speaking on behalf of the millions of doubters, the Assassination Information Bureau puts it in its best Bicentennialese: "an elemental cleansing of the political process is an essential first step if the people...are to have any chance of reestablishing the rule of law in a country that now seems incapable of coping with economic recession, domestic repression and foreign entanglements."

The rule of law is, of course, paramount. It was violated from the minute the Dallas Police arrested Lee Harvey Oswald at 1:51 p.m. on November 22, 1963, and in a very real sense, it's been in suspension since then.

Perhaps it will be too much to expect of a Congressional investigation, but a searching examination of all the "evidence" that the Government amassed against the late Lee Harvey Oswald may find it to be as unworthy as that which the French used to condemn Captain Alfred Dreyfus in 1895. It would take twelve years for the French Government to admit to *its* crime of high treason. In 1906, Dreyfus returned from Devil's Island, to live out the rest of his life.

Oswald will not be similarly rehabilitated, nor will John F. Kennedy be restored to life. But there is a striking parallel in the Oswald and Dreyfus cases. In both instances, the prosecution's case was so shoddy to start with that it became necessary for the government prosecutors to fabricate the "evidence"—and then, to stamp it "top secret" on grounds that publication would endanger the "national security".

Now that our "national security" barriers are turning out to be as contrived as those erected by the French Ministry of War, perhaps a good place to start might be to apply some candor. It is generally agreed that *ex post facto* proof of conspiracy will now be impossible to obtain; it can only be suggested—and that would not be enough to overturn the official government verdict. But suppose the Government were to frankly admit that—in retrospect—the case *was* contrived in order to allow Kennedy's successor to govern? That had the crime not been "solved" in the way it was, the country would have almost surely been in an open-ended state of anarchy?

At least, such openness would be no less traumatic than to persist in the fiction that Lee Harvey Oswald pulled the trigger that killed the 35th President—when 82% of the people now believe this to be a bald lie.

David W. Belin who, more than any other, helped perpetuate the fraud of the Warren Report for more than eleven years, now says that a reinvestigation will by itself restore governmental

298

credibility. But as the *New York Times* declared editorially at the close of 1975:

> "...that is hardly likely. Few Americans were prepared a decade ago to believe in official cover-ups and murder plotting; yet, even then they grew increasingly skeptical of the Warren Commission's findings. Having learned to their horror of all those hitherto unthinkable revelations, they are unlikely to have their damaged faith entirely repaired by one or more investigations."

We are, observes Richard M. Nixon from his exile in San Clemente, "a compromised country...so cynical, so disbelieving." The alienation process began with the Warren Report, not Watergate, as the self-pitying former President would like us to believe. Like the cover-ups, it too is still in place—witness the frantic efforts on the part of the Ford Administration to try and suppress the Church Committee's report on CIA-sponsored assassinations.

It will take more than a Congressional investigation into JFK's death to undo the cynicism, the disbelief. But one can think of no better way to at least start repairing the damage than to let Congress grapple with the questions the people are asking. As the *Times* noted:

> "The American system of self-government can hardly be deemed to be working effectively so long as major questions relating to cover-ups in the investigation of a Presidential murder remain unanswered."

Regardless of what Congress will learn about what really happened in Dallas on November 22-24, 1963, one thing is certain: it's time to restore to the American people their inalienable right to elect their political leaders by ballot, and not by bullet.